The Report Writer's Handbook

Paul Georgiou

Published by Panarc International Ltd in 2014

Copyright Paul Georgiou

First Edition

The author asserts the moral right
under the Copyright, Design and Patents Act, 1988
to be identified as the author of this work.

All Rights reserved.
No part of this publication may be reproduced,
stored in a retrieval system or transmitted, in any form or by any means
without the prior written consent of the author,
nor be otherwise circulated in any form of binding or cover
other than that which is published
and without a similar condition being imposed on the subsequent purchaser.

www.panarcpublishing.com

Panarc International Ltd
(www.panarc.com)

ISBN: 978-0-9931103-0-6
Ebook: 978-0-9931103-1-3
Kindle: 978-0-9931103-2-0

Table of Contents

1 INTRODUCTION...1
2 BASIC PRINCIPLES..5
    2.1 Clarity...6
    2.2 Simplicity...6
    2.3 Brevity...6
    2.4 Quality Control...7
3 GROUPING..8
    3.1 Compare and Contrast..9
    3.2 Criteria for Grouping..9
    3.2.1 Grouping words and objects..9
    3.2.2 Grouping ideas...12
    3.3 The Grouping Principle..17
4 ORDERING..19
    4.1 Alphabetical..20
    4.2 Causal..20
    4.3 Chronological..21
    4.4 General to Particular...23
    4.5 Ranking...23
5 LINKING..29
    5.1 Causal..30
    5.2 Combining..31
    5.3 Consequential...32
    5.4 Contrasting...33
    5.5 Conditional...33
    5.6 Elucidating..34
    5.7 Exceptional...34
    5.8 Purpose..35
    5.9 Temporal...36

    5.10 Link Analysis..36
    5.11 Final thoughts on Linking..39
6 STRUCTURING..41
    6.1 How to build a structure..42
    6.1.1 Bottom up construction...42
    6.1.2 Top Down Construction..45
    6.1.3 Building a hierarchy in practice....................................46
    6.2 A couple of hierarchy guidelines.....................................51
    6.2.1 Status Equivalence..51
    6.2.2 Symmetry...53
    6.3 A note on types of hierarchy...54
    6.3.1 Homogeneous Hierarchy...54
    6.3.2 Hybrid Hierarchy...55
7 SUMMARY CHART..58
8 A NOTE ON MIND MAPPING.....................................61
9 REFRESHER COURSE ON SOME BASICS................62
    9.1 The Sentence..62
    9.1.1 Recognizing a sentence...63
    9.1.2 Structuring a sentence to achieve the right emphasis......64
    9.1.3 Sentence cohesion..65
    9.1.4 Key Questions..68
    9.1.5 Bullet Points...68
    9.2 Paragraphs..69
    9.3 Punctuation..70
    9.3.1 Apostrophes...70
    9.3.2 Colons..70
    9.3.3 Commas...70
    9.3.4 Exclamation Marks...71
    9.3.5 Full Stops...71
    9.3.6 Hyphens...72
    9.3.7 Question Marks...72
    9.3.8 Quotation Marks...72
    9.3.9 Semi-colons...72
    9.4 Vocabulary...73
    9.4.1 Register..73
    9.4.2 Alternatives for over-worked words...............................74
    9.5 FIGURES OF SPEECH...92
    9.5.1 Alliteration...92
    9.5.2 Ambiguity..92
    9.5.3 Assonance..92
    9.5.4 Euphemism..93
    9.5.5 Hyperbole..93
    9.5.6 Irony...93
    9.5.7 Litotes..94
    9.5.8 Metaphor...94

- 9.5.9 Metonymy..94
- 9.5.10 Onomatopoeia..94
- 9.5.11 Oxymoron..95
- 9.5.12 Paradox..95
- 9.5.13 Personification..95
- 9.5.14 Rhetorical Question..95
- 9.5.15 Pun..96
- 9.5.16 Simile..96
- 9.5.17 Syllepsis..96
- 9.5.18 Synecdoche..96
- 9.5.19 Zeugma...97

10 THOUGHTS ON FURTHER ASPECTS OF WRITING..........................98
- 10.1 HUMOUR...98
- 10.2 PROVERBS/APHORISMS...98
- 10.3 TRICKY WORD GUIDE..105
- 10.3.1 Criteria for advice on tricky words.............................105
- 10.3.2 Tricky Words and Verbiage..107
- 10.4 QUIRKY WORDS..191
- 10.4.1 One-hit words...191
- 10.4.2 Un-Positive words...192
- 10.5 GRAMMATICAL/VERBAL HAZARDS...................................193
- 10.5.1 Ambiguity..195
- 10.5.2 Dangling Participles..196
- 10.5.3 False Ellipsis..197
- 10.5.4 Mispositioning..198
- 10.5.5 Problems with Negatives..202
- 10.5.6 Problems with Pronouns...203
- 10.5.7 Mixed up Figures of Speech......................................204
- 10.5.8 Number errors..204
- 10.5.9 Prepositions...205
- 10.5.10 Split Infinitives...207
- 10.5.11 Tautology...207

11 ADVANCED TECHNIQUES...210
- 11.1.1 Emphasis...210
- 11.1.2 Digressions..212
- 11.1.3 Bending the rules..213

12 PREPARING BUSINESS DOCUMENTS......................................218
- 12.1 General guidelines for reports......................................218
- 12.2 Components of a report...219
- 12.3 Proposals..220
- 12.4 Checking and revising...221
- 12.5 Common Business Terms...221
- 12.6 Business Clichés and Jargon..230

13 CHECKLIST TEMPLATES..237
- 13.1 Concept Proposal...237

13.2 Curriculum Vitae..241
13.3 House Buying Questionnaire..245
13.4 MARKETING PLAN..249
13.5 Product Marketing Plan..250
13.6 Renting a house checklist..251
14 TERMINOLOGY FOR DOCUPRAXIS USERS...................................256
15 BIBLIOGRAPHY...258

1 Introduction

We all have to write documents of some sort.

Everyone has to put together a letter or an email. Many of us have to produce formal business or administrative reports. Others may spend their working lives researching and writing novels or factual books.

Some people are lucky. They have a natural talent for organising and expressing their thoughts in written form. For them, I hope this book will be an interesting exposé of some of the techniques which, consciously or unconsciously, they routinely employ.

Others are not so lucky. They do not find it easy to organise and express themselves clearly and succinctly. And, it has to be said, the educational system applied over the last two or three decades has done little to help them.

So my main purpose is to explain the four simple techniques that enable anyone to express what they have to say in clear, coherent and persuasive written form. These are:

grouping; ordering; linking; structuring.

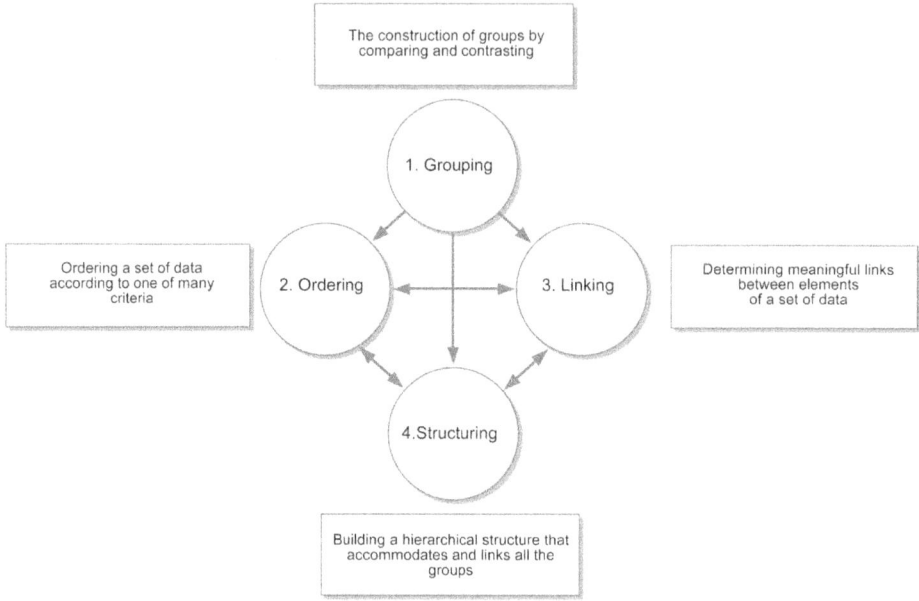

Now I'm well aware that, when writing a book of this type, a book that might be thought to reveal the secrets of any technique, the worst thing you can do is set out on the first page the key elements of what you have to say. You are supposed to titillate the reader with the promise of a great truth but you must avoid at all costs revealing the truth itself until 'your mark is hooked'.

I'm not going to do that, partly because I find that kind of manipulation irritating but mainly because I have no secrets to impart. Grouping, ordering, linking and structuring are fundamental to all activities involving any kind of planning, from preparing a shopping list to composing a document setting out a corporate strategy. All I can offer is some help in understanding and applying these fundamental processes.

Given the importance of these four activities, it is odd that probably the last time you heard them discussed, if ever, was at primary school. **That's a pity because, as I hope to show, skill in performing grouping, ordering, linking and structuring in a determined and disciplined manner will help anyone to improve their written work, whether writing a letter to a friend, composing a business letter, constructing a marketing plan or publishing a Utopian masterpiece.**

As further help in document preparation, the later sections of this book:
- summarise some of the basic rules of good writing
- help the reader to identify and avoid some of the more common mistakes in written work
- explore some of the more interesting aspects of language

in the hope that, in some small way, it will increase the reader's sensitivity, finesse and pleasure in reading and writing.

DocuPraxis®

While this book is intended to stand on its own, the author has created a computer program designed to help those who wish to follow the approach set out in this book in preparing any kind of document.

This program is **DocuPraxis®**.

The DocuPraxis® program is a sophisticated outliner which provides the user with a range of **document construction** and **PIM** (personal information management) applications:

DOCUMENT CONSTRUCTION: The primary purpose of the DocuPraxis® program is to assist the user in constructing any type of document:
- books (fiction and non-fiction)
- essays (academic or journalistic)
- letters
- manuals
- reports
- research papers

enabling the user to structure, reorder and refine documents, secure in the knowledge that the DocuPraxis® program is holding the document together throughout.

PIM APPLICATIONS: The DocuPraxis® program also fulfils the requirements for:
- address books
- to do lists
- diaries
- purchase records
- decision tree / 'what if?' projects

providing editable and, in some cases, dynamic, forms.

TEMPLATES: To help the user and to give examples of how to use the program, DocuPraxis® provides templates for many different types of document, from simple letters:
- general business letter
- personal letter
- job application letter
- complaint letter
- praise letter

to more complex proposals and reports:
- concept proposal
- curriculum vitae
- product marketing plan

There is also a selection of **checklists** of subjects to be covered or points to be made in common types of situation:
- holiday luggage checklist
- house buying checklist
- flat/house renting checklist

And you can also use the program simply as a database for any project.

The uses of the **DocuPraxis® program** are limitless.

How to purchase the DocuPraxis® program

The current version of the **DocuPraxis** program can be downloaded from the **DocuPraxis®** website; www.docupraxis.com.

The **DocuPraxis® program** can also be downloaded from the Panarc International website at www.panarc.com.

2 Basic Principles

Before we start to discuss techniques, it is worth explicitly stating three basic principles. In every instance, in composing any type of written document, the aim should be **clarity, simplicity and brevity.**

So far, most people would agree but before moving on, we had better make clear exactly what we mean. Clarity and simplicity require precision. And precision means using words correctly and structuring sentences so that they obey the rules of grammar. Unfortunately, although most people agree that clarity and simplicity are excellent goals, it is not so easy to develop an appreciation of the precise use of words or the value of a firm grasp of grammar. You have only to read the mass of material sent to us by government and commercial companies to find abundant examples of ambiguity, vagueness and, on occasions, complete unintelligibility

When we advocate careful structuring of even simple documents, when we recommend certain forms of sentence construction and criticise others, when we list common grammatical errors, censure verbiage and condemn tautological expressions, we are basing our judgement on these three primary requirements - clarity, simplicity and brevity.

Why do we propose brevity in report-writing as one of the three basic principles? Because it means we are using verbal communication as efficiently as possible. Brevity does not mean that all words and sentences should be short; it does not preclude sophisticated style, subtle nuances or even rhetorical devices. But it does demand that you always write as simply and clearly as possible; that you don't use long words just for the sake of it; that you should never disguise muddled thinking under a cloak of confusing verbiage.

The three principles together (clarity, simplicity and brevity) demand that what you write should mean what you want it to mean; **and, at least as important, that it could not possibly mean anything other than what you want it to mean.**

2.1 Clarity

We aim for clarity because we wish to communicate - and the more clearly we express ourselves, the more likely it is that we will communicate effectively. Always read through what you have written and ask yourself the following questions:

- Is there a way to rearrange each sentence to make my meaning clearer?
- Is there any way the reader could misinterpret or misunderstand what I have written?
- Have I used any jargon unnecessarily? In particular, have I used any terms which my target audience is unlikely to understand? Technical terms have their place, in that they allow authors to express themselves succinctly, but that is true only if the audience knows the meaning of such technical terms.

2.2 Simplicity

As a general principle, you should aim to express your meaning as simply as possible. It is always counter-productive to use longer words and more complex sentences than are necessary. Such practices will not impress your reader; rather they will suggest that you are desperately trying to appear more intelligent than you are (assuming that is possible) and that you are covering up with verbiage a lack of clarity in your thought processes (heaven forbid!).

Ask the following questions:
- Could I say exactly the same thing in fewer words?
- Could I use shorter, simpler words to replace longer words without losing meaning?
- Could I simplify my sentence structure and still convey the same meaning?

Of course, some thoughts are more complex than others so, even when such thoughts have been expressed as simply as possible, they may still be difficult to grasp. 'As simply as possible' does not always mean simple. Nevertheless, the principle is sound and most ideas, however complex, can be broken down into fairly simple, comprehensible elements.

2.3 Brevity

It follows from the principles of clarity and simplicity that we should aim for brevity - in the sense that the document should be no longer than is necessary to convey the meaning clearly and simply. Whatever the motivation behind it, verbosity generally impedes understanding and, for that reason alone, brevity is a worthy objective.

There is another reason to aim for brevity, a reason with which anyone who presents to an audience will probably be familiar. We live in a multi-media world where most people have a strictly limited attention span. Unless the audience is interested and entertained, eyes glaze over very quickly.

At home, we are all offered a splendid choice of information, education and entertainment but, if we become bored, even if the presenter has a brain the size of the planet and is expressing an insight for which Einstein would have given his eye teeth, at the press of a button, we can and will dismiss him from our presence.

So be warned and be brief.

2.4 Quality Control

If we have made sure our document is clear, simple and brief, as defined above, we should find that we have conveyed our meaning as well as we can - but it is worth checking once again:

- Could I say exactly the same thing in fewer words?
- Could I use shorter, simpler words to replace longer words without losing meaning?
- Is there a way to rearrange the sentence to make my meaning clearer?
- Is there any way the reader could misinterpret or misunderstand what I have written?

Finally, we should ask:

- Am I sure I know the precise meaning of the words I have used and that I have used them correctly? (See section on **Tricky Words**.)
- Within what I have written, have I used *all* the available resources (grouping, ordering, linking, structuring, punctuation, etc.) to convey my meaning?

Precisely what is meant by this last question will become clear in subsequent sections of this handbook.

PROOF-READING: Always read through what you have written. I have yet to write a document, whether a business report, a novel or a poem, that I cannot improve on a second and third reading.

If possible, get someone else to read through what you have written. You may be surprised how often a fresh pair of eyes can spot the odd solecism or error.

Creativity without skills and discipline is like archery without a bow and an arrow.

Without skills and discipline, you will not hit the target.

3 Grouping

Grouping is a fundamental skill which every writer of documents needs to exercise (in both senses). It enables the individual to comprehend and manage large quantities of information which, at first sight, might seem formless or chaotic. It provides the basis for developing structures which is the subject of a later section and central to the approach we recommend.

For many people in business the ability to group data is second nature. Nevertheless, it is still worth setting out some basic rules and giving some examples. For those who already enjoy and employ this skill routinely, this section may serve only to elicit the occasional, muttered "of course", or "that's obvious". For others, it may furnish some useful guidelines on how to grasp, order and, indeed, add meaning to those floods of information about which everyone in business is forever complaining.

We should perhaps emphasise **the adding of meaning**. In any set of data, there is of course meaning in each of the units that make up the set, but grouping allows you to add meaning simply by the act of grouping. Grouping tells the reader the criterion the writer is applying in order to construct the group. That criterion is itself an additional unit of meaning.

3.1 Compare and Contrast

How do we constitute groups? We compare and contrast. We look for characteristics or features which some items have in common and which are not shared by other items.

In its simplest application, the compare and contrast technique enables us to divide things into groups on the basis of physical characteristics: e.g. size, weight, shape.

At a more sophisticated level, we can compare and contrast ideas and arguments, identifying features of each so that we can see similarities and differences, and the links within each group.

3.2 Criteria for Grouping

When constructing a group or groups from any set of data, you must first decide the criterion for grouping.

Of course the quality or characteristic that is to form the basis for the grouping must inhere in the members of the group - but which of the various qualities or characteristics the 'grouper' chooses for any particular grouping process is very much a 'grouper' decision.

3.2.1 Grouping words and objects

Let us take a really simple example:

animals, apples, bicycle, boats, car, copper, cows, earth, farmer, fruit, gardener, horse, iron, miner, minerals, sheep, tomatoes

There are many different ways of creating groups from the list. In some cases, the classification system is comprehensive (i.e. all items on the list fall into one of the categories created by the chosen grouping criterion); in other cases, the classification system is eclectic (i.e. it selects those items which fall into the category or categories created by the chosen criterion, and ignores the rest - or classifies them simply as outside the available categories).

In some cases, the criterion is coincidental (e.g. whether the words are monosyllabic or polysyllabic); in other cases, it may be significant (in the sense that the categories are based on the *meaning* of the words). In the latter case, the grouping criterion is an indicator of the grouper's thinking or intention.

The essential point is this - with any set of data, there will be many ways of grouping the elements. This is true of sets of words, factual data and ideas. The skilled report writer needs to be able to explore different ways of grouping elements in the set to find the best way of presenting his case.

Here are some examples of the various types of grouping, using the set of data above:

Grouping by Word

Here we are grouping the items based on the characteristics of the words themselves:

Words starting with a vowel	Words starting with a consonant
animals, apples, earth, iron	bicycle, boats, car, copper, cows, farmer, fruit, gardener, horse, miner, minerals, sheep, tomatoes

Singular words	Plural words
bicycle, car, copper, earth, farmer, fruit, gardener, horse, iron, miner, sheep (singular)	animals, apples, boats, cows, minerals, sheep, tomatoes, sheep (plural)

One syllable	Two syllables	Three syllables
boats, car, cows, earth, fruit, horse, sheep	apples, copper, farmer, iron, miner	animals, bicycle, gardener, minerals, tomatoes

Origin				
French	Greek	Latin	Old English	Spanish
garden, miner, mineral	bicycle	animal, car, copper, farmer, fruit	apple, boat, cow, earth, horse, iron, sheep	tomatoes

Grouping by Sense

Here are some ways of grouping the words on the basis of what they mean (i.e. the characteristics of the things which they denote).

Animate	Inanimate
animals, apples, cows, farmer, fruit, gardener, horse, miner, sheep, tomatoes	bicycle, boat, car, copper, earth, iron, minerals

Human	Animal	Fruit	Mineral	Manufactured
farmer, gardener, miner	animals, cows, horse, sheep	apples, fruit	copper, earth, iron, minerals	bicycle, boats, car

Group words	Non-group words
animals, fruit, minerals	apples, bicycle, boats, car, copper, cows, earth, farmer, gardener, horse, iron, miner, sheep, tomatoes

Note that what may be a non-group word on one grouping criterion can be a group word when grouping is based on a different criterion: e.g. in another hierarchy, 'apple' could be the group word for all the different varieties of 'apple'. So, while the rules of any particular grouping exercise should be rigidly observed, the role played by each word can vary from one exercise to another.

Or we may go through the list and simply pick out those that meet a single criterion, ignoring the rest or putting them into an "Other" category.

Means of transport	bicycle, boats, car, horse

or

Things to eat	animals (only some), apples, cows, fruit, horse (in some places), sheep, tomatoes

One of the most important functions of grouping is to enable the grouper to hierarchise the data. In the examples above, we see examples of simple hierarchies.

Animals		
cows	horse	sheep

or

Mineral	
copper	iron

At the higher level of the hierarchy, we use a group word to indicate the common features of all members of the group, and to identify them.

The point we are making is this. Given a set of data, there are many different ways of grouping and hierarchising. Each criterion for grouping and each imposition of a hierarchical level adds meaning to the data because it indicates the thinking of the 'grouper' (the author). **Use every opportunity to add meaning to data.**

All this sounds obvious but it is often given a low priority by inexperienced authors of business reports and other types of document. The ability to form logical groups is crucial if the report writer hopes to organise his material and present his case coherently.

Author's footnote
To illustrate the importance of re-reading what we have written and looking for ways to make sure the logic, balance and flow of the sentence are as clear and precise as possible, we show the text of the previous paragraph as it was written **before** a second critical reading:

> All this sounds simple and obvious but the ability to form logical groups that enable the report writer to organise his material and present his case coherently is crucial. Yet it is often given a low priority by inexperienced authors of business reports and other types of document.

The price of clarity is eternal vigilance.

3.2.2 Grouping ideas
We can apply exactly the same technique with arguments. Let's look at the issue of capital punishment and list some of the arguments presented in any debate of the subject.

1. Capital punishment, after due legal process, is a legitimate punishment.
2. Capital punishment degrades those who administer it.
3. Capital punishment denies the possibility of redemption.
4. Capital punishment gives closure to the relatives of the victim.
5. Capital punishment is a cruel and inhumane punishment.
6. Capital punishment is an effective deterrent.
7. Capital punishment is barbaric.
8. Capital punishment is cheaper for the state/taxpayer than keeping murderers in prison.
9. Capital punishment is justified on the 'eye for an eye' principle.
10. Capital punishment is state murder.
11. Capital punishment is the only proportionate punishment for murder.
12. Capital punishment is too kind to the murderer.
13. Capital punishment violates and individual's human rights.

14. Capital punishment precludes the possibility of repeat offending.
15. Hundreds of innocent lives have been lost when released murderers re-offend.
16. Some murderers are so evil they defile the world and should be exterminated.
17. The murder rate increases in societies where capital punishment has been abolished.
18. The murder rate is unaffected by the abolition of capital punishment.
19. There are proven cases of the execution of innocent individuals.
20. There is always the risk that you execute an innocent person.
21. "'Vengeance is mine', saith the Lord."

The list is not ordered, or rather it is in alphabetical order which is meaningless in this case because it all depends on how each sentence has been formulated. (We could move the 21st argument to the top slot, simply by expressing it thus: As the bible says, "'Vengeance is mine', saith the Lord'")

So how can we bring order out of chaos? There are many ways but first we must decide on our aim.

If we wish to analyse the issue as a whole, we would probably begin by dividing the list into arguments for and arguments against:

Arguments for Capital Punishment
1. Capital punishment, after due legal process, is a legitimate punishment.
2. Capital punishment gives closure to the relatives of the victim.
3. Capital punishment is an effective deterrent.
4. Capital punishment is cheaper for the state/taxpayer than keeping murderers in prison.
5. Capital punishment is justified on the 'eye for an eye' principle.
6. Capital punishment is the only proportionate punishment for murder.
7. Capital punishment precludes the possibility of repeat offending.
8. Hundreds of innocent lives have been lost when released murderers re-offend.
9. Some murderers are so evil they defile the world and should be exterminated.
10. The murder rate increases in societies where capital punishment has been abolished.

Arguments against Capital Punishment
1. Capital punishment degrades those who administer it.
2. Capital punishment denies the possibility of redemption.
3. Capital punishment is a cruel and inhumane punishment.
4. Capital punishment is barbaric.
5. Capital punishment is state murder.
6. Capital punishment is too kind to the murderer.
7. Capital punishment violates and individual's human rights.
8. The murder rate is unaffected by the abolition of capital punishment.
9. There are proven cases of the execution of innocent individuals.
10. There is always the risk that you execute an innocent person.
11. "'Vengeance is mine', saith the Lord."

On the other hand, we might wish to distinguish between those arguments based on **evidence** and those based on other **non-evidential drivers** (e.g. emotion, religion):

Evidence-based Arguments
1. Capital punishment degrades those who administer it.
2. Capital punishment gives closure to the relatives of the victim.
3. Capital punishment is an effective deterrent.
4. Capital punishment is cheaper for the state/taxpayer than keeping murderers in prison.
5. Hundreds of innocent lives have been lost when released murderers re-offend.
6. The murder rate increases in societies where capital punishment has been abolished.
7. The murder rate is unaffected by the abolition of capital punishment.
8. There are proven cases of the execution of innocent individuals.
9. There is always the risk that you execute an innocent person.

We are assuming that it would be possible to gather evidence on whether those who administer capital punishment are degraded and that we could find evidence of the extent to which capital punishment gives the relatives of victims closure.

Non-evidence based Arguments
1. Capital punishment, after due legal process, is a legitimate punishment.
2. Capital punishment denies the possibility of redemption.
3. Capital punishment is a cruel and inhumane punishment.
4. Capital punishment is barbaric.
5. Capital punishment is justified on the 'eye for an eye' principle.
6. Capital punishment is state murder.
7. Capital punishment is the only proportionate punishment for murder.
8. Capital punishment is too kind to the murderer.
9. Capital punishment violates an individual's human rights.
10. Capital punishment precludes the possibility of repeat offending.
11. Some murderers are so evil they defile the world and should be exterminated.
12. "'Vengeance is mine', saith the Lord."

Or again, we might wish to distinguish between those arguments which are **incontrovertibly true** and those that are **open to debate**:

Arguments incontrovertibly true
1. Capital punishment, after due legal process, is a legitimate punishment.
2. Capital punishment denies the possibility of redemption.
3. Capital punishment is cheaper for the state/taxpayer than keeping murderers in prison.
4. Capital punishment violates an individual's human rights.
5. Capital punishment precludes the possibility of repeat offending.
6. Hundreds of innocent lives have been lost when released murderers re-offend.

7. There are proven cases of the execution of innocent individuals.
8. There is always the risk that you execute an innocent person.

Argument 1 is true in its own terms because it is circular. Capital punishment must be legitimate (i.e. legal) if it is endorsed by due legal process.

Argument 4 is true if we accept Amnesty International's interpretation of the UN's definition of human rights (which recognises each person's right to life and categorically states that "No one shall be subjected to torture or to cruel, inhuman or degrading treatment or punishment").

Arguments open to debate
1. Capital punishment degrades those who administer it.
2. Capital punishment gives closure to the relatives of the victim.
3. Capital punishment is a cruel and inhumane punishment.
4. Capital punishment is an effective deterrent.
5. Capital punishment is barbaric.
6. Capital punishment is justified on the 'eye for an eye' principle.
7. Capital punishment is state murder.
8. Capital punishment is the only proportionate punishment for murder.
9. Capital punishment is too kind to the murderer.
10. Some murderers are so evil they defile the world and should be exterminated.
11. The murder rate increases in societies where capital punishment has been abolished.
12. The murder rate is unaffected by the abolition of capital punishment.
13. "'Vengeance is mine', saith the Lord."

Or yet again, we might want to be more precise in our analysis of all the different drivers that lie behind the various arguments. Now we will find arguments falling in to more than one category:

Rational arguments
1. Capital punishment, after due legal process, is a legitimate punishment.
2. Capital punishment denies the possibility of redemption.
3. Capital punishment is an effective deterrent.
4. Capital punishment is cheaper for the state/taxpayer than keeping murderers in prison.
5. Capital punishment precludes the possibility of repeat offending.
6. Hundreds of innocent lives have been lost when released murderers re-offend.
7. There is always the risk that you execute an innocent person.

Arguments from authority
1. Capital punishment, after due legal process, is a legitimate punishment.
2. Capital punishment is a cruel and inhumane punishment.
3. Capital punishment is justified on the 'eye for an eye' principle.
4. "'Vengeance is mine', saith the Lord."

Emotional arguments
1. Capital punishment degrades those who administer it.
2. Capital punishment gives closure to the relatives of the victim.
3. Capital punishment is a cruel and inhumane punishment.
4. Capital punishment is barbaric.
5. Capital punishment is state murder.
6. Capital punishment is the only proportionate punishment for murder.
7. Capital punishment is too kind to the murderer.
8. Some murderers are so evil they defile the world and should be exterminated.

Moral arguments
1. Capital punishment degrades those who administer it.
2. Capital punishment denies the possibility of redemption.
3. Capital punishment gives closure to the relatives of the victim.
4. Capital punishment is a cruel and inhumane punishment.
5. Capital punishment is barbaric.
6. Capital punishment is justified on the 'eye for an eye' principle.
7. Capital punishment is state murder.
8. Capital punishment violates an individual's human rights.
9. The murder rate increases in societies where capital punishment has been abolished.
10. There are proven cases of the execution of innocent individuals.
11. There is always the risk that you execute an innocent person.

Practical/economic arguments
1. Capital punishment is an effective deterrent.
2. Capital punishment is cheaper for the state/taxpayer than keeping murderers in prison.
3. Capital punishment precludes the possibility of repeat offending.
4. Hundreds of innocent lives have been lost when released murderers re-offend.
5. The murder rate increases in societies where capital punishment has been abolished.
6. The murder rate is unaffected by the abolition of capital punishment.

Evidence-based arguments
1. Capital punishment degrades those who administer it.
2. Capital punishment gives closure to the relatives of the victim.
3. Capital punishment is an effective deterrent.
4. Capital punishment is cheaper for the state/taxpayer than keeping murderers in prison.
5. Hundreds of innocent lives have been lost when released murderers re-offend.
6. The murder rate increases in societies where capital punishment has been abolished.
7. The murder rate is unaffected by the abolition of capital punishment.
8. The murder rate increases in societies where capital punishment has been

abolished.
9. The murder rate increases in societies where capital punishment has been abolished.
10. There are proven cases of the execution of innocent individuals.
11. There is always the risk that you execute an innocent person.

Arguments 7 and 8 contradict each other but both are evidence-based: i.e. they must be justified on the basis of evidence.

ooo

So here we have four ways in which our 21 propositions can be grouped. In each case, the criteria for and the objective of the grouping are different. In the first example, we might simply wish to assess the number and validity of arguments for and against capital punishment. In the second example, we might well wish to emphasise the superiority of the arguments based on evidence compared with arguments based on emotion or other drivers. In the third case, we might be attempting to expose the extent to which emotional/irrational arguments confuse the issue. In the fourth case, we might be trying to identify the different constituencies that participate in the argument with a view to presenting arguments to each of the groups that would be most likely to persuade them to our point of view.

In other words, our purpose is an important factor in determining how we group. Whether we realise it or not, the act of grouping adds meaning to the data and, if we know what we are doing when we group, we can make sure it is ***our meaning*** which will be added.

Given that most readers will agree with the nature and function of grouping as here defined, we have to ask why the technique is so often poorly applied in the preparation of business documents. Public relations departments seem particularly inept in analysing issues in this way for which, I suppose, we should all be grateful. After all, if they applied and exploited the technique fully, they would be much better able to target arguments at different audiences in such a way as to influence opinion far more effectively.

Footnote: It is a good exercise to pick on one or two contentious issues: e.g.
- fox hunting
- the welfare state

and draw up your own ordered lists of arguments according to different criteria: e.g.
- evidence-based / morality-based
- for and against
- rational versus emotional.

3.3 The Grouping Principle

So what has all this got to do with preparing business documents?

In preparing any document, we have to determine the main sections of the document and then to fit into those sections all the sub-sections. Although this is generally the most effective way of preparing a document and certainly the best way of ensuring that the final document is comprehensive and coherent, it is often not what happens.

In deciding on the number and nature of the main sections, it is necessary to group the sub-sections so that they fit. In formal terms, we might end up with a structure such as this:

DOCUMENT					
Section 1		Section 2		Section 3	
Subsection 1.1	Subsection 1.2	Subsection 2.1	Subsection 2.2	Subsection 3.1	Subsection 3.2

Here we have six Subsections (the basic units in this set of data) and have divided them into three groups of two (the Sections), checking that each pair of Subsections sits comfortably within its own Section. The structure, a simple hierarchy, accommodates all the data (the Subsections), is balanced and is neatly symmetrical. Balance and symmetry are two desirable attributes for any hierarchy (see 'A couple of hierarchical principles' in the section on Structure).

Grouping and hierarchising do not end here. Beneath each Subsection, we can apply the same principles to the smallest structural units of a document - the paragraphs. At each level, we will be looking for balance; i.e. some degree of equivalence amongst all the units at the same level of the structure and, in many cases, some degree of symmetry.

Consciously or unconsciously, much human thinking takes this form. To grasp complex data, we need to group and hierarchise.

Whatever the subject of a document, you can organise and manage the data in this way; identify all the units of information, and then group them.

This may sound a bit theoretical and perhaps even unnecessarily laborious - but what is meant and why it is important will become clearer in the section on Structure.

4 Ordering

Whenever you wish to list a group of similar items, you should consider the order in which you intend to present them.

We may use the order to add meaning or we may wish to present the items in a completely neutral way. The intelligent reader will look for significance in the order of the items. If you intend the order to be neutral, give a clear indication of your intention.

While imposing order on lists may seem a relatively unimportant part of communicating, it should not be underestimated. In managing sentences, paragraphs and sections or chapters, ordering is crucially important (see section Refresher Course on Some Basics). Lists are simply the lowest level at which order should be imposed but that is a good reason to ensure that, at this simplest and most obvious level, you apply the ordering principle.

"Cheese, steak, apple pie and soup - but not necessarily in that order."

4.1 Alphabetical

Alphabetical ordering is the standard way of presenting items in a neutral order (i.e. in a way that adds no meaning to the list).

If you are sending a memo to a list of people, you can use alphabetical ordering in order to say: "There is no significance in the order in which the names on this list appear".

If you do not present the names in alphabetical order, the reader may assume you have placed the names in order of importance – or conclude you are sloppy in your thinking and have not bothered to consider the question of order at all.

4.2 Causal

Where there is a causal relationship between the items in the list, it makes sense to present them in order of cause and effect. If, for example, you are writing a report on economic conditions and you wish to discuss:

- inflation
- interest rates
- labour disputes
- quantitative easing
- recession

and you believe there are causal relationship between these items:

e.g. quantitative easing > inflation > interest rate increases > labour disputes > recession

you should deal with them, as far as possible, in the order which allows you to trace these causal relationships and thus present your case most cogently.

Order can, of itself, *imply* causation and thus can affect meaning. By placing the economic factors listed above in the order shown, we may well imply to the reader that there is a causal relationship, even if we lack strong supporting evidence.

For any reader who thinks we are exaggerating the importance of ordering, consider this. When two warring countries are involved in a series of incidents, the order in which the incidents are reported in newscasts can determine which act is perceived as provocative and which as retaliatory. As a result, one country will be thought of as the aggressor and the other as simply responding to aggression. In such instances, order can be a matter of life or death, determining governmental policy and, possibly, prompting military intervention.

4.3 Chronological
Chronological order can be neutral or significant.

If we were drawing up a comprehensive list of conflicts around the world since the end of the Second World War, we might well decide to present them in chronological order. This would obviously tell us the order in which these conflicts occurred - but nothing else. The chronological order might be used as a neutral way of presenting such conflicts: e.g.

Start	Location	Type	Detail	Continent	Fatalities
1948	Burma	Internal		Asia	210,000
1953	Nigeria	Religious	Shariah	Africa	15,000
1978	Afghanistan	Political		Asia	1,750,000
1991	Somali	Civil War		Africa	500,000
1992	Yemen	Religious	Al Qaeda insurgency	Middle East	3,700
2004	N-W Pakistan	Political		Asia	48,000
2006	Mexico	Criminal	drug war	N. America	86,400
2009	Sudan	Political	nomadic conflicts	Africa	7,400
2011	Syria	Political	also sectarian/religious	Middle East	80,000
2011	Sudan	Internal		Africa	2,400
2011	Iraq	Insurgency	after allied withdrawal	Middle East	6,100
2012	Mali	Political		Africa	3,500

http://en.wikipedia.org/wiki/War_today

In this case, the chronological order is neutral and would be taken as such. It shows the sequence of conflicts but in this example there is no implication that one conflict caused a subsequent conflict. (Of course, we could change the order of these conflicts to bring out certain aspects of these conflicts. See Ranking below).

Events can also be ordered chronologically when describing a series of connected events. In such cases chronological ordering can be easily used to accommodate, if not to imply, a causal relationship between the events. Let's take the example of the Suez crisis:

Year	Date	Event
1948		State of Israel established despite Palestinian and general Arab opposition. The first Arab Israeli war takes place. Israel effectively defeats the Arab forces but the conflict is unresolved.
1954		President Nasser of Egypt, a nationalist, adopts a neutralist policy during the Cold War. Egypt announces plans to sell cotton to China and negotiates with Czechoslovakia for arms in exchange for cotton.
1956	19 Jul	USA unhappy with Nasser's neutralist policies and his hostility to Israel. USA withdraws funding for Egypt's Aswan Dam.
	26 Jul	Nasser announces he intends to nationalise the Suez Canal.
	28 Jul	Britain freezes Egyptian assets.
	29 Oct	Israel invades Sinai Peninsula.
	5 Nov	British and French airborne forces invade Egypt.
	7 Nov	UN General Assembly calls on Britain, France and Israel to withdraw from Egyptian territory.
	29 Nov	Pressure from UN compels Britain and France to withdraw.
	24 Dec	British and French troops leave Egypt.

This chronology illustrates three points:
1. As noted elsewhere, the reader's understanding of the chronology will be crucially affected by which events are included in the chronology and with which event we begin. (Many accounts of the Suez crisis begin with Nasser's decision to nationalise the Suez Canal.)
2. Because this is a sequence of connected events, the reader is predisposed to see one event as the effect of a preceding cause and the cause of a succeeding effect.
3. This type of chronology cannot help but be seen as a narrative. It has a beginning, a middle and an end. It invites us to make sense of the series of events so that by the end, we feel we have 'the whole story'.

While most reports do not deal with events as momentous as those that made up the Suez Crisis, the features of chronological ordering are all available to the report writer. The selection and ordering of events adds meaning to the series, and can be used to illustrate or imply causal relations between the events.

4.4 General to Particular

Ordering on the basis of 'from the general to the particular' is a useful and very common way of conducting the reader through a complex set of data by leading with the top level and working progressively down through lower levels of the data, one section and one level at a time. It is the favoured form for factual books and is an ingredient in almost all business reports.

For example, a guide book on a continent might begin with a general description of the land mass which makes up the continent; then list the countries in the continent; and then, within each country, list the main cities and towns.

This form of ordering is very useful when you need a readily understood means of organising and presenting complex data. When used in conjunction with other forms of neutral ordering (i.e. alphabetical), this is a form of ordering which intentionally foregoes the opportunities to 'add meaning' which ordering causally, chronologically or by rank provides.

4.5 Ranking

There are two categories of ranking, both of which add meaning to data and focus the reader's attention on a particular aspect of a set of data:
- qualitative (eminence, importance, qualifications, seniority, etc.)
- quantitative (amount, size, speed, volume, etc.)

The ways of ranking are almost limitless. For example, we might rank a company's product range by:
- length of time on the market
- price
- profitability (gross profit % and actual annual gross profit)
- quality control scores
- returns
- sales

Given such a set of data, we can produce a number of tables which focus our attention on different aspects of the product range.

Years on the Market Ranking

Product	Years on market	Price £	Gross Profit %	Annual Gross Profit £000	QC Scores out of 10	Returns %	Sales £ 000
A	10	3	40	200	9	0.1	500
B	8	2	35	210	6	0.3	600
C	6	6	40	180	8	0.1	450
D	4	4	30	90	9	0.2	300
E	1	9	50	100	7	0.2	200

Gross Profit % Ranking

Product	Years on market	Price £	Gross Profit %	Annual Gross Profit £000	QC Scores out of 10	Returns %	Sales £ 000
E	1	9	50	100	7	0.2	200
A	10	3	40	200	9	0.1	500
C	6	6	40	180	8	0.1	450
B	8	2	35	210	6	0.3	600
D	4	4	30	90	9	0.2	300

Annual Gross Profit Ranking

Product	Years on market	Price £	Gross Profit %	Annual Gross Profit £000	QC Scores out of 10	Returns %	Sales £ 000
B	8	2	35	210	6	0.3	600
A	10	3	40	200	9	0.1	500
C	6	6	40	180	8	0.1	450
E	1	9	50	100	7	0.2	200
D	4	4	30	90	9	0.2	300

QC Scores Ranking

Product	Years on market	Price £	Gross Profit %	Annual Gross Profit £000	QC Scores out of 10	Returns %	Sales £ 000
A	10	3	40	200	9	0.1	500
D	4	4	30	90	9	0.2	300
C	6	6	40	180	8	0.1	450
E	1	9	50	100	7	0.2	200
B	8	2	35	210	6	0.3	600

Returns % Ranking

Product	Years on market	Price £	Gross Profit %	Annual Gross Profit £000	QC Scores out of 10	Returns %	Sales £ 000
B	8	2	35	210	6	0.3	600
D	4	4	30	90	9	0.2	300
E	1	9	50	100	7	0.2	200
A	10	3	40	200	9	0.1	500
C	6	6	40	180	8	0.1	450

Sales £000 Ranking

Product	Years on market	Price £	Gross Profit %	Annual Gross Profit £000	QC Scores out of 10	Returns %	Sales £ 000
B	8	2	35	210	6	0.3	600
A	10	3	40	200	9	0.1	500
C	6	6	40	180	8	0.1	450
D	4	4	30	90	9	0.2	300
E	1	9	50	100	7	0.2	200

In each case, the ranking criterion, changing the order of the products in the first column, focuses our attention on a particular aspect of the product range. **The order *adds meaning* to the table.**

□□□

Although this section is about ranking, we began with a chronological arrangement (Years on the Market). It seems only fair to take the example we gave in the Chronological section and give it the 'ranking' treatment.

In the section on chronological ordering, we listed major conflicts since 1948. We showed them in chronological order, as a means of presenting the information in a 'neutral' way.

We could, however, re-order the list, ranking the conflicts by various features, to focus attention on various aspects of the set of data.

If we wanted to make the point that Afghanistan had been by far the costliest war in terms of human lives lost we would rearrange the order, ranking the conflicts in order of fatalities:

Start	Location	Type	Detail	Continent	Fatalities
1978	Afghanistan	Political		Asia	1,750,000
1991	Somali	Civil War		Africa	500,000
1948	Burma	Internal		Asia	210,000
2006	Mexico	Criminal	drug war	N. America	86,400
2011	Syria	Political	also sectarian/religious	Middle East	80,000
2004	N-W Pakistan	Political		Asia	48,000
1953	Nigeria	Religious	Shariah	Africa	15,000
2009	Sudan	Political	nomadic conflicts	Africa	7,400
2011	Iraq	Insurgency	after allied withdrawal	Middle East	6,100
1992	Yemen	Religious	Al Qaeda insurgency	Middle East	3,700
2012	Mali	Political		Africa	3,500
2011	Sudan	Internal		Africa	2,400

If we wanted to draw attention to the regional nature of conflicts, we might use alphabetical order applied to the Continent column:

Start	Location	Type	Detail	Continent	Fatalities
1991	Somali	Civil War		Africa	500,000
1953	Nigeria	Religious	Shariah	Africa	15,000
2009	Sudan	Political	nomadic conflicts	Africa	7,400
2012	Mali	Political		Africa	3,500
2011	Sudan	Internal		Africa	2,400
1978	Afghanistan	Political		Asia	1,750,000
1948	Burma	Internal		Asia	210,000
2004	N-W Pakistan	Political		Asia	48,000
2011	Syria	Political	also sectarian/religious	Middle East	80,000
2011	Iraq	Insurgency	after allied withdrawal	Middle East	6,100
1992	Yemen	Religious	Al Qaeda insurgency	Middle East	3,700
2006	Mexico	Criminal	drug war	N. America	86,400

Or if we wanted to put the emphasis on the causes of such conflicts, we might use alphabetical order but apply it to the type of conflict:

Start	Location	Type	Detail	Continent	Fatalities
1991	Somali	Civil War		Africa	500,000
2006	Mexico	Criminal	drug war	N. America	86,400
2011	Iraq	Insurgency	after allied withdrawal	Middle East	6,100
1948	Burma	Internal		Asia	210,000
2011	Sudan	Internal		Africa	2,400
2012	Mali	Political		Africa	3,500
1978	Afghanistan	Political		Asia	1,750,000
2004	N-W Pakistan	Political		Asia	48,000

Start	Location	Type	Detail	Continent	Fatalities
2009	Sudan	Political	nomadic conflicts	Africa	7,400
2011	Syria	Political	also sectarian/religious	Middle East	80,000
1953	Nigeria	Religious	Shariah	Africa	15,000
1992	Yemen	Religious	Al Qaeda insurgency	Middle East	3,700

All very straightforward. In all three tables, we are using order to focus the reader's attention on a particular aspect of the set of data that we wish to emphasise.

5 Linking

Perhaps the most crucial process in the building of a report structure is determining the appropriate links - links between one chapter and the next; one section and the next, between one paragraph and the next; between one sentence and the next.

In the simplest cases, linking may be essentially a question of ordering. But in most documents, the author has a more difficult task. There may be a logic to the case he is presenting. There may be causal links. The author may have to qualify statements by expressing conditions. There may be links determined by temporal sequence. Statements may have to be qualified by exceptions. There may be a need for links designed to contrast opposites.

It is easy, when writing a business report, to forget to express the links between propositions. While these links may be obvious to the author, they may well be less clear to the reader. It is, in any case, a good discipline to consider the nature of the links in any document at every level to ensure we are packing in as much meaning as possible, as economically as possible.

As skill and confidence increase, writers will often omit the linking words, secure in the knowledge that the way in which they have ordered and presented their material makes explicit links redundant. They know that their audience has embarked with them on the train of their thought and will remain on track.

Those with less expertise and/or confidence should at least check to see whether there is a link, expressed or not, to connect each part of the document to what went before and what follows.

We will now review each of these links in their simplest forms, giving examples of linking words and phrases; proposing symbols to represent each type of link; and illustrating each link with examples.

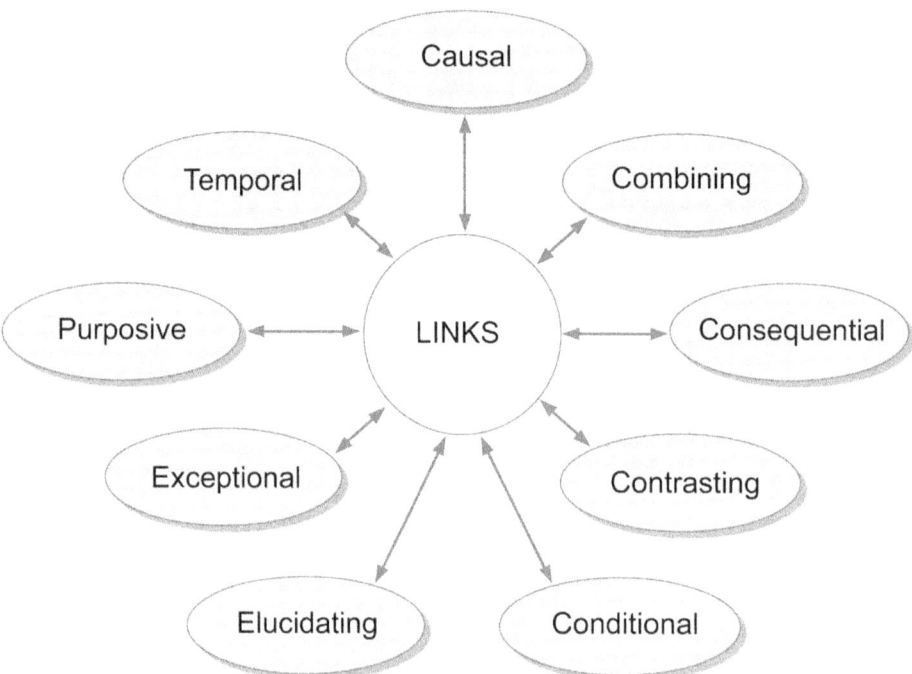

5.1 Causal

Causal links show that one thing is the result of another.

Key Words/Phrases
- as a result of
- because
- due to
- for this reason
- on account of

Symbol: ▽
e.g.
- "He was promoted as a result of his dedication to the company's interests."
- "He resigned from his post because he feared failure."
- "Because the product was well-designed, it enjoyed considerable success."
- "His dismissal was due to his bungling incompetence."
- "For this reason alone, you have forfeited your right to any respect."
- "He withdrew the product on account of the adverse publicity."

Causal links can be used at every level of a document structure. They are particularly important as an option for connecting paragraphs, where the second paragraph is used to explain what caused the events or results described in the first.

We should note in passing that causal links involve a temporal dimension, simply because a cause precedes an effect (it's that 'river of time' thing). On the other hand, temporal links do not necessarily involve a causal link, although they can be used to imply one.

5.2 Combining

Key Words/Phrases
- also
- and
- furthermore
- in addition
- moreover
- not only ... but also

Symbol: &
e.g.
- "Love and marriage go together like a horse and carriage."

In addition to illustrating the simplest form of combining, we might in passing note that this proposition implies an analogical simile (love is to marriage as horse is to carriage), a not entirely happy implication since it might suggest that love is harnessed to marriage and has to drag marriage along behind it - not, presumably, a meaning the librettist intended. (Sorry. I digress. Not good in a section on linking.)

Here are two more examples of this type of linking:
- "We have prepared the marketing plan. **In addition**, the sales force has been fully trained."
- "We guarantee to work hard. **Furthermore**, we will allocate the financial resources necessary for investment and success."

Semantic problems can arise with the use of 'and' within a poorly constructed sentence.
- "He argued against the plan which had been prepared by the committee and

won the approval of the board."

If it was the plan that had previously won the approval of the board, we would need to insert 'which had' after the 'and' for the meaning of the sentence to be clear. Otherwise, we must assume he not only argued against the plan but also won the support of the board.

Always check to make sure what you have written doesn't just mean what you want it to mean **but also that it cannot be taken to mean anything else.** (See the later section on Grammatical and Verbal Hazards.)

5.3 Consequential

Key Words/Phrases
- so that
- therefore
- consequently
- as a result

Symbol: ∆

Consequential links are about causality and purpose. Use consequential indicators when you wish to make it clear that something ensued from something else.
- "The manager seemed to be in a perpetual state of irritation. The staff were totally demoralised."

These are two statements. We cannot be sure (although it seems likely) that the writer thinks the demoralisation ensued from the manager's irritability. After all, there could be separate reasons for the manager's irritation (e.g. chronic indigestion) and for the staff's demoralisation (e.g. low pay, appalling work conditions) but, if the point the writer wished to make is that the manager's manner was causing the low morale, he should put in an explicit link indicator:
- "The manager seemed to be in a perpetual state of irritation. As a result, the staff were totally demoralised."

or, more emphatically:
- "The staff were totally demoralised by the manager's perpetual state of irritation."

In this example, the emphasis is on the consequence. We can assume it was not the manager's intention to demoralise his staff. If, however, the sentences had read:
- "The manager seemed to be in a perpetual state of goal-orientated enthusiasm. The staff were highly motivated."

we might justifiably attribute some degree of purpose to the manager's attitude as well as consequence to the outcome amongst the staff.

5.4 Contrasting

Key Words/Phrases
- but
- in contrast
- instead of
- on the other hand
- unlike
- whereas

Symbol: X

In any form of analysis, contrasting is a valuable technique. We have already noted the usefulness of 'compare and contrast' in grouping. Contrasting helps the reader to see more clearly not only distinctions between the two subjects being contrasted but also the criterion on which the contrasting is based.
- "Smith tended to appeal to his subordinates' better nature; whereas Jones had a stricter, more dictatorial approach."

Here two styles of management are being contrasted, with an implicit contrast between the views of the two managers on human nature and how to get the best results from employees.

Here are a couple more formulations of the same thought, using contrasting links.
- "Instead of adopting Jones' more dictatorial approach, Smith tended to appeal to his subordinates' better nature."
- "Smith tended to appeal to his subordinates' better nature, unlike Jones who adopted a stricter, more dictatorial approach."

5.5 Conditional

Key Words/Phrases
- if...then
- on condition that
- prerequisites
- preconditions

Symbol: /

The 'If...then' link can be temporal or consequential or, most frequently, both.
- "If winter comes, can spring be far behind?"
- "If you try hard, then you will succeed."
- "If it rains today, flowers will bloom tomorrow."
- "A prerequisite of success in marketing is careful, thorough planning."

The conditional link is related to the causal link. The difference is that, with the conditional link, the cause/effect relationship is dependent on the fulfilment of the 'if' clause:
- **Conditional:** "If you try hard, then you will succeed." (Success is not guaranteed unless you fulfill the condition.)

- **Causal:** "Because you try hard, you will succeed." (Success is certain.)

5.6 Elucidating

Key Words/Phrases
- thus
- for example
- in the case of

Symbol: <

This is one of the commonest forms of linking and often appears without a link indicator. The writer is developing his subject by expanding the content of the previous paragraph. This may take the form of explaining a point made in the previous paragraph, or it may be a development of, or an addition to, such a point.

In terms of giving a document coherence, this tends to be one of the weaker forms of linking, in the sense that it is often simply adding new information without stipulating a tighter connection (logical, temporal, etc.) between the new and the preceding material.

These two paragraphs above are connected by an elucidating link. 'In terms of giving a document coherence' refers back to the previous paragraph and introduces further thoughts about the nature of elucidating links.

5.7 Exceptional

Key Words/Phrases
- although
- despite
- except

Symbol: ∉

Some care is needed in composing propositions with exceptions. Here is an example and analysis of muddled use of the exception link.

> e.g.
> - "There was intense competition in the market in December, although four of the products in our range showed a fall in sales and only two showed an increase. Despite this, overall, sales were up by 2%."

Here the author presumably means:
- "There was intense competition in the market in December. Although four of the products in our range showed a fall in sales and only two showed an increase, sales were up by 2%."

In the first version, the author has attached the 'exception' clause to the wrong element of the proposition.

If the author is eager to put emphasis on the reason for the decline in sales of four of the company's products, the following formulation carries the meaning more clearly:

- "Because of intense competition in the market in December, four of the products in our range showed a fall in sales and only two showed an increase. Despite this, overall, sales were up by 2%."

Or if the author wishes to emphasise the achievement of the 2% increase in sales, he might write:

- "Despite the intense competition in the market in December, which drove down sales of four of the six products in our range, overall sales were up 2%."

All this might seem rather picky but it is important to be as precise as possible when deciding what you want to say and where you want to put the emphasis.. If your main intention is to explain why something happened, use a causal link (e.g. because). If your main purpose is to point out that the outcome of a situation is unexpected, use an exception indicator (e.g. despite). The facts may be the same but the point you are making about the facts is different - and that's what links are for.

5.8 Purpose

Key Words/Phrases
- in order to
- so that
- to

Symbol: ⊕

Given that many business and administrative documents are about defining and fulfilling objectives, it is not surprising that 'to' and 'in order to' are well worked.

- "We must spend more on advertising to increase sales."
- "We must reduce unemployment benefits if we are to/in order to persuade youngsters to embark on apprenticeships."

To and **in order to** can mean the same thing and, in the interest of brevity, where there is no ambiguity, to is to be preferred.

Where there is ambiguity, if you want to convey purpose, use **in order to**. In the following example, there is the possibility of ambiguity:

- "We need more evidence to prosecute Smith for alleged sexual harassment."

This could mean:

- "We need more evidence **in order to** prosecute Smith for alleged sexual harassment."

or it could mean:

- "We need more evidence **if we are to** prosecute Smith for alleged sexual harassment."

So, if we are to be clear, we need the 'in order to' and the 'if we are to'.

5.9 Temporal

Key Words/Phrases
- after
- before
- meanwhile
- then
- subsequently
- whereupon
- finally

Symbol: →

Temporal words are essentially words to establish chronological order. They allow you to say what happened 'before' or 'after' or, with 'meanwhile', what happened at the same time.

We have previously mentioned the importance of ordering. The order in which we present items in a list offers an opportunity to add meaning to the list. The order can indicate seniority, or importance, or chronology.

Ordering is just as important in sequencing thoughts in sentences and paragraphs. At the least, temporal words can tell the reader the sequence of events; more subtly they can prepare the reader to accept causal/consequential relations between thoughts and/or events. The English language allows the writer to use word order to change the meaning, or at least the emphasis, in statements involving temporal links and to introduce by implication various levels of causation.
- "After the terrorist outrage of 9/11, the United States decided to invade Afghanistan."

This formulation strongly implies that it was because of the terrorist attack that the United States decided to invade Afghanistan. It is very close in meaning to:
- "Because of the terrorist outrage of 9/11, the United States decided to invade Afghanistan."

If we turn the sentence round:
- "The United States decided to invade Afghanistan after the terrorist outrage of 9/11."

we are still justified in assuming a causal link between the terrorist attack and the invasion, but the causal link is weaker than in the first version and the chronological information (the sequence of events) is stronger.

Of course, in both, the only explicit link is temporal.

5.10 Link Analysis

So far, the examples of linking have been based on one or two sentences but as we noted earlier you can apply exactly the same linking strategy to whole paragraphs.

In analysing any factual report, it is possible to identify the links that the author has used to give the document coherence and direction. You will have noticed in the description of each link that we proposed a symbol. Here are all the symbols in list form:

LINK	SYMBOL	LINKING WORDS
Causal	∇	because
Combining	&	and
Consequential	∆	consequently, so that, therefore
Contrasting	X	but, on the other hand, in contrast
Conditional	/	if, on condition that, with the prerequisite, with the precondition, when
Elucidating	<	thus
Exceptional	∉	despite, except
Purposive	⌽	in order to, to
Temporal	→	subsequently, then, when, whereupon

We can use these symbols to represent the structure of a sentence but it is when we are dealing with paragraphs that the usefulness of identifying and marking links becomes most apparent.

Below we give an example of how to apply this form of analysis to an extended comment piece, taken from The Guardian. Here the links relate to paragraphs. Links are shown within paragraphs only where the author changes direction.

Friday January 11, 2002
The Guardian

1. Jack and Chloe are going to school. They're packing their satchels and pulling on their John Lewis uniforms. When once these children may have walked up the road to their local state primary, now they're driving to a private pre-prep. The number of children going to "independent" schools has risen in the last year, to about 7% of the total school population, despite record fee increases outstripping inflation. The government itself predicts that the private school sector will grow steadily for the next 10 years. Already, more than half a million middle class children are opting out of the state school system.

∆

2. The government response is to try to tempt them back. This week the education secretary, Estelle Morris, announced a "£100m schools for the future" scheme. One purpose of the "launch pad" schools is to encourage more professional people to put their sons' and

daughters' names on the register. Other carrots to those opting-out middle classes, still a minority, have included city academies, city technology colleges, and specialist status schools.

X

3. But the point of no return has been passed, and no amount of bribes will bring the likes of Jack and Chloe back. Even some families with distinctly modest middle class salaries now struggle to fork out fees, averaging £6,250 per annum, for their child's education.

&

4. This belief in bought-for education is not rational, so nothing can counter it. No amount of "proof" that they've got a good chance of getting three straight As at the excellent local comprehensive will make these families enrol Jack and Chloe there. Some parents don't even make a perfunctory tour of their local state school before deciding upon which - often distant - independent institution they'll send their child to. The presumption is that if it's state, it can't possibly be good enough.

∆

5. In a bid to counter the "my Jack's too bright for an ordinary school" argument, the government introduced a £29m programme for "gifted and talented" children, appropriately known as "G&Ts". There are after-school clubs, master-classes, and summer schools for the exceptionally able. X But the government is wasting its time trying to second guess what would make these parents commit themselves to state education, throwing away millions on initiatives which mainly benefit the majority of middle-class families who do refuse, or are unable, to opt out. Instead, children should be brought back into the state system by pulling away the safety net. Private schools should be abolished.

<

6. It doesn't have to happen in one fell swoop. First, charitable status could be removed from Britain's 2,400 private schools. This has given the independent sector considerable tax benefits, including no income tax, no corporation tax, no capital gains tax, no inheritance tax and preferential business rates on properties. Without these benefits, parents would have to pay a realistic price for the small class sizes and swimming pools they expect. It would no longer be a case of simply sacrificing that winter skiing holiday for the sake of Chloe's education; the house in Hampstead or the Wirral would have to go as well. And, as a bonus, state education would benefit from the new tax raised.

X

7. There is huge reluctance by government (double the national average of privately-educated) to implement even this simple measure. Presumably the risk of alienating the middle-class electorate is felt to be too great. X But as with the gradual removal of tax relief from mortgage interest payments, measures that seem to be directly targeted against

the middle classes rarely produce the feared suburban semi-detached backlash. With the prospect of private fees at least doubling, many of those who have recently flown from the state system would simply be forced to rejoin for financial reasons. Slowly, the private sector would wither away.

X

8. There might be a reactionary rump, a few dedicated to allowing their children to exercise the Harry Potter option whatever the cost and whatever the alternatives. Such entrenched attitudes are difficult to shift. Electronic whiteboards, cyberspace libraries and a laptop for each teacher will not buy them over to the wonders of the local secondary. X But such a tiny minority holding on to such an outdated view on the right to exclusivity would increasingly appear absurd, as redundant as the royal family. Once private schools were reduced to such insignificant numbers, they could be easily, quietly closed down.

→∆

9. The benefits would be enormous. Education would become something we all shared, equal stakeholders in its quality and worth. Education could be effectively and efficiently planned on a national basis, in the knowledge that every child would go to a local school.

<∆

10. Early this year, Estelle Morris announced that tackling social divisions in education would be her priority. But as long as there's a subsidised fee-paying option, those divisions will flourish. Half a million mostly white, well off children will not be schooled alongside their peers, a form of educational apartheid. It's no longer any good just offering carrots. It's time to reach for the stick.

∆, &, ∆, <, X - X , X - X , →∆, <∆

This is the typical profile of a comment article which depends more on emotion than reason. The number of Xs suggest that the author's convictions are continually interrupting the flow of the argument. Paragraphs 5, 7 and 8 contain internal Xs which indicate that the author finds it difficult to present the things she disapproves of, without immediately countering or dismissing them. This might well be an effective piece if addressed to those who agree with the author (which may well be the case in this instance) but it is likely to be ineffective if it is intended to persuade those who either have no view on this issue or disagree.

We are not suggesting you should spend a great deal of time analysing how journalists and other writers connect their thoughts (although it can be illuminating to see how they use, or sometimes abuse, links to move their narrative forward). No, the point is to suggest that, whenever we write a document, we should think about the paragraph structure we use and how best to connect the paragraphs together.

5.11 Final thoughts on Linking

Some types of links are related to each other in varying degree: e.g.:
- Causal, Consequential, Temporal
- Combining, Elucidating
- Conditional, Purposive
- Contrasting, Exceptional

but it is always worth deciding within each group of links which link is precisely the right one to move your narrative forward.

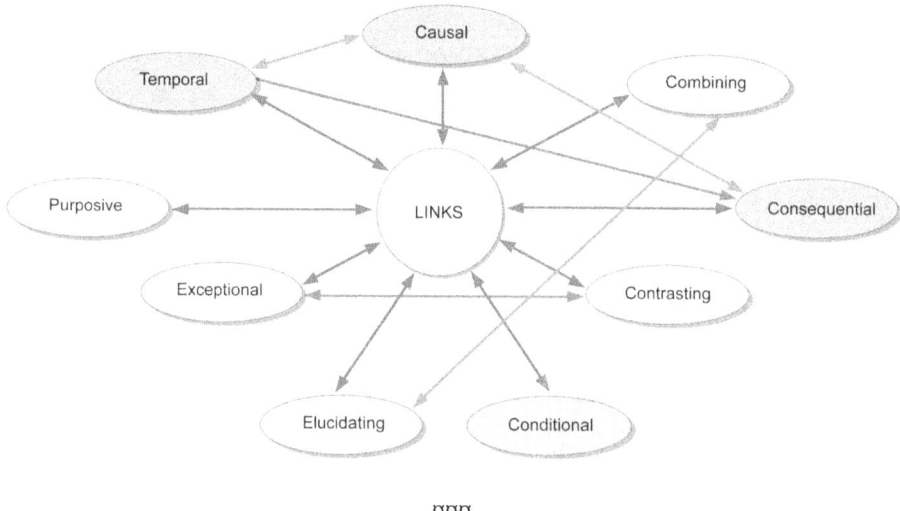

By now it will be apparent that grouping, ordering and linking all make use of a small set of underlying principles. We use comparing and contrasting to construct groups; we often use grouping in ranking and ordering; and we use causal and chronological criteria in ordering and linking; etc. In other words, when writing any document, we have at our disposal a few simple methods of imposing order on data and, once we are aware of them and apply them, we can be confident that what we write is comprehensive, coherent and comprehensible.

6 Structuring

Dictionaries describe hierarchy as a system of persons or things arranged in ranks or graded order.

Here we use hierarchy to mean rather more. For us, hierarchy means:
- the arrangement of a set of information in a graded order
- which shows the relationship between all the parts which make up the set and
- which adds meaning to the set by virtue of the principles on which the hierarchy is formed.

We will explore here the rules that govern hierarchical structures in our sense of the term. (There are other ways of seeking to impose order on raw data but hierarchies have proved to be the most powerful and widely applicable system.)

We should emphasise that, while the rules we set out here are fundamental, there is no need for the experienced practitioner to follow them rigidly on all occasions. Indeed the skilled writer will sometimes intentionally deviate from the rules in order to achieve a particular effect or to avoid unnecessary complexity. Nevertheless, awareness of the rules and the reasons for them are invaluable as guidance and control mechanisms in preparing any written document.

NOTE FOR DOCUPRAXIS® USERS: In building projects, the DocuPraxis® program uses hierarchical structures as the most effective form for organising complex, multi-layered material.

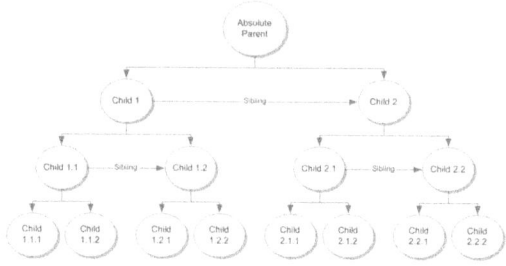

Please note we use the 'parent, sibling, child' convention to describe the structuring process.

6.1 How to build a structure

To build a structure for a report, you need to fit all your material into a hierarchical framework. To achieve this, you will use grouping, ordering and linking in order to take control of the content and to make sure you know the path you will follow from 'Introduction' to 'Conclusion'. Please make sure your structure is thoroughly thought through and completed before you start to write.

6.1.1 Bottom up construction

STAGE 1: When building from the bottom up, you collect all the elements of your structure together and then sort them into groups.

The element you use as the parent of any group may be one of the elements already in your collection of elements or, if there is no suitable parent amongst your elements, you will have to add an element to serve as a parent for the 'orphan' group.

The name of this new element will be determined by the criterion you used to compile the group.

Of course, some elements may resist grouping, standing on their own.

STAGE 2: You now apply the grouping process to the parents of all the groups and any 'stand alone' elements, looking for ways in which to construct one or more groups at this 'higher' level. The elements you use to head these 'groups of groups' are the parents of the groups and the grandparents of the lowest level elements.

You continue the process until all your elements (those you had as your original collection and any you have added in order to give an orphan group a parent) have been fitted into the structure at some level under the absolute parent which is, in effect, the title of the report, essay or document you are planning to compose. (If this is confusing, even after a second reading, I apologise. .All will become clear in the example that follows.)

As you build the structure, you may wish to promote or demote any of the elements. You may realise that one of the grandchildren is not being given sufficient prominence (i.e. it should at least have the same status as a parent or even a grandparent); or is in the wrong group (i.e. it fits more easily in another group); or is less important than you thought and would fit more appropriately as the child of another parent.

Sometimes, when you are halfway through constructing your hierarchy, you will realise you have set out on entirely the wrong path and you need to start again. Life can be hard.

Example of the bottom up approach.
Let us assume you have been asked to prepare a marketing plan. You have been supplied with an impressive store of information on your product and the market:
- Competitor Advertising/Promotional Activity/Costs
- Competitor Sales
- Definition of the Market
- Main Competitors
- Market Research Programme
- Market Statistics
- Product Description
- Product Positioning
- Product-related PR
- Profit Forecast
- Sales Forecast
- Sales/Promotion Plan
- Strengths and Weaknesses of main competitors
- Strengths and Weaknesses of the product
- Total Marketing Costs

This information resource may be impressive - but it is also intimidating. It needs sorting.

Below is one way of organising the available information. We have six group headings. Of the 15 'elements' with which we began, 14 have fitted into five of our group headings. The 15th 'element' (Market Research Programme), we have promoted to group heading level, because it stood alone and certainly does not seem out of place amongst the other group headings.

1. **Market Data**
    1.1. Definition of the Market
    1.2. Market Statistics
2. **Competitor Data**
    2.1. Main Competitors
    2.2. Strengths and Weaknesses of main competitors
    2.3. Competitor Advertising/Promotional Activity/Costs
    2.4. Competitor Sales
3. **Product Data**
    3.1. Product Description
    3.2. Strengths and Weaknesses of the product
4. **Product Marketing Strategy**
    4.1. Product Positioning
    4.2. Sales/Promotion Plan

    4.3. Product-related PR
    4.4. Total Marketing Costs
5. **Sales/Profit Forecast**
    5.1. Sales Forecast
    5.2. Profit Forecast
6. **Market Research Programme**

There are of course other ways of grouping this material - some simpler and some more complex. Below we show a simple variant:

1. **Product Description**
2. **Market Data**
    2.1. Definition of the Market
    2.2. Market Statistics
    2.3. Market Research Programme
3. **Competitor Data**
    3.1. Main Competitors
    3.2. Strengths and Weaknesses of main competitors
    3.3. Competitor Advertising/Promotional Activity/Costs
    3.4. Competitor Sales
4. **Product Strengths and Weaknesses**
5. **Product Marketing Strategy**
    5.1. Product Positioning
    5.2. Sales/Promotion Plan
    5.3. Product-related PR
    5.4. Total Marketing Costs
6. **Sales/Profit Forecast**
    6.1. Sales Forecast
    6.2. Profit Forecast

In each case, we have already imposed some order on to the data, have made the data easier to grasp and, to some extent, given an indication of our thinking and priorities. The first structure suggests we have started with the market and the product has emerged out of our analysis of the market. In the second structure, there is a suggestion that understanding the product itself is key to understanding the market at which it is aimed. In the first structure, the market research function is seen as a major component of the plan (it has a main section of its own) and, coming at the end of the plan, prepares us to expect it is to be an ongoing activity. In the second structure, it simply forms part of the main section on market data and implies the market research results are in and already incorporated into the plan.

Each plan may carry the same information but the way in which the information is organised becomes additional information. We need to understand this because otherwise the way in which the document is organised may inadvertently convey additional information that we do not intend or that contradicts our own thinking.

Note on the DocuPraxis® program: The DocuPraxis® program has been specifically designed to assist writers in organising and manipulating the structure of reports. Users can start by listing all the points they intend to make or the topics they wish to cover. They can then group them according to any criteria; they can order and reorder them until they feel the sequence makes the most sense and fits best with how they wish to deal with them; they can experiment with various links to see which sequence of links fits best with their objectives; they can promote or demote an entry, moving it up or down the hierarchy as their ideas on how to organise the material develop. Whether the document is short or long, simple or complex, the DocuPraxis® program will help users to experiment and test various options until they have achieved complete mastery of the content of their report.

Remember that grouping, ordering and linking add meaning by indicating to your readers your line of thinking, so make full use of these techniques to create a structure that best suits your purpose. **Creating a good structure is critical, and is at least as important as the writing of the report.**

6.1.2 Top Down Construction

The top down approach starts with the gathering of the main elements of the document. Many companies have a standard format for various types of report and these provide the report writer with a useful template to follow, at least in determining the main sections of the report.

Most business documents have the following form:
1. **Introduction**
2. **Body of the report**
3. **Conclusion**

We might add a synopsis or a summary as the first element.
   Summary
1. **Introduction**
2. **Body of the report**
3. **Conclusion**

The body of the report might have the following elements
- Objectives
- Research
- Methods
- Results
- Discussion

We now have as our top down structure;
   Summary
1. **Introduction**
2. **Body of Report**
    2.1. Objectives
    2.2. Research
    2.3. Methods
    2.4. Results

  2.5. Discussion
3. **Conclusion**

We can now break down each of these elements (parents) into a number of sub-elements (children).

  The Structure might end up looking something like this;

Summary
1. **Introduction**
2. **Body of Report**
  2.1. **Objectives**
    2.1.1. **Product Development**
    2.1.2. **Product Launch**
    2.1.3. **Sales Targets**
    2.1.4. **Breakeven**
  2.2. **Research**
    2.2.1. **Technical Resources**
    2.2.2. **Market Research**
      2.2.2.1. Desk Research
      2.2.2.2. Survey Research
  2.3. **Methods**
    2.3.1. **Launch Conference**
    2.3.2. **Advertising**
    2.3.3. **Public Relations**
      2.3.3.1. National Media
      2.3.3.2. Regional Media
  2.4. **Results**
    2.4.1. Costs
    2.4.2. Sales
    2.4.3. **Forecast Breakeven**
  2.5. Discussion
3. **Conclusion**

We can now develop and refine the structure, making sure that it accommodates all the information we wish to impart and that each piece of information appears in the 'right' place.

6.1.3 Building a hierarchy in practice
The best hierarchical structures for report-writing are usually a combination of the bottom-up and top-down approaches. Whichever method you start with (and it really doesn't matter which you prefer), you are likely to find you have used both techniques before the construction process is completed.

  We put a great deal of emphasis on Structuring, partly because it is the key to composing a well-ordered, persuasive report but mainly because, whatever people say, it is rare to find business report-writers who give the application of structuring anything like enough energy or commitment. It seems the urge to start writing as quickly as possible often proves irresistible. Why? Perhaps because the author wants to feel a start has been made on producing the finished document. Or perhaps because the author hopes that the structure will somehow emerge as the writing proceeds (a pretty forlorn hope, if we're honest). As a result, business reports are often disjointed and discursive. (This tendency is at least as pronounced amongst students preparing essays for course work or in exams as it is amongst the writers of administrative and business reports.)

"I had no plans so I had to start somewhere."

It's rather like building a house. Of course, you can have some bricks delivered and start laying them - but if you did, you'd be a fool. Obviously, you need firm foundations and you need an architect. Only when you have the architect's drawings should you start to think about laying some bricks and, by then, you may have found you don't have sufficient bricks or you don't have the right type of bricks for the house you now know you wish to build.

Only when you know the plans are good, the foundations are solid and all the necessary materials are available should you start to build. Then you will appreciate all the effort that has gone in to the structuring stage. You will know you have all the materials you need. You will know how they fit in, so you will know where to put them.

If you apply the structuring technique to document preparation, writing the report becomes much easier because, before you start to write, you know where you're going and how to get there. And the report will be a much better document because the fact that you have known where you were going and how to get there will shine through in the text and the way in which the report flows from section to section and point to point.

ααα

Here's another exercise. In this one, we will use both a bottom up and a top down approach.

This issue is alcohol pricing (AP). By alcohol pricing we mean setting a minimum price per unit of alcohol as one way of influencing the consumption of alcohol. We will assume we have to write a report for government, analysing the issue of Alcohol Pricing.

We might start with a mixture of propositions and issues:
- Accident and Emergency (A&E) in many towns is swamped with drunks at weekends
- Alcohol abuse affects others as well as the abuser
- Alcohol is a drug
- AP interferes with the freedom of the individual
- AP is another example of the Nanny State
- AP is politically unacceptable in a recession
- AP is social engineering
- AP penalises moderate drinkers
- AP penalises the poor unfairly
- AP prevents the poor from drinking too much
- AP prevents the young from drinking too much
- AP reduces drinking of alcohol
- AP will save the NHS money
- AP won't discourage binge drinking
- Drunk driving is a major cause of road accidents
- Heavy drinking often leads to antisocial behaviour
- Much crime is associated with alcohol abuse
- Much domestic violence is caused by alcohol abuse
- The drinks industry opposes AP
- The Government enjoys substantial revenues from taxes on alcohol
- The medical profession backs AP
- The pub industry depends on a lightly regulated trade in alcohol
- Town centres are off limits to all but the drinkers at weekends
- We need to change the British drinking culture

Our first step might be to divide the list of arguments into three groups;
- those for AP
- those against AP
- practical concerns

For AP
- A&E in many towns is swamped with drunks at weekends
- AP prevents the poor from drinking too much
- AP prevents the young from drinking too much
- AP will save the NHS money
- Drunk driving is a major cause of road accidents
- Heavy drinking often leads to antisocial behaviour
- Much crime is associated with alcohol abuse
- Much domestic violence is caused by alcohol abuse
- Town centres are off limits to all but the drinkers at weekends

Against AP
- AP interferes with the freedom of the individual
- AP is another example of the Nanny State
- AP is social engineering
- AP penalises moderate drinkers
- AP penalises the poor unfairly
- AP won't discourage binge drinking
- Pub industry will be damaged by AP
- The Government enjoys substantial revenues from taxes on alcohol

Practical Considerations
Alcohol abuse affects others as well as the abuser
- AP is politically unacceptable in a recession
- The drinks industry opposes AP
- The Government enjoys substantial revenues from taxes on alcohol
- The medical profession backs AP
- The pub industry depends on a lightly regulated trade in alcohol

We have two propositions left over:

Alcohol is a drug
This invites us to consider alcohol in the context of other drugs, many of which are illegal but which cause far less damage to the individual user and society.

We need to change the British drinking culture
This raises an even broader issue, inviting comparison with the drinking culture of other societies.

We might well decide to save these two propositions for some broad discussion at the end of the exercise.

Assuming we are happy with our three main categories, we may now undertake a combination of top down and bottom up grouping:

For AP
Protecting the User
- AP prevents the poor from drinking too much
- AP prevents the young from drinking too much

Protecting other Citizens
- A&E in many towns is swamped with drunks at weekends
- Drunk driving is a major cause of road accidents
- Heavy drinking often leads to antisocial behaviour
- Much crime is associated with alcohol abuse
- Much domestic violence is caused by alcohol abuse
- Town centres are off limits to all but the drinkers at weekends

Saving Money
- AP will save the NHS money

Against AP
Individual Freedom
- AP interferes with the freedom of the individual
- AP is another example of the Nanny State
- AP is social engineering

Fairness Argument
- AP penalises the poor unfairly

Effectiveness Argument
- AP won't discourage binge drinking

Financial Argument
- The Government enjoys substantial revenues from taxes on alcohol
- Pub industry will be damaged by AP

Practical Considerations
Social Considerations
- Alcohol abuse affects others as well as the abuser

Political Considerations
- AP is politically unacceptable in a recession
- The drinks industry opposes AP

Economic Considerations
- The Government enjoys substantial revenues from taxes on alcohol
- The medical profession backs AP
- The pub industry depends on a lightly regulated trade in alcohol

Broader Issues
- Alcohol is a drug
- We need to change the British drinking culture

We now have a structure for our report. It is, of course, just one way of organising the material that makes up the content of our subject but it meets the criterion of accommodating all the data. And it seems to provide a logical form which will facilitate a smooth transition from one section to the next.

Now we might refine it by imposing a standard report format: e.g.

1. **Introduction**
    1.1. Definition of Alcohol Pricing
    1.2. Objectives of the Report
2. **Arguments for**
    2.1. Protecting the User

2.2. Protecting other Citizens
   2.3. Saving Money
3. **Arguments against**
   3.1. Individual Freedom
   3.2. Fairness Argument
   3.3. Effectiveness Argument
   3.4. Financial Argument
4. **Broader Issues**
   4.1. Alcohol in the context of drug legislation
   4.2. Alcohol abuse in Britain seen as a cultural issue
5. **Conclusion**

When we write the report, we will have a mass of statistics to incorporate and many examples we will need to cite but now, because we have a comprehensive, coherent structure, we will know where to put the statistics and when to introduce the examples.

Just as important, because we have a structure, the reader will see where we are going, the precise path we are following and why we are going there.

6.2 A couple of hierarchy guidelines
There are a couple of guidelines to be kept in mind when developing hierarchical structures:
- **Status Equivalence**
- **Symmetry**

6.2.1 Status Equivalence
The principle of status equivalence requires that you should aim to place each element in an hierarchical structure at the same level in the structure as every other element **of equal importance.** The justification for this rule is both logical and aesthetic.

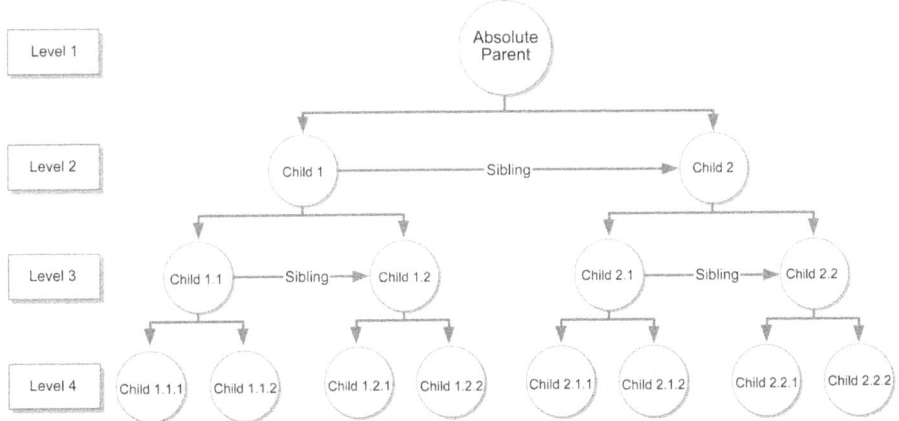

The level at which you decide to put each element of the structure determines the relative importance of each element and how they relate to the whole.

Let us return to our example of a marketing plan, but this time we will assume we need to compile the plan from scratch, without the benefit of a mass of detailed information on specific topics. The first task will be to list the main sections of the report. We would be aiming to:
- cover all the activities which we need to perform
- break the activities down into sensible categories
- arrange them in a sensible order
- ensure each section is of approximately equal importance.

We might well end up with the following section headings:
1. Introduction
2. Market Data
3. Competitor Data
4. Product Data
5. Product Marketing Strategy
6. Sales/Profit Forecast
7. Market Research Programme

These sections are of approximately equal importance and are therefore set at the same level in the structure.

We will now follow the same procedure within each of the sections.

1. **Introduction**
2. **Market Data**
    2.1. Definition of the Market
    2.2. Market Statistics
        Total Sales
        Total Advertising Spend
3. **Competitor Data**
    3.1. Main Competitors
    3.2. Strengths and Weakness of main competitors
    3.3. Competitor Advertising/Promotional Activity/Costs
    3.4. Competitor Sales
4. **Product Data**
    4.1. Product Description
    4.2. Strengths and Weakness
5. **Product Marketing Strategy**
    5.1. Product Positioning
    5.2. Sales/Promotion Plan
        Activities
        Schedule
        Costs
    5.3. Product-related PR
        Activities
        Schedule
        Costs
    5.4. Total Marketing Costs

6. **Sales/Profit Forecast**
   6.1. Sales Forecast
   6.2. Profit Forecast
7. **Market Research Programme**

At every level in the structure, we are aiming to place elements of approximately equal importance. In the case of a marketing plan, the relative importance of each element is fairly easy to determine. Even so, there is still the opportunity to add meaning to your structure by promoting or demoting a section to a higher or lower level in the structure to indicate your own sense of the relative importance of each element.

How do we determine the relative importance of each element? Well, that is largely a matter for you to decide. How you arrange your structure should reflect your own view of the relative importance of the elements; and the way your structure is arranged will communicate that judgement to your reader. In other words, use the hierarchy to communicate your view of the relative importance of each element.

Note on the close relationship between grouping and hierarchising

In this instance, we have performed the exercise set out in Grouping - but in reverse.

In Grouping we were organising a mass of information (sub-sections) into groups, in effect preparing the basic elements of a hierarchy from the bottom up. Here we have devised our section headings first, and then broken each section heading down into its constituent elements (a top down approach).

In other words, grouping and hierarchies are two sides of the same coin and proficiency in both guarantees control and cohesion in any document.

6.2.2 Symmetry

While we are organising our material in a hierarchy, there is another principle which can help us to ensure the underlying coherence of the way in which we have organised our material shows through.

For example, if we wish to propose three measures (let's call them M1, M2 and M3) and we plan to give two reasons for each measure (R1 to R6), we can organise our document in one of three ways, all of which conform to the principle of symmetry. In these examples, each line is a separate paragraph:

Three paragraph solution
1. M1 + R1 and R2
2. M2 + R3 and R4
3. M3 + R5 and R6

or

Six paragraph solution
1. M1
2. R1 and R2
3. M2

    4. R3 and R4
    5. M3
    6. R5 and R6

or

    Nine paragraph solution
    1. M1
    2. R1
    3. R2
    4. M2
    5. R3
    6. R4
    7. M3
    8. R5
    9. R6

In each case, the reader will see there is symmetry in the structure of the document.

In the first solution, the measure and the reasons for it are kept in a single paragraph.

In the second solution, the measure is given a paragraph of its own - which is then followed by another paragraph containing the two reasons for the measure. This pattern is repeated for the second and third measure.

In the third solution, each measure and each supporting reason is given a paragraph of its own.

Which of the solutions is most appropriate is a matter of judgement and depends on:
    a. factors such as length and complexity of each measure and each reason
    b. the level of importance you wish to accord each element.

Whichever option is chosen, the reader will:
- quickly discern the logic behind the author's structure
- be helped to understand the measures and the reasons for them because he/she will know what to expect
- will recognise the author's clarity of thought as an indication of intelligence and discipline.

6.3 A note on types of hierarchy
There are two types of hierarchy;
- homogeneous hierarchies
- hybrid hierarchies

6.3.1 Homogeneous Hierarchy
This is the simplest form of hierarchy and is familiar to everyone in the form of the traditional family tree.

If you are constructing a family tree, all elements in the structure (i.e. all the nodes) should be people. You may, for example, wish to show the companies for which each of the people work, but, in a homogeneous hierarchy you will not enter companies as "children" of the individual. If you do, you could end up with individual children and companies on the same level of the hierarchy with the same parents - which will destroy the homogeneity of the structure.

NOTE FOR DOCUPRAXIS® USERS: If you wish to develop a homogenous hierarchy, there are two ways to handle this type of problem when using the DocuPraxisT program.
1. You can enter the companies in the associated Workpage. Indeed, you can add any amount of additional information, since there is no limit to the size of the Workpage. In this way you can enter any amount of diverse data without undermining the integrity of the homogeneous structure. If you are using the Workpage in this way, remember to make full use of the various insert templates.

or

2. Right-clicking on any node will open up a window which includes a 'Details' option. There you can record further information about the subject of the node without compromising the homogeneity of your hierarchy.

6.3.2 Hybrid Hierarchy

A hybrid hierarchy is a hierarchy in which elements *of different kinds* are accommodated in the structure. When writing reports, there are many occasions when you will find a hybrid hierarchy is the only way to contain all the elements of your subject in an organised from.

If you are developing a structure for a complex issue, you may find it useful to enter a large number of aspects of the issue into a draft structure, either singly or in groups, without a clear idea as to how the elements should finally be arranged. For example, if you were preparing a document on Welfare Reform, you might create the following major sections:
- **Government Policy**
- **Pressure Groups**
- **Media Input**
- **Economic Factors**

You might then list under these main headings, the elements (sub-headings) you know you need to cover:

Government Policy
- Children
- People of Working Age
- Pensioners

Pressure Groups
- Age Concern

- CBI
- Help the Aged
- IOD
- NSPCC
- Trades Unions

Media Input
- Press
- Broadsheets
- Mid-Market Press
- Popular Press
- Broadcast
- TV
- Radio
- Internet

Economic Factors
- Inflation
- Unemployment

Clearly government policy, pressure groups, the media and economic factors are different in kind, but all four are relevant to the subject. In a hybrid hierarchy you accommodate all these groups in a draft structure so that you can then arrange and rearrange them until you find the best way of organising your report. You can move individual items or whole groups up or down the structure (i.e. change the order); you can promote or demote individual items or whole groups (i.e. change the level). How best to arrange them will be heavily influenced by the links you intend to use to explain how these different groups are related. The arrangement set out above might be the simplest way to present all the data in a straightforward structured form.

Alternatively you may have an argument you wish to present, and this argument will almost certainly have a bearing on how you arrange the elements. It will also affect the grouping process, including the naming of groups. For example, you may wish to draw attention to how each of the factors (pressure groups, media and economic factors) contributes to the formulation of government policy towards a) children, b) those of working age and c) pensioners. In this case, you might find the following structure appropriate.

1. **Government Policy for Children**
    - Pressure Groups
    - Media
    - Economic Factors
2. **Government Policy for People of Working Age**
    - Pressure Groups
    - Media
    - Economic Factors
3. Government Policy for Pensioners
    - Pressure Groups

- Media
- Economic Factors

As it happens, this arrangement produces a semi-homogeneous hierarchy. All the main headings concern government policy; all the children (sub-sections) are factors affecting government policy.

Alternatively, you might wish to put the emphasis on the different ways in which each of the influencing factors affects the different areas of government policy. In this case you could find the following structure more appropriate;

1. **Pressure Groups**
    - Government Policy for Children
    - Government Policy for those of Working Age
    - Government Policy for Pensioners
2. **Media**
    - Government Policy for Children
    - Government Policy for those of Working Age
    - Government Policy for Pensioners
3. **Economic Factors**
    - Government Policy for Children
    - Government Policy for those of Working Age
    - Government Policy for Pensioners

NOTE FOR DocuPraxis® USERS: While experimenting with various ways of arranging your data, you can work on any part of the Structure at any time, knowing that, whatever changes you make to the Structure (changing the order or the level of any node), the Workpage and any attachments associated with the node, will move with the node.

And when you come to export your **DocuPraxis®** project to an .html or .rtf file, the output will be correctly formatted, numbered and indented according to your default or project settings.

7 Summary Chart

In terms of constructing a document, that's it:
- Grouping
- Ordering
- Linking
- Structuring

As I said in the Introduction, there is no secret. The principles are simple and obvious.
- To make sense of any set of data you need to organise the data into **groups**.
- To present a list of any type, you should consider the **order** in which you present it.
- To connect the elements of your document together, you need to decide at every level (chapter, section, paragraph, sentence) how best to **link** each element to what goes before and what comes after.
- And before you write any document, you should have a clear and detailed **structure** so that you know, before you start to write, how you can move smoothly from the beginning to the end.

Here we have divided the four activities into separate chapters in order to identify and illustrate the different processes involved. In practice, you will not use these techniques one at a time in isolation. You will use all four processes all the time. When you make your first attempt at building your structure, you will think about linking, because how you connect the nodes in the structure will have a bearing on their order and even which group you put them in. When you are organising your material into groups, you will consider the order in which you place the items in each group, where they might fit in the structure and how you can link them. And so on.

All the time, you will be mastering your material and adding information and meaning to it.

All very reasonable, if not obvious! So why is it that so few business reports and academic essays observe these principles consistently?

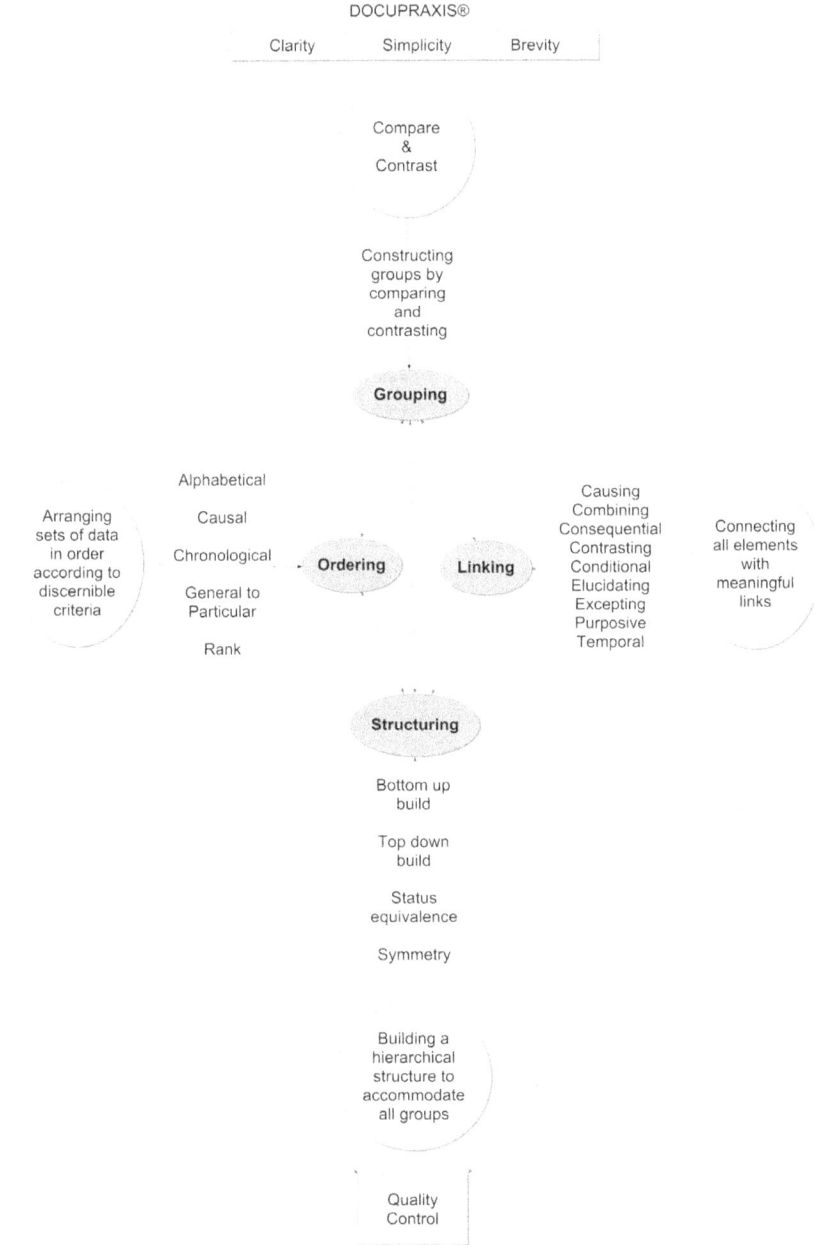

The four techniques of grouping, ordering, linking and structuring are four tools in a toolbox, tools you can use at any time in any situation to create order and communicate clearly.

The rest of this book focuses on the actual writing of a document, the putting of verbal clothes on the conceptual structure. Some of it is very basic advice - but nonetheless useful in a world where much basic advice is hard to come by. Other sections take a look (sometimes a fairly light-hearted look) at some of the pitfalls that any writer can slip into (or should I say 'into which any writer can slip').

8 A Note on Mind Mapping

Mind mapping has become popular in recent years as a technique that offers an alternative to the rigidity of hierarchies. Correctly used, it is a powerful tool for exploring issues and for suggesting previously unidentified, unsuspected connections.

Unfortunately, too often mapping has been hi-jacked by woolly thinkers who use it as a device for presenting a chaotic jumble of thoughts in an apparently organised form. Many of the better so-called 'mind maps' are simply hierarchical structures presented in chart form. They have the limitation that they cannot comfortably accommodate complex projects or any but the simplest of texts, simply because of space considerations.

On balance, DocuPraxis® provides a better solution. By ensuring that the outline of any project can be viewed, adjusted and manipulated easily at any point and that each node, with its associated content, is always on display, the DocuPraxis® program provides a powerful document construction tool which can handle any project, whether simple or complex. It also accommodates any amount of text alongside each node in the structure at every level.

9 Refresher Course on Some Basics

This section, which runs through some basics of grammar and syntax, is intended as a helpful reminder, for any who need it, of those half-forgotten school lessons on the English language.

9.1 The Sentence

The sentence is the basic unit of any written document. It is therefore important to observe the rules of sentence composition. As always, we are aiming for clarity and simplicity.

In grammatical terms there are three main types of sentence:
- simple (one main clause)

He seized the opportunity.
- compound (two or more main clauses joined by conjunctions)

He seized the opportunity and enjoyed considerable success.
- complex (main clause plus one or more **subordinate clauses**)

He **who seizes the opportunity** will enjoy success.
Whenever you seize the opportunity, you will enjoy success.
Success comes to him **who seizes the opportunity**.

In terms of function, sentences fall into one of the following categories:
- declarative (e.g. John is going.)
- interrogative (e.g. Is John going?)
- imperative (e.g. John, go.)
- exclamatory (e.g. John has gone!)

Whatever the type of sentence, it must make complete sense. When a set of words makes complete sense, we have the option to end the sentence with a punctuation mark (a full stop, a question mark or an exclamation mark) which indicates the sentence has finished or to continue, by using a conjunction (thus creating a compound sentence) or other linking word (thus creating a complex sentence).

With simple sentences, it should be obvious when the sentence has reached an end.

"The most common mistake amongst learners is to run two or more sentences together this is not a good idea readers can easily become confused."

Sometimes the answer is simply to break the passage into individual sentences:

"The most common mistake amongst learners is to run two or more sentences together. This is not a good idea. Readers can easily become confused."

In many cases, a linking word and the creation of a subordinate clause is the answer:

"The most common mistake amongst learners is to run two or more sentences together. This is not a good idea because readers can easily become confused."

When writing sentences, it is always worth asking two key questions:
- What are the thoughts I am trying to convey?
- How can I best link these thoughts together?

In the example given above there are three thoughts. The first is a simple statement. The second is a judgement. The third is a justification for the judgement. It makes sense to join the second and third thoughts together in one sentence by using "because", so that the judgement and its justification are securely linked.

Of course, we could incorporate all three thoughts into one sentence;

"The most common mistake amongst learners is to run two or more sentences together which is not a good idea because readers can easily become confused."

but this is cumbersome and is probably overloading a single sentence with too many thoughts for most modern audiences.

9.1.1 Recognizing a sentence

To someone brought up at a time when grammar was an essential element of primary school education, it is surprising to see CVs from graduates with first class degrees in arts subjects who really don't know where and when to use a full stop.

It is quite difficult to give a complete definition of a sentence but it's not hard to recognise one when you see it. A sentence is the smallest grammatical construction of words that makes complete sense. When the construction makes sense, it is ready for a full stop or, at the least, one of its close relatives (a question mark or an exclamation mark); or, at the very least, one of its children - a colon or a semicolon. (Okay, so I'm addicted to familial analogies!)

"When the sun shines" is not a complete sentence. If someone enters a room and, out of the blue so to speak, announces "When the sun shines", we are going to ask, "What? What 'when the sun shines'?" If the answer is "The sky is at its best when the sun shines", we may not be particularly impressed by the content but we will recognise what has been said as a complete sentence.

The most common fault in the use of the full stop is to deploy too few, rather than too many. When the sense is complete, the sentence should end. Frequently, those who have problems with sentences run two or more sentences together. Apart from being syntactically incorrect, it makes it more difficult for the reader to understand the writer and, for this reason more than any other, is a serious flaw.

Traditionally, sentences are seen as composed of two major elements:
- subject (i.e. who or what the sentence is about)
- predicate (i.e. the rest of the sentence which includes the verb and tells you something about the subject)

In the example above, 'the sun' is the subject and 'is at its best when the sun shines' is the predicate.

As noted above, there are three main types of sentence. In order of increasing complexity, they are:
- **Simple:** a single subject and a single, simple predicate (e.g. The sun is shining):
- **Compound:** in effect two sentences joined together by a conjunction (e.g. The sun is shining but the wind is cold)
- **Complex:** a sentence consisting of a main clause and one or more subordinate clauses (e.g. The sun, the star around which the planets orbit, is going to blow up in about four billion years when it becomes a red giant because, by then, it will have burnt up most of its fuel.)

Simple and compound sentences are pretty straightforward. They allow the writer to make clear, unambiguous statements. Complex sentences are more sophisticated and enable the writer to shift the emphasis of a statement in innumerable and sometimes extremely subtle ways. Complex sentences are therefore more challenging and, if used by those who have not fully marshalled their thoughts or mastered their material, can lead to unintended consequences and grammatical errors.

As always, keep things simple. If simple or compound sentences will say what you mean, use them.

9.1.2 Structuring a sentence to achieve the right emphasis

Another aspect of ordering a sentence involves ensuring that the structure of the sentence puts the emphasis in the right place. (One way to check whether the emphasis is right is to ask what question the statement in your sentence is answering.)

"Peter proposed a cut in the workers' pay because he wished to provoke a confrontation."
This is an answer to the question: "Why did Peter propose a cut in the workers' pay?"

"Peter provoked a confrontation because he proposed a cut in workers' pay."
This is an answer to the question: "How did Peter provoke a confrontation?" or "Why was there a confrontation?"

In the first version, it was clearly Peter's intention to provoke a strike. In the second version, all we know is what triggered the strike. We do not know whether Peter intended to provoke a confrontation.

Here is a rather complicated example:
"The strike which Peter provoked by suggesting a cut in the workers' pay resulted in the closure of the business which was, as it turned out, his original aim."

The main clause is:
"The strike resulted in the closure of the business."

There are two subordinate clauses:
"which he provoked by suggesting a cut in workers' pay"
"which was, as it turned out, his original aim"

If we recast the sentence as follows:
"As it turned out, Peter's original aim in provoking a strike, by suggesting a cut in workers' pay, was to close the business."

we have shifted the revelation about Peter's aim from the subordinate clause at the end of the sentence to the main clause at the start. This has the effect of emphasising the element of premeditation in Peter's actions.

When composing complex sentences (sentences with at least one subordinate clause), it is generally best to express the dominant thought in the main clause.

See also Advanced Techniques.

9.1.3 Sentence cohesion
Proximity

The first guideline in sentence composition is that words and phrases that are related to each other should be arranged as close to each other as is practical. If connected words or phrases become separated from their close relatives, the result can be ungainly or ambiguous.

Here is an example of an ungainly sentence:
"He launched the new range of products quickly which meant we kept ahead of the competition which I think was a good idea."

This sentence has not been 'composed'. The writer did not know how the sentence would end when he started to write.

Try:
"I approved of his move to launch the new range of products quickly. As a result of the launch, we have kept ahead of the competition."

Or, if you wish to express the content in one sentence:
"I approved of his move to launch the new range of products quickly in order to keep us a head of the competition."

In this version, we have explicitly stated what was implied in the original sentence (i.e. that his purpose in launching quickly was to keep ahead of the competition). This is an example of enhanced linking. Instead of having three thoughts loosely held together:

a. He launched the new range of products quickly

b. This meant we were ahead of the competition
  c. I think was a good idea

we have presented b) as the reason for a) and encompassed the now tightly linked a) and b) in the approval expressed in c). But note we have promoted the 'approval' to the main clause, thereby shifting the emphasis of the thought. If we now feel we are putting too much emphasis on the approval, we can recast the sentence as follows:
  "His decision to launch the new product range quickly, of which I approved, kept us ahead of the competition."

Of course this formulation is open to the objection that it is not entirely clear whether the approval relates primarily to the decision or to the prompt launch of the new product range. If we wish to make it clear the approval was directed primarily at the decision, the ambiguity can easily be removed by yet another formulation:
  "His decision, of which I approved, to launch the new product range quickly, kept us ahead of the competition."

There is a further complication in one of the above formulations.
  "I approved of his move to launch the new range of products quickly in order to keep us a head of the competition."

This could be read to mean: "I gave my approval of his decision quickly in order to keep us ahead of the competition." The credit for 'keeping us ahead of the competition' is now claimed, at least in part, by the author. If that is the author's intended meaning, he should move the 'quickly' closer to the verb it qualifies:
  "I quickly approved of his move to launch the new range of products in order to keep us a head of the competition."

And so on. The point is this. If you are going to compose complex sentences, be very aware of the order in which you present the elements of meaning and how you link them. Complex sentences allow you to place the emphasis precisely where you want it. On the other hand, if not handled with care, they can convey meanings you did not intend. In general, keep it simple and, if it is difficult to achieve precisely the right balance in a complex sentence, break it down into simple or compound sentences.

For further details on linking, see Links.

Avoiding muddle
Another common problem arises when there is a sudden and unnecessary shift in the structure of the sentence:
  "I am aware of all your efforts and you should be rewarded for your hard work."

The subject of the first part of this sentence is 'I' and it would read more easily if the 'I' was also the subject of the second part of the sentence. We could recast the sentence as follows:

"I am aware of all your efforts and am confident you will be rewarded for your hard work."

Yet again we are applying the principle of simplicity. The original sentence involved a change of subject in the second half of the sentence (from 'I' to 'you') and a change of the mood of the verb (from active to passive). Both changes were unnecessary, as the second version of the sentence shows.

Losing the thread
Another common mistake can arise when a more complex sentence structure is attempted:
"I have never, nor will I ever admit, any responsibility for this fiasco."

The form of the verb which goes with 'I have never' is 'admitted'. The 'admit' which appears later as part of the future form of the verb cannot stand in for the missing 'admitted'. We would have to say:
"I have never admitted, nor will I ever admit, any responsibility for this fiasco."

On the other hand, the following sentence works well:
"I was not then, nor am I now, guilty of any offence."
because 'guilty' works with 'was' and 'am'.

Dangers of Ambiguity
Here is an example of an ambiguity generated by a lack of cohesion in the sentence:
"I attended the meeting yesterday on alleged sexual excesses amongst the staff in the Managing Director's office."

If it was only the meeting that took place in the MD's office, the phrase 'in the Managing Director's office' should come a good deal closer to 'meeting'.
You could try:
"Yesterday, in the Managing Director's office, I attended the meeting on alleged sexual excesses amongst the staff."

or

"I attended the meeting, held yesterday in the Managing Director's office, at which we discussed alleged sexual excesses amongst the staff."

or

"Alleged sexual excesses amongst the staff were discussed at the meeting I attended yesterday in the Managing Director's office."

Here is another example:
"He made a number of enquiries about lack of discipline amongst the parents."

Is it the parents who lack discipline? It might be. It is ambiguous. This one is easily resolved:

"He made a number of enquiries amongst the parents about lack of discipline."

The threat of ambiguity is always present. It is often helpful to ask "To what specific question would this statement be a clear and precise answer?" You should then be able to see whether the statement means what you intend.

Watch these Words
Whenever we compose a sentence, we need to be on our guard against "tricky words" (For much more on this subject see section on Tricky Words).

The proud chemist who proclaimed: "We dispense with accuracy" clearly ignored this advice.

A misplaced 'only' can create ambiguities:

"Our cashflow problems can only be relieved by a rights issue."

Does this mean our cashflow problems will be reduced, but not solved, by a rights issue - or does it mean that a rights issue is the only way to solve our cashflow problems? If the latter is the case, we should say:

"Our cashflow problems can be relieved only by a rights issue."

The building contractor who comes up with a concrete proposal may not win the contract but he should get a laugh, as should the apple-seller who is looking for a quick turnover. And we may even have reservations about the possibly homicidal family butcher.

Always be alert to the meaning and the connotations of words. Words need watching but they are not uncontrollable. The more you use them and assert your authority over them, the more comfortable you will be in their company. A bit like training a dog!

9.1.4 Key Questions
Perhaps the best advice in checking and refining sentences is to ask the following question:

Is there any way in which anyone could, with justification, misinterpret my meaning?

It is not sufficient that the sentence carries your meaning. It should also be the case that your meaning is the only meaning it could possible carry.

One trick for checking whether what you have written is precisely what you mean is to ask:

What is the question to which what I have written is the answer?

9.1.5 Bullet Points
Bullet points are popular in business reports, and rightly so. They allow the writer to state succinctly a series of related propositions. It hardly need be said that bullet

points should be short and clear. They should also be presented in the correct order; i.e. the order which corresponds with the line of thought the writer wishes the reader to follow.

In considering the order in which to present bullet points, the writer can use any of the ordering criteria described in the chapter on Ordering. The most useful forms of ordering for bullet points are:
- rank
- temporal
- causal

Rank is probably the most common form of ordering because readers tend to assume that whatever appears at the top of the bullet list is the most important point and that the other points have been ranked in order of importance.

Temporal bullet points show the order in which events or processes occur

Causal ordering is not relevant in all cases but, where it is applicable, it can be used to convey the writer's thinking implicitly. See Causal under Ordering.

9.2 Paragraphs

It is relatively easy to determine when a sentence is complete. It is slightly more difficult to determine where to end one paragraph and start another.

A paragraph should have two structural characteristics:
- it should be separate from what precedes and what succeeds it for a discernible reason
- it should be connected to what precedes it and what succeeds it in a discernible way

In other words, there should be a reason why the paragraph starts and ends as it does, and there should be clear links from the paragraph to what goes before and what comes after.

There is no fixed rule to determine how to divide a long passage of text into paragraphs. The key to good paragraphing is a sense of structure. Here are just some of the criteria you may use to determine when to end one paragraph and start another:
- you have completed a particular point and intend to go on to a new point
- you are about to move from a particular point to a general point, or vice versa
- you are about elaborate at some length on a point just made
- you are about to draw a conclusion from the preceding text
- you are about to change the direction of your discourse

Whatever the criterion, it is generally advisable to apply it consistently within a single document. For example, if you are moving on from one paragraph to the next because you have completed a single point, then move on to yet another paragraph when you have completed your next point.

It is not generally a good enough reason to break up a passage of text into paragraphs simply because the text is too long. Closer examination of long passages will generally (although not always) reveal a sound criterion for splitting the text into paragraphs.

NOTE FOR DOCUPRAXIS® USERS: In business reports, it can sometimes be useful to set individual paragraphs as the lowest level of your outline. If, when you do this, you follow the guidelines set out in Hierarchies and Links, you will find, on printing your work, that your document is already sorted into discrete paragraphs which connect one with another.

9.3 Punctuation

The purpose of punctuation is to make the meaning of what is written as clear as possible. It fulfils in writing the functions of inflexion, intonation and pauses in speech.

In the following sub-section we give some guidelines on how to use each of the punctuation marks, but there is no need to follow every rule slavishly. Expert opinions vary on some points, and, on others, more than one approach is regarded as correct.

The two best aids in determining punctuation, once the essential function of each punctuation mark has been grasped, are logic and consistency.

9.3.1 Apostrophes

The main use of the apostrophe ['] is to indicate the possessive case.

"This is the company's best product."

NB: As noted elsewhere, there is no apostrophe in the possessive adjective "its".

The apostrophe is also used to indicate the omission of a letter; e.g. It's = It is.

"It's (i.e. It is) the best product of its (possessive adjective) kind."

Other examples of this use of the apostrophe to indicate the omission of one or more letters are given below:

can't, couldn't, didn't, haven't, he's, I'm, isn't, she's, they're, wasn't, we're, won't, wouldn't, you're

9.3.2 Colons

The colon [:] is used at the end of what would otherwise be a finished sentence to explain or expand on what has already been written.

"He provided everything for the project: brains, money, personnel and nerves of steel."
"He provided the brains for the project: his own and the computer program he had devised."

In both cases the post-colon section of the sentence explains and expands upon the pre-colon section. In many cases what follows the colon is some form of list.

The colon is also used:
- to introduce quotations, especially extended ones
- to express ratios, between numbers (e.g. 2:1).

9.3.3 Commas

The comma [,] is a means of separating units within a sentence in order to make clear where words and phrases belong and where their sense begins and ends.

Commas are used:
- to separate items listed within a sentence

"He took personal responsibility for the research, development, production, quality control and marketing of the product."
(NB: Some would add another comma after 'control')

- to separate a series of adjectives before a noun

"It turned out to be a difficult, expensive, time-consuming, risky venture."

- to mark the start and end points of a descriptive subordinate clause

"The Managing Director, who had recently joined us from the United States, was eager to assert his authority."

- to mark the end of a subordinate clause which precedes the main clause

"When the new Managing Director rose to speak, we all fell silent."

- to separate main clauses joined by a conjunction in the same sentence

"The Managing Director spoke, and the General Manager took copious notes."

- before 'please', when please is at the end of a sentence
- generally to separate words, phrases or clauses from the rest of the sentence to increase clarity or to achieve the right emphasis

"That, I have to say, is just about the lamest excuse I have ever heard.
"That's rubbish, isn't it?"

9.3.4 Exclamation Marks

The exclamation mark [!] denotes the end of a sentence which the author considers exclamatory: i.e. abrupt, exciting or surprising, or a peremptory command.

e.g.
"Watch it!"
"What a good idea!"
"Really!"
"Go away!"

In many contexts, it is up to the author to determine whether such sentences merit an exclamation mark. "We shall succeed" could end with a full stop ("We shall succeed.") or an exclamation mark ("We shall succeed!"), depending on sense and the emphasis the author wishes the sentence to carry.

In other cases, the choice might be between an exclamation mark and a question mark:

"Aren't they beautiful!" or "Aren't they beautiful?"

9.3.5 Full Stops

The full stop [.] is one of the punctuation marks that brings a sentence to an end. (Others are the question mark and the exclamation mark.)

The full stop is also used to terminate some abbreviations: e.g. A.D., e.g., etc.

NB: A sentence must make complete sense in itself. It must therefore contain at least one main clause.

In general, in business documents, short sentences are preferable to long ones. In particular, the use of long sentences, like the use of long words, to disguise a lack of clarity in thought, is always counter-productive.

9.3.6 Hyphens

The hyphen [-] is used to mark the break point in a word which is split between the end of one line and the start of the next. The break point is at the end of one of the syllables:

> allit-eration, ambig-uity, employ-ment, pronunc-iation

The hyphen may also be used in words such as co-operation, where the absence of the hyphen (cooperation) could lead to problems of pronunciation.

The hyphen is also used to link numbers between 21 and 99 when they are written in letters:

> twenty-one, ninety-nine

NB: In business documents, it is common practice to write the numbers one to ten in letters and to express numbers above ten in numbers.

9.3.7 Question Marks

The question mark [?] denotes the end of a direct question. In other words, we place a question mark at the end of a sentence which expects an answer.

> "Shall we succeed?"

NB: We do not use a question mark at the end of an indirect question.

> "He asked whether we intended to support his candidacy." (no question mark).

9.3.8 Quotation Marks

There are two forms of quotation marks
- 'single inverted commas'
- "double inverted commas"

One of these forms is used to denote quotations within direct speech, the other to denote direct speech itself. Which fulfils each role seems to be a matter of personal preference.

> The speaker declared: 'When John Donne said "No man is an island", he spoke for all of us'.

or

> The speaker declared: "When John Donne said 'No man is an island', he spoke for all of us".

9.3.9 Semi-colons

The symbol for the semi-colon [;] is a full stop on top of a comma and it may be useful to think of the semi-colon as a half-way house between the two.

The semi-colon's most common use is to join together two sentences when, because of the sense, a full stop at the end of the first sentence would seem unnecessarily abrupt and yet the use of a conjunction to join them together would create a lengthy, cumbersome construction.

> "Mary proved herself an expert motivator of staff; Peter managed the administration most effectively."

In this example, we could make two sentences, simply by replacing the semi-colon with a full stop, or make it one sentence without a semi-colon by using a conjunction to join the two clauses together.

> "Mary proved herself an expert motivator of staff, while Peter managed the administration most effectively."

(In passing, note the ambiguity that can arise with the use of 'while'. In the sentence above, 'while' can simply mean 'whereas' but it could also mean 'during the period that' or 'for as long as', suggesting that Mary's motivational success depended at least to some extent on Peter's administrative efficiency.)

9.4 Vocabulary
9.4.1 Register

We have mentioned elsewhere the need to make sure that you address your audience in a form of language with which they are familiar and comfortable. This rule applies to oral presentations as well as to written reports.

Here we are talking about **register**, that is the type of language (vocabulary and syntax) used. There are three criteria for assessing register, although there is some overlap.

Field of Discourse

This is primarily about the type of vocabulary used. Every specialist area develops its own jargon, its own technical terms, on the assumption that the audience is literate in that vocabulary. It is not appropriate to use this vocabulary when communicating with a lay audience.

The following example appearing on the Digital Marketing Show website (2013) is an example of text which would be perfectly intelligible to the audience for which it is intended but which would probably leave the lay person little the wiser:

> "Interactive ads served before video content (pre-rolls) are twice as popular in the UK as they are globally, according to new data from AdoTube, the in-stream video advertising specialist owned by Exponential Interactive. Interactive pre-rolls accounted for twice the share of in-stream video ads in the UK (72%) in 2012 than they did globally (36%). In contrast, standard pre-rolls accounted for 25% in the UK – almost half the global share (46%)".

Mode of Discourse

This is about the medium of communication being used. The syntax of the spoken word is different from the syntax used in writing. The form of expression on BBC2 will tend to be different from that used on BBC1. Those communicating on Radio 4 will certainly use a different vocabulary and syntax from those working on Radio 1. The quality press will use a different vocabulary and syntax from the mid-market and popular press.

Here is an example of the different ways of headlining a news story:

"BEEB's £22m on 'gagging pay-off' deals" (The Sun, 20/06/2013)

"BBC spends £28million on gagging orders: 500 staff silenced using licence fee money" (Daily Mail)

"BBC spent £28m of licence-fee payers' money gagging 500 staff" (The Telegraph).

The Sun uses the colloquial 'Beeb', even though in written form it is longer than 'BBC'. The headline is short, in keeping with the preference (and the likely attention span) of the average Sun reader.

The Daily Mail's headline is the longest, containing more information than the Sun headline but no more than the Daily Telegraph headline.

The Daily Mail and the Telegraph headlines carry the same information but while the Telegraph composes all the information in one sentence, the Daily Mail chooses to use two.

Manner of Discourse

This is about the social and possibly hierarchical relationship between the communicator and the audience. The register for a boss talking to an employee will generally be different from the register of the employee talking to the boss.

ααα

The real point here is that communication does not exist in a vacuum, nor is it a narcissistic or solipsistic activity. It is a process that takes place between a communicator and an audience. It is not enough to say what you mean. It is not even enough to say what you mean in such a way that what you say cannot be taken to mean anything else. You also have to say what you mean in a way that enables your audience to understand what you mean.

In many cases in business, you will be addressing your peers, so problems of register are much less likely to arise but, even amongst your peers, there will be different levels of knowledge and expertise so it is always better to err on the side of clarity and simplicity, even if, on occasions, that policy militates against brevity.

9.4.2 Alternatives for over-worked words

There are some words, especially in business documents, which are over-worked. Their repetition is tedious and stylistically regrettable.

Where possible, it is a good idea to vary the words used. Sometimes we can even convey a more precise meaning by careful selection of an alternative word.

Below we list some of the words which fall into this category, with suggestions for possible alternatives. These alternatives are not necessarily synonyms. They are words which, ***in particular contexts,*** might serve as well as, or better than, the word they replace. For example, under 'observe' you will find 'accept'. 'Observe' does not mean 'accept', but in the sentence "He observed the rules I had laid down", 'observed' could reasonably be replaced by 'accepted'.

WORD	ALTERNATIVES
ability	aptitude, capability, control, efficacy, facility, faculty, skill, talent
Able	accomplished, capable, clever, competent, effective, proficient, talented
accede	(v) agree, allow, comply, concur, consent, permit
accept	agree, embrace, receive, take
achieve	accomplish, attain, complete, execute, finish, fulfil, perform, realise
accidentally	inadvertently, unintentionally
accurate	correct, exact, faultless, precise, punctilious
accomplished	able, adroit, expert, practised, proficient
acquaint	advise, apprise, enlighten, inform, notify, tell
administer	arrange, conduct, control, manage, organise, order, oversee, run, supervise
advance	(v) amplify, develop, elaborate, expand, foster, progress, promote
advice	counsel, recommendation
advise	acquaint, apprise, enlighten, inform, notify, prescribe, propose, recommend, suggest, tell
Affirm	assert, declare, express, speak, say, tell
Agree	accede, allow, comply, concur, consent, permit
agreement	approval, assent, consent, permission
aim	(n) goal, intention, objective, purpose, target
aim	(v) attempt, endeavour, seek, strain, strive, try
Alert	astute, awake, discerning, sharp, shrewd, understanding
allow	accede, agree, comply, concur, consent, permit
allowable	lawful, legal, legitimate, permissible
ambiguity	equivocation, uncertainty
ambiguous	confusing, doubtful, equivocal, uncertain, undefined
amend	correct, improve, rectify, redress, remedy
analyse	(v) assess, deconstruct, dissect, evaluate

WORD	ALTERNATIVES
analysis	(n) appreciation, assessment, criticism, critique, evaluation, judgement
answer	(n) rejoinder, reply, response, retort
answer	(v) rejoin, reply, respond
apart from	analysis, appreciation, assessment, criticism, critique, evaluation, judgement
appreciation	acknowledgement, analysis, appraisal, approval, assessment, criticism, critique, evaluation, judgement, recognition
apprise	acquaint, advise, enlighten, inform, notify, tell
appropriate	fitting, proper, right, suitable
approval	(n) agreement, assent, consent, permission
argue	contend, debate, imply, plead, present, suggest
argument	conflict, difference, disagreement, dispute, dissension, dissent, divergence, quarrel
arrange	align, catalogue, categorise, co-ordinate, manage, marshall, organise, order
arrangement	configuration, constitution, construction, fixtures, formation, framework, organisation, plans
assent	(n) agreement, approval, consent, permission
assess	analyse, deconstruct, dissect, evaluate
assessment	analysis, appreciation, criticism, critique, evaluation, judgement
assumption	belief, conjecture, guess, hypothesis, speculation, supposition, surmise, theory
astute	discerning, perceptive, perspicacious, sharp, shrewd, understanding
attain	accomplish, achieve, complete, execute, finish, fulfil, perform, realise
attempt	(n) effort, endeavour, enterprise, project, undertaking, scheme, venture
attempt	(v) aim, endeavour, seek, strain, strive, try
attention	care, focus, mindfulness, regard

WORD	ALTERNATIVES
authority	control, influence, jurisdiction, power, sway
background	circumstances, context, environment, history
barring	apart from, except, excluding, other than
basic	crucial, essential, important, key, major, principal
belief	assumption, conjecture, guess, hypothesis, speculation, supposition, surmise, theory
bias (v)	incline, influence, predispose, prejudice, skew, sway
bring about	achieve, accomplish, act, conduct, do, effect, execute, implement, perform, transact
bring to light	elicit, bring out, draw out, evoke, produce
bring out	bring to light, draw out, elicit, evoke, produce
broach	commence, inaugurate, initiate, institute, start
cancel	abolish, abort, annul, conclude, discontinue, end, finish, stop, terminate
capable	competent, effective, efficient, qualified, skilful
category	class, division, part, portion, section, segment
celebrate	accept, extol, honour, keep, laud, observe, praise
chance	contingency, fortune, opportunity, opening, possibility
choose	adopt, designate, elect, opt for, pick, select, single out
circulate	disseminate, promulgate, publish, spread
circumstance	case, instance, plight, position, predicament, scenario, situation, state, status
clarification	definition, elucidation, explanation, explication, exposition, illumination, simplification
class	category, division, part, portion, section, segment
clever	able, capable, gifted, smart, talented
cogent	compelling, conclusive, convincing, persuasive, potent, powerful
coherent	coherent, connected, consistent, intelligible, logical, rational, well-organised
commence	broach, inaugurate, initiate, institute, start

WORD	ALTERNATIVES
commission (v)	appoint, contract, engage, select
communicate	air, announce, circulate, disseminate, impart, proclaim, promulgate, publish, reveal, spread, transmit
competent	able, capable, fit, qualified
compliance	acquiescence, agreement, assent, conformity, consent
complete (v)	accomplish, attain, execute, finish, fulfil, perform, realise
complex	difficult, exacting, hard, intricate, involved, obscure, perplexing
comply	accede, agree, allow, concur, consent, permit
comprehend	discern, grasp, perceive, understand
concept	design, hypothesis, idea, invention, notion, view
conclude	cancel, decide, deduce, determine, discontinue, end, finish, judge, stop, terminate
conclusion	consequence, effect, outcome, result
conclusive	convincing, decisive, indisputable, irrefutable
concur	(v) accede, agree, allow, comply, consent, permit
conducive	contributing, instrumental
conduct	(v) achieve, accomplish, act, bring about, effect, execute, implement, perform, transact
configuration	arrangement, constitution, construction, formation, framework, organisation
confirm	assure, authenticate, endorse, establish, ratify, reinforce, substantiate, validate, verify
conflict	argument, difference, disagreement, dispute, dissension, dissent, divergence, quarrel
conjecture	assumption, belief, guess, hypothesis, speculation, supposition, surmise, theory
consent	(n) agreement, approval, assent, permission
consent	(v) accede, agree, allow, comply, concur, permit
consequence	conclusion, effect, outcome, result
consistent	coherent, connected, intelligible, logical, rational, well-organised

WORD	ALTERNATIVES
constitution	arrangement, configuration, construction, formation, framework, organisation, structure
construction	arrangement, building, configuration, constitution, explanation, fabrication, formation, framework, interpretation, organisation, version
contend	argue, debate, imply, plead, present, suggest
contentious	controversial, debatable
context	background, frame of reference, framework
contingency	chance, event, incident, occurrence
controversial	contentious, debatable
co-ordinate	arrange, manage, marshall, organise, order
correct	(adj.) accurate, exact, faultless, precise, punctilious
correct	(v) amend, improve, rectify, redress, remedy
criticism	analysis, appreciation, assessment, critique, evaluation, judgement
critique	(n) analysis, appreciation, assessment, criticism, evaluation, judgement
crucial	basic, critical, decisive, essential, fundamental, indispensable, key, necessary, principal, requisite, vital
cycle	(n) period, season, term, time, duration
data	facts, information, intelligence
debatable	contentious, controversial
decent	equitable, fair, honest, honourable, straight, straightforward, true, trustworthy, upright
decision	conclusion
decisive	conclusive, incisive
declare	assert, affirm, express, speak, say, tell
deconstruct	analyse, assess, dissect, evaluate
define	delineate, detail, determine, explain, outline
definition	clarification, elucidation, explanation, explication, exposition

WORD	ALTERNATIVES
deny	disallow, discard, dismiss, exclude, reject, repudiate, spurn, veto
describe	define, delineate, depict, detail, draw, illustrate, narrate, recount, trace
design	(n) aim, plan, project, scheme, undertaking
design	(v) conceive, draft, draw, invent, originate, outline, plan
designate	(v) allot, assign, call, choose, define, denote, entitle, label, name, select
destroy	annihilate, crush, demolish, devastate, eradicate, extirpate, raze, smash
determine	ascertain, choose, conclude, decide, discover, establish
develop	advance, amplify, elaborate, expand, foster, progress, promote
devise	concoct, contrive, invent
difficult	complex, exacting, hard, obscure, perplexing
disagreement	argument, conflict, difference, dispute, dissension, dissent, divergence, quarrel
disallow	deny, discard, dismiss, exclude, reject, repudiate, spurn, veto
discern	comprehend, grasp, perceive, understand
discontinue	cancel, conclude, discontinue, end, finish, stop, terminate
disinclined	loath, reluctant, unwilling
dismiss	disregard, reject
dispute	argument, conflict, difference, disagreement, dissension, dissent, divergence, quarrel
dissect	assess, analyse, deconstruct, evaluate
disseminate	circulate, promulgate, publish, spread, transmit
dissent	argument, conflict, difference, disagreement, dispute, dissension, divergence, quarrel
division	category, class, part, portion, section, segment
do	achieve, accomplish, act, bring about, conduct, effect, execute, implement, perform, perpetrate, pursue, transact

WORD	ALTERNATIVES
document	(n) paper, proposal, record, report, submission, thesis
document	(v) detail, minute, note, record, report
draw out	bring to light, bring out, elicit, evoke, produce
effect	(n) conclusion, consequence, outcome, result
effect	(v) achieve, accomplish, act, bring about, conduct, do, execute, implement, perform, transact
effective	competent, cogent, convincing, efficacious, forceful, potent, powerful
efficacy	ability, competence, potency, power
efficient	capable, competent, effective, focused, potent
elaborate	(v) advance, amplify, develop, embellish, enhance, expand, foster, progress, promote, refine
elicit	bring to light, bring out, draw out, evoke, produce
embellish	elaborate, enhance, expand, foster, progress, refine
employ	apply, commission, enlist, make use of, use
endeavour	aim, attempt, seek, strain, strive, try
endorse	advise, prescribe, propose, recommend, suggest
enlighten	acquaint, advise, apprise, inform, notify, tell
enterprise	attempt, effort, endeavour, project, undertaking, scheme, venture
environment	background, conditions, context, milieu, scene, situation, surroundings
episode	circumstance, contingency, event, happening, incident, occurrence
equal	equivalent, even, level, tantamount
equitable	disinterested, even-handed, fair, impartial, just, reasonable
erroneous	inaccurate, false, imprecise, incorrect, inexact, unsound, wrong
error	fault, inaccuracy, miscalculation, mistake
essential	basic, crucial, fundamental, indispensable, key, necessary, principal, requisite, vital

WORD	ALTERNATIVES
establish	confirm, demonstrate, prove, show, substantiate, validate, verify
evaluate	analyse, assess, deconstruct, dissect, gauge, judge, rank, rate, value
evaluation	analysis, appraisal, appreciation, assessment, criticism, critique, judgement
event	chance, contingency, incident, occurrence
evince	display, establish, exhibit, indicate, make evident, manifest, prove, show
evoke	bring to light, bring out, draw out, elicit, produce
exact	accurate, faultless, precise, punctilious
examine	explore, investigate, probe, research, study
except	apart from, barring, excluding, other than
exclude	deny, disallow, discard, reject, repudiate, veto
excluding	apart from, barring, except, other than
execute	achieve, accomplish, act, bring about, conduct, do, effect, implement, perform, transact
expand	amplify, develop, elaborate, embellish, enhance, foster, grow, increase, progress, promote
explanation	clarification, definition, elucidation, explication, exposition
exposition	clarification, definition, elucidation, explanation, explication
express	assert, affirm, declare, speak, say, tell
facts	data, information, intelligence
fail	be unsuccessful, crash, fall short, founder, sink
failure	collapse, defeat, fiasco
fair	decent, equitable, honest, honourable, straight, straightforward, true, trustworthy, upright
false	erroneous, inaccurate, imprecise, incorrect, inexact, unsound, wrong
fault	error, inaccuracy, miscalculation, mistake

WORD	ALTERNATIVES
finish	accomplish, attain, complete, end, execute, finalise, fulfil, perform, realise
fitting	appropriate, proper, right, suitable
foster	advance, amplify, develop, elaborate, encourage, enhance, expand, progress, promote, refine
framework	arrangement, configuration, constitution, construction, formation, organisation, outline, structure
fulfil	accomplish, attain, complete, execute, finish, perform, realise
fundamental	basic, crucial, critical, essential, indispensable, key, necessary, principal, requisite, vital
goal	aim, objective, purpose, target
grasp	comprehend, discern, perceive, understand
gifted	able, capable, clever, smart, talented
happen	occur
hard	complex, demanding, difficult, exacting, obscure, perplexing
honest	decent, equitable, fair, honourable, straight, straightforward, true, trustworthy, upright
honourable	decent, equitable, fair, honest, straight, straightforward, true, trustworthy, upright
hypothesis	assumption, belief, conjecture, guess, speculation, supposition, surmise, theory
idea	concept, inspiration, notion, thought
ill-advised	ill-conceived, ill-judged, imprudent, injudicious, unwise
ill-judged	ill-advised, ill-conceived, imprudent, injudicious, unwise
impact	effect, hit, impression
implement	achieve, accomplish, act, bring about, complete, conduct, do, effect, execute, perform, transact
important	grave, major, momentous, notable, serious, significant (of), urgent, valuable
imprecise	erroneous, inaccurate, false, incorrect, inexact, unsound, wrong

WORD	ALTERNATIVES
improve	amend, correct, rectify, redress, remedy
imprudent	foolhardy, ill-advised, ill-conceived, ill-judged, injudicious, reckless, unwise
inaccuracy	error, fault, miscalculation, mistake
inaccurate	erroneous, false, imprecise, incorrect, inexact, unsound, wrong
inadvertently	accidentally, unintentionally, serendipitously
inaugurate	broach, commence, initiate, institute, start
incessant	ceaseless, constant, continuous, perpetual, unceasing, unending, unremitting
incident	chance, circumstance, contingency, episode, event, happening, incident, occurrence
incline	(v) bias, influence, predispose, prejudice, skew, sway
include	add, comprehend, comprise, embrace, encompass, incorporate, subsume
including	comprising, embracing, encompassing, inclusive of, incorporating
incorrect	erroneous, inaccurate, false, imprecise, incorrect, inexact, unsound, wrong
indicate	betoken, demonstrate, denote, evince, illustrate, intimate, make evident, prove, show, suggest
indispensable	basic, crucial, critical, decisive, essential, fundamental, key, necessary, principal, requisite, vital
inexact	erroneous, inaccurate, false, imprecise, incorrect, unsound, wrong
influence	(n) affect, bias, control power, sway, weight
influence	(v) affect, bias, move, persuade, skew, sway
inform	acquaint, advise, apprise, enlighten, inform, notify, tell
information	data, intelligence, knowledge
initiate	broach, commence, inaugurate, institute, start
injudicious	foolhardy, ill-advised, ill-conceived, ill-judged, reckless, unwise
institute	(v) broach, commence, inaugurate, initiate, start

WORD	ALTERNATIVES
instrumental	conducive, contributing
integrity	coherence, cohesion, honesty, honour, probity, rectitude
intelligent	alert, astute, clever, discerning, shrewd, understanding
intelligible	coherent, connected, consistent, intelligible, logical, rational, well-organised
intention	aim, design, end, goal, plan, purpose
invent	concoct, contrive, design, devise, originate
investigate	(v) consider, examine, explore, inspect, probe, research, scrutinise, study
issue (n)	(n) concern, point, problem, question, subject, topic
judgement	analysis, appreciation, assessment, criticism, critique, evaluation
key	(adj.) basic, crucial, essential, important, major, principal
lawful	allowable, legal, legitimate, permissible
legal	allowable, lawful, legitimate, permissible
loath	disinclined, reluctant, unwilling
legitimate	allowable, lawful, legal, permissible
list	(n) catalogue, index, record, register, schedule
list	(v) catalogue, enumerate, itemise, record, register, tabulate
logical	coherent, connected, consistent, intelligible, rational, well-organised
manage	administer, arrange, control, co-ordinate, effect, engineer, govern, manipulate, marshall, organise, order, oversee, plan, run
manner	means, method, procedure, process, scheme, system, technique, way
method	manner, means, procedure, process, scheme, system, technique, way
miscalculation	error, fault, inaccuracy, mistake
mistake	error, fault, inaccuracy, miscalculation
necessary	basic, crucial, essential, fundamental, indispensable, requisite, vital

WORD	ALTERNATIVES
notify	acquaint, advise, apprise, enlighten, inform, tell
objective	aim, goal, purpose, target
observe	accept, celebrate, comply with, keep, mark, note, notice, perceive, see, remark, watch
occur	chance, happen
occurrence	chance, circumstance, contingency, episode, event, happening, incident
opportunity	chance, contingency, gap, occasion, opening
order	(n) arrangement, array, layout, pattern, plan, system
order	(v) align, arrange, categorise, manage, marshall, organise, plan
originate	concoct, design, devise, invent
organise	align, arrange, catalogue, categorise, co-ordinate, manage, marshall, order, plan
organisation	arrangement, company, configuration, constitution, construction, formation, framework, institution, structure
other than	apart from, barring, except, excluding
outcome	conclusion, consequence, effect, result
part	category, class, division, portion, section, segment
pattern	arrangement, design, motif
perceive	comprehend, discern, grasp, understand
perception	apprehension, understanding
perceptive	astute, discerning, perspicacious, shrewd, understanding
perform	achieve, accomplish, act, attain, bring about, complete, conduct, do, effect, enact, execute, finish, implement, transact
period	cycle, duration, season, term, time
permissible	allowable, lawful, legal, legitimate
permission	(n) agreement, approval, assent, consent
permit	(v) accede, agree, allow, comply, concur, consent
perpetrate	act, bring about, effect, execute, implement, perform, transact (all in a negative sense)

WORD	ALTERNATIVES
perspicacious	astute, discerning, perceptive, shrewd, understanding
plan	approach, design, means, procedure, process, programme, scheme, system, technique, way
plead	argue, beg, contend, debate, imply, present, suggest
potent	effective, cogent, powerful, strong
potential	(adj.) capable, latent, possible
potential	(n) ability, capability, possibility, power
power	ability, authority, capability, command, control, efficacy, might, potency, strength
practice	conduct, custom, habit, manner, method, procedure, usage
practise	apply, do, enact, exercise, perform, perpetrate, train
praise	(n) acclamation, approbation, approval, congratulations
praise	(v) acclaim, applaud, approve, commend, congratulate, laud
precise	(adj.) accurate, exact, faultless, punctilious
predispose	bias, incline, influence, prejudice, skew, sway
prejudice	bias, incline, influence, predispose, skew, sway
prescribe	advise, endorse, propose, recommend, suggest
present	(v) display, exhibit, express, give, grant, introduce, show
problem	difficulty, dilemma, dispute
procedure	manner, means, method, process, scheme, system, technique, way
process	manner, means, method, procedure, system, technique, way
produce	(v) accomplish, achieve, bring to light, bring out, conceive, draw out, effect, elicit, engender, evoke, exhibit, furnish, generate, show, yield
progress	(n) advance, amelioration, gain, headway
progress	(v) advance, amplify, develop, elaborate, embellish, enhance, expand, foster, improve, promote, refine
project	attempt, effort, endeavour, enterprise, undertaking, scheme, venture

WORD	ALTERNATIVES
promote	advance, amplify, boost, elaborate, encourage, enhance, expand, foster, nurture, progress, refine, stimulate, support
promulgate	circulate, disseminate, publish, spread
proper	appropriate, fitting, right, suitable
proposal	bid, idea, offer, plan, proposition, scheme, suggestion
propose	move, present, recommend, submit, suggest
prove	ascertain, demonstrate, establish, substantiate, verify
publish	air, announce, communicate, circulate, disseminate, proclaim, promulgate, reveal, spread, transmit
purpose	aim, design, end, goal, objective, target
quarrel	argument, conflict, difference, disagreement, dispute, dissension, dissent, divergence
rational	coherent, connected, consistent, intelligible, logical, well-organised
reasonable	equitable, fair, just, proper, rational, sensible
receive	accept, acquire, gain, greet, take, welcome
reckless	foolhardy, ill-advised, ill-conceived, indiscrete, ill-judged, injudicious, reckless, unwise, volatile, wild
recommend	advise, endorse, prescribe, propose, suggest
recommendation	advice, counsel
record	(n) account, evidence, history, list, log, memorandum, register
record	(v) document, log, minute, note, register
rectify	amend, correct, improve, redress, remedy
redress	amend, correct, improve, rectify, remedy
reject	(v) deny, disallow, discard, dismiss, exclude, reject, repudiate, spurn, veto
reluctant	disinclined, loath, unwilling
remedy	amend, correct, improve, rectify, redress
repudiate	disallow, discard, dismiss, exclude, reject, spurn
reply	(n) answer, rejoinder, response, retort

WORD	ALTERNATIVES
reply	(v) answer, rejoin, respond
report	(n) account, document, statement
report	(v) announce, declare, describe, detail, state
research	(n) analysis, examination, inquiry, investigation, scrutiny, study
research	(v) examine, explore, investigate, probe, study
respond	(v) answer, rejoin, reply
response	(n) answer, rejoinder, reply, retort
result	(n) conclusion, consequence, effect, end, issue, product, outcome
reveal	announce, disclose, divulge, expose, show, uncover
right	(adj.) appropriate, fitting, proper, suitable
say	acquaint, affirm, declare, express, speak, tell
scenario	case, circumstance, instance, plight, position, predicament, situation, state, status
scheme	attempt, effort, endeavour, enterprise, project, undertaking, venture
scrutinise	examine, explore, investigate, probe, research, sift, study
significant	expressive, indicative
season	cycle, duration, period, term, time
section	category, class, division, part, portion, segment
seek	aim, attempt, endeavour, strain, strive, try
segment	category, class, division, part, portion, section
show	illustrate, demonstrate, evince, indicate, make evident, prove
simplification	clarification, elucidation, explanation
simplify	abstract, clarify, deconstruct, elucidate, facilitate, make less complicated, précis, summarise
situation	case, circumstance, instance, plight, position, predicament, scenario, state, status
skew	bias, incline, influence, predispose, prejudice, sway

WORD	ALTERNATIVES
speak	assert, affirm, declare, express, say, tell
speculation	assumption, belief, conjecture, guess, hypothesis, supposition, surmise, theory
start	broach, commence, inaugurate, initiate, institute
stimulate	arouse, encourage, foment, incite, prompt, provoke, spur on
strain (v)	aim, attempt, endeavour, seek, strive, try
status	circumstance, position, rank, ranking, reputation, situation
strive	aim, attempt, endeavour, seek, strain, try
structure	arrangement, configuration, constitution, construction, formation, framework, organisation, structure
succeed	excel, overcome, triumph, win
success	triumph, victory, win
suitable	appropriate, fitting, proper, right
suggest	advise, argue, endorse, prescribe, propose, recommend
supervise	administer, conduct, control, direct, oversee, run
supposition	assumption, belief, conjecture, guess, hypothesis, speculation, surmise, theory
system	manner, means, method, plan, procedure, process, scheme, technique, way
talented	able, capable, clever, gifted, smart
tell	acquaint, advise, affirm, apprise, declare, enlighten, express, inform, notify, say
terminate	abort, cancel, close, conclude, discontinue, end, finish, stop
time	cycle, duration, period, season, term
transact	achieve, accomplish, act, bring about, conduct, do, effect, execute, implement, perform
trustworthy	decent, equitable, fair, honest, honourable, straight, straightforward, true, upright
try	aim, attempt, endeavour, seek, strain, strive
result	conclusion, consequence, effect, outcome
sway	bias, incline, influence, predispose, prejudice, skew

WORD	ALTERNATIVES
technique	manner, means, method, procedure, process, system, way
theory	assumption, belief, conjecture, guess, hypothesis, speculation, supposition, surmise
train	(v) coach, direct, educate, exercise, instruct, teach
training	(n) education, coaching, instruction, teaching
try	aim, attempt, endeavour, seek, strain, strive
understand	comprehend, discern, grasp, perceive
understanding	comprehension, intelligence
undertaking	(n) attempt, effort, endeavour, enterprise, project, scheme, venture
unintentionally	accidentally, inadvertently
unwilling	disinclined, loath, reluctant
upright	decent, equitable, fair, honest, honourable, straight, straightforward, true, trustworthy
Use	exercise, employ, practise, utilize
useful	beneficial, conducive, effective, helpful, practical, suitable, serviceable, valuable
Valid	cogent, logical, powerful, sound
validate	authenticate, certify, confirm, endorse, ratify, substantiate
venture	attempt, effort, endeavour, enterprise, project, undertaking, scheme
Vital	crucial, critical, essential, fundamental, indispensable, key, requisite
well-organised	coherent, connected, consistent, intelligible, logical, rational
wrong	erroneous, inaccurate, false, incorrect, unsound

NB: The use of alternatives can enrich and enliven the text of any document, enabling the writer to avoid tedious repetition. When writing manuals of any kind, however, it is important to use the same word or phrase for each feature consistently throughout. The manual writer can cause great confusion by using two, or even three, different terms for the same thing. The reader may justifiably but wrongly assume that the text is referring to two or three different features.

9.5 FIGURES OF SPEECH

This section contains information that could be helpful to some users. It explains and provides examples of a number of figures of speech which can be employed to enrich the texture of writing.

For most business-writing purposes, this section can safely be ignored.

9.5.1 Alliteration

Alliteration is the repetition, close together, of a letter (usually a consonant) at the beginning of a word, or a syllable within a word:

"Peter Piper picked a peck of pickled pepper."

Business Writing: While a writer may at any time decide to embellish his work with alliteration, the primary use of alliteration in a business context is in advertising:

"Put a **t**iger in your **t**ank."
"**G**uinness is **g**ood for you"

Creative Writing: Both prose and, especially, poetry make frequent and effective use of alliteration which, like rhythm and rhyme, are pleasing to the ear.

9.5.2 Ambiguity

Ambiguity allows a single formulation of words to carry more than one meaning.

Business Writing: Ambiguity is almost always to be avoided in business communications where the general aim is simplicity, clarity and precision. In this Guide, we have therefore dealt with ambiguity under Grammatical & Verbal Hazards.

Journalism: Newspaper headlines are a fertile field in which to spot ambiguities (usually unintentional).

"Camouflaged army vehicle disappears."
"Children make great meals".
"Homicide victims rarely talk to the police."
"Prostitute appeals to judge"
"Iraqi head seeks arms."
"Miners refuse to work after death."
"Reagan wins on budget, but more lies ahead."

And in normal writing, the author always needs to be aware of the possibility of ambiguity. Seemingly straightforward statements can be open to misinterpretation:

"The MD didn't reject the plan because Sabrina was the author",

leaves us guessing whether the MD did or did not reject the plan and, if he did or didn't, why?

Creative Writing: Intentional ambiguity is a powerful tool in the poet's workshop. (See "Seven Types of Ambiguity" by William Empson.)

9.5.3 Assonance

Assonance is the repetition, close together, of vowel sounds:

"no pain, no gain"
"time and tide wait for no man"
"I caught this morning morning's minion
kingdom of daylight's dauphin, dapple-dawn drawn falcon".
Gerald Manley Hopkins "The Windhover"

(The last two examples illustrate alliteration as well as assonance)

9.5.4 Euphemism
A euphemism is a gentle, oblique way of alluding to something that, if expressed more bluntly, might give offence or cause distress:

e.g.
- collateral damage (for civilian casualties in war)
- friendly fire (for accidentally firing on your own troops or allies in war)
- pass on (for die)
- pass wind (for belch)
- put to sleep (for humanely killing animals)
- surplus to requirement (for redundant)

Some 'politically correct' expressions are euphemistic:
- friends with benefits (friendship enhanced with occasional, non-romantic sex)
- significant other = sexual partner
- vertically challenged = short

Euphemisms are to be avoided unless there is justification for disguising the precise nature of the thought by understatement. To tell someone they are "surplus to requirement" may make the employer feel better but it is unlikely to soften the blow for the employee.

9.5.5 Hyperbole
Hyperbole is overstatement or exaggeration used as a means of emphasis.
"Age cannot wither her."
"He took infinite care in preparing his presentation."
"His performance was out of this world."

Hyperbole is to be avoided in business documents, with the possible exception of motivational presentations to salespersons.

9.5.6 Irony
Irony consists of saying the opposite of what is meant, with humorous or critical intent, or discerning irony (the opposite of what is meant or intended) in a situation:
"For Brutus is an honourable man
So are they all, all honourable men." *Julius Caesar; Act 3 Sc. 2; Shakespeare*
"It was ironic that the Chief Executive fired the only manager who had supported him in the secret ballot."

9.5.7 Litotes
Litotes consists of understatement, usually involving the use of a negative.

"He was not entirely surprised by the reaction of the shareholders" is an example of litotes, being an understatement for what is meant: i.e. "He was not (or even "not at all") surprised by the reaction of the shareholders."

The most common form of litotes involves the use of a double negative. Examples are:

"not infrequent" (i.e. quite frequent)
"not uncommon" (i.e. fairly common)
"not unusual" (i.e. usual)

but many adjectives, especially those referring to states of mind, can be used in litotes:

"I am not unaware of the seriousness of our predicament."
"We are not insensitive to the loss you have suffered."

9.5.8 Metaphor
A metaphor describes something as something else in order to bring out a particular quality.

e.g.
"He was the **light** of the world."
"He was a **lion** in battle."
"He was a **wolf** amongst sheep."
"She was a **rock** in a sea of uncertainty."

Language is full of metaphors, many of which are so familiar that their metaphorical origins are no longer recognised in everyday speech:

e.g.
- a **sterile** debate
- she **threw** him a glance
- she tried to **build** his self-confidence
- the idea **struck** him
- to **catch** sight of

9.5.9 Metonymy
Using one aspect or part of a person or thing to stand for the person or thing: e.g.
- the Crown (i.e. the Queen or the Monarchy)
- the Cloth (i.e. the Church)
- Dickens (the novels of Charles Dickens)
- the Press (editors and journalists)
- the Turf (for horse-racing)
- the pen is mightier than the sword (ideas are more powerful than violence).

9.5.10 Onomatopoeia
The formation of words to represent the sounds made by the thing they denote:

e.g.
- buzz
- fizz
- ping-pong

9.5.11 Oxymoron
The combining of contradictory terms to produce, through surprise, a striking effect:
e.g.
"He suffered a **glorious defeat**.."
"He unleashed a **storm of apathy**."
"It was a **living death**."
"He was a very **professional amateur**."
"The play was **sensationally boring**."

9.5.12 Paradox
A seeming nonsense which nevertheless reveals a deeper meaning or truth:
e.g.
"I must be cruel to be kind." *Hamlet, William Shakespeare*
"The child is father of the man." *William Wordsworth*
"What a pity that youth must be wasted on the young." *George Bernard Shaw*
"Careless she is with artful care, Affecting to seem unaffected." *William Congreve*
"All animals are equal, but some animals are more equal than others." *Animal Farm, George Orwell*
"Tough love."
"The sound of silence."
"The fool doth think he is wise, but the wise man knows himself to be a fool." *As You Like It, V.i, William Shakespeare*

9.5.13 Personification
To represent an abstract entity or an inanimate object as a human being or as having human characteristics:

"The sea does battle with the rocky shore,"
personifies the sea.

"Famine stalked the land."

Countries are often referred to as male or female (e.g. the German Fatherland, the Russian Motherland). This is a form of personification.

9.5.14 Rhetorical Question
A rhetorical question is a question for which the answer is obvious. It is used to elicit a nod of agreement rather than a reply from the audience.
"If you break every rule in the book, can you complain if they throw the book at you?"
(i.e. you can't complain)

9.5.15 Pun

Pun is a play on words. One word is made to carry two, usually conflicting and amusing, meanings. Shakespeare and the headlines of any contemporary newspaper are good sources of puns.

"Now is the winter of our discontent

Made glorious summer by this sun [son] of York." *Opening line of Richard III, William Shakespeare*

"A chicken crossing the road is poultry in motion."

"If you find yourself in a cul-de-sac, you need a backup plan."

"He who thinks he can walk on burning coals will know the agony of defeat."

"Sugar substitutes can make you feel full of sweetness and light."

9.5.16 Simile

A simile likens one thing to another in order to illustrate or emphasise a quality of the former by focusing on that same quality which is clearly evident in the latter. Typically it introduces the comparison with the words 'as' or 'like'.

e.g.

"Why man he doth bestride the world like a Colossus!" *Act 1, Scene II, Julius Caesar, William Shakespeare.*

"He was as useful as an ashtray on a motorbike."

"His idea was about as practical as an ejector seat on a helicopter."

"It was just about as sensible as a catflap on a submarine."

9.5.17 Syllepsis

Syllepsis is the figure of speech in which two or more words, usually nouns, are linked to a single verb which creates a striking incongruity by shifting its meaning when it is related to each of the nouns.

e.g.

"He arrived in a limousine and a filthy temper."

"He drove a Rolls Royce and a hard bargain."

"He lost his fortune and his sanity."

"First her tears dropped; then her guard."

"Having drunk too much, the man got into his car. He then left the public house, the road and a widow."

(i.e. he drove away from the public house; he skidded off the road; and was killed).

"The litigious tailor pressed his suit and then his case."

9.5.18 Synecdoche

Synecdoche is figure of speech in which the whole stands for the part, or the part for the whole. In the latter circumstance it is closely related to metonymy.

Examples of synecdoche are:

"England beat Germany five nil" (i.e. the English national football team beat the German national football team five nil)

"Man cannot live by bread alone" (where bread represents the material world).

9.5.19 Zeugma
Zeugma is the figure of speech in which two or more words, usually nouns, are linked to a single adjective or verb which is appropriate to only one of the words.
  "Be still my beating heart and soul!".
Presumably souls don't beat.

  "He was struck by the idea and the encouragement."
Presumably he was inspired, rather than struck, by the encouragement.

10 Thoughts on Further Aspects of Writing

10.1 HUMOUR

In most business reports there is not much room for humour, although the occasional flash of wit can help to enhance a point and re-awaken interest.

In business speeches, humour is probably second in importance only to content.

Humour should be relevant to the subject of the speech. Ideally it should form an integral part of the speech. The use of jokes which have no relevance to the speaker's subject generally seem forced.

10.2 PROVERBS/APHORISMS

There are many common expressions which an educated person may be expected to know and understand. Here we provide a selection of some of the best known, expressions and proverbs which you may come across in business life. Where the meaning of the expression may not be immediately clear, or where it is not infrequently misunderstood or misused, we provide a definition or notes.

EXPRESSION	MEANING
A bad workman blames his tools	Someone who is incompetent will excuse poor work by blaming the facilities he has used.
A bird in the hand is worth two in the bush	It is better to be satisfied with what you have than to hanker after more and risk losing what you have.
A chain is no stronger than its weakest link	The weakest component in any system, the weakest person in any team, determines the strength of the whole.

EXPRESSION	MEANING
A man is known by the company he keeps	The friends and associates that a man chooses will tell you the type of person he is. It has also been said that "You can tell a company by the men it keeps".
A man who is his own lawyer has a fool for a client	Never try to represent yourself in a legal dispute.
Attack is the best form of defence	When under attack, the best way to defend yourself is to attack. Another version is "Get your retaliation in first".
Better to travel hopefully than to arrive	This saying has two meanings. First it suggests that the real reward is in the journey, not in arriving at the destination. Secondly, it implies that many journeys end in disappointment and that, while on the journey, one can at least enjoy the hope that the journey will end happily.
Brevity is the soul of wit	Verbosity takes the edge off wit.
Buyer beware	A warning to purchasers to be on their guard. The Latin version 'caveat emptor' is in common use.
Circumstances alter cases	As a situation develops or changes, it is necessary to review one's attitude.
Clogs to clogs in three generations	Clogs are wooden shoes which were worn by the poorer people in the north of England. A poor man works hard and makes money; his son builds on his father's foundations; his grandson spends the accumulated wealth; the great grandson is poor and, if he is to succeed, must work hard again.
Credit where credit is due	Although one may have reservation in other respects, where a person has shown merit, it is only fair to acknowledge it.
Cut your coat according to your cloth	Plan your expenditure according to your available resources. (A problem for individuals and governments alike.)
Discretion is the better part of valour	However brave you are, there are many situations in which confrontation can be unnecessarily and dangerously rash.

EXPRESSION	MEANING
Divide and rule/ Divide and conquer	If you can split any group into factions, they will tend to fight with each other, providing you with the perfect opportunity to take control. Even if they remain at peace with each other, they will be weaker individually than united.
Don't change horse in mid-stream	When you are half way through implementing a particular plan, it is unwise to decide to change direction.
Don't count your chickens before they are hatched	Don't assume success until you know for certain you have succeeded.
Don't cross the bridge till you come to it	Don't anticipate problems; wait until it is necessary to deal with them. A common variant is: "We will cross that bridge when we come to it."
Don't let the urgent take precedence over the important	Beware of delaying the important because less important matters are more urgent. (Easier said than done.)
Don't put all your eggs in one basket	Don't risk everything on one venture. Or as a master at my school once quipped when recounting the story of a fire in a cinema in northern Spain; "Don't put all your Basques in one exit."
Don't teach your grandmother to suck eggs	Don't offer advice to those who are wiser or more experienced than you.
Falling between two stools	Failure to choose between alternatives can mean that, although you avoid the risks of choice, you also ensure you have no chance at all of success, and therefore are certain to fail.
Fool me once, shame on you; fool me twice, shame on me.	If you trick me once, I blame you; but if I let you trick me again, I blame myself. Another version is: "You diddle me once, shame on you; you diddle me twice, shame on me." Yet another: "Once bitten; twice shy".
Forewarned is forearmed	If you know what is going to happen, you can prepare for it.
From little acorns, mighty oak trees grow	From small beginnings, great things can come.

EXPRESSION	MEANING
Garbage in, garbage out	If your input is rubbish, you will get a rubbishy output. Originally a computer term, it now enjoys wider applications.
He who pays the piper calls the tune	Whoever is paying has the final decision on everything.
He who sups with the devil should have a long spoon	Show great caution when dealing with a dangerous or evil person.
Hoist with one's own petard	Caught out by one's own scheme. A petard was an explosive device, used by engineers in the 16th and 17th century to breaching walls in sieges. If detonated prematurely, the device would blow up the engineer rather than the wall.
If anything can go wrong, it will	This is variously known as Murphy's Law (after an American aircraft engineer) and Sod's Law.
If it ain't broke, don't fix it	This expression came from America. The English equivalent, which has brevity to recommend it, is "Let well alone".
If you can't stand the heat, get out of the kitchen	If you don't like the more challenging aspects of your job or the situation you find yourself in, don't complain - quit. Attributed to US Senator and then President Harry S Truman.
If you pay peanuts, you get monkeys	If you pay a low price, you will get a poor product or service.
If you're in a hole, stop digging	When in a difficult situation, further activity, especially of an excavational type, will often make things worse rather than better.
If you're not part of the solution, you are part of the problem	You are either helping us to solve the problem or you are obstructing us. This is close in meaning to: "You are either with us or against us".
In for a penny, in for a pound	If you have embarked on a course, you might as well see it through to the end. Indeed, you might as well be hanged for a sheep as a lamb.
In the country of the blind, the one-eyed man is king	When no one is fully able to deal with a situation, the one who has a little more competence than the others becomes pre-eminent. *"In regione caecorum rex est luscus."* Desiderius Erasmus, 1500.

EXPRESSION	MEANING
It is no use crying over spilt milk	Don't waste time regretting something which has already happened and which you cannot reverse.
It does what it says on the tin	It does exactly what it claims to do. This was originally an advertising slogan used by Ronseal, the wood stain and preservative manufacturer.
It's a pity to spoil the ship for a ha'porth of tar	One should not ruin an entire enterprise by stinting on a relatively small additional effort or expenditure. 'Ha'porth = 'halfpenny-worth'. Tar was used to make ships water-tight. Stinting on waterproofing could have disproportionately disastrous consequences.
It's all grist to the mill	Whatever is available will be put to good use. Grist is corn ready for grinding.
It's an ill wind that blows nobody any good	Bad news for one person is generally good news for someone else.
It's the early bird that catches the worm	Whoever gets in first has the advantage.
It's the last straw that breaks the camel's back	Because of the cumulative effect of previous factors, the next factor, although relatively small in itself, can bring a situation or a person to breaking point.
Know thyself	A recommendation of self-knowledge. See Alexander Pope's: "Know then thyself, presume not God to scan The proper study of Mankind is Man."
Make haste slowly	You will finish more quickly if you take the time to be careful along the way. The Latin is "festina lente".
Moore's Law	Moore's Law originated with the observation that integrated circuits tended to double in capacity every two years. Moore's Law has evolved to cover the exponential nature of development in computer hardware so it is now generally expressed as: "Computing capacity of hardware (i.e. computer chip performance) tends to double every 18 months."

EXPRESSION	MEANING
No pain, no gain	If you want to benefit, you have to put in the effort. This expression goes back to the 16th century.
Nothing is certain but death and taxes	The meaning is clear. Daniel Defoe paired death and taxes as perfectly certain and Benjamin Franklin couched the sentiment in the form of words best known today.
Nothing ventured, nothing gained	If you don't take any risks, you won't enjoy any profit.
One picture is worth a thousand words	In stimulating emotion, a picture can be far more effective than a verbal description.
Occam's Razor	The proposition that, given competing explanations for any phenomenon, the simplest explanation is the best and most likely to be correct (cf. the geocentric and the heliocentric explanations of planetary orbits). William of Ockham (c1287 –1347) was an English Franciscan friar and scholastic philosopher.
Parkinson's Law	Work expands to fill the time available for its completion.
Putt's Law	Putt's Law states that technology is dominated by two types of people: those who understand what they do not manage and those who manage what they do not understand.
Rogers' Diffusion of Innovations	Everett Rogers identified five categories of people in the process of accepting new technologies: • innovators • early adopters • early majority • late majority • laggards
Second thoughts are best	A period of reflection enables one to improve on one's first reaction to any situation.
Success has many fathers; failure is an orphan	Everyone is happy to claim responsibility for success; no one is prepared to take responsibility for failure.

EXPRESSION	MEANING
The end justifies the means	A good result can excuse dubious methods employed to achieve such a result. More frequently, the opposite is asserted: i.e. the ends cannot justify the means.
The exception that proves the rule	The original meaning, and the only one that makes any sense, is that an exception 'tests' the rule. Presumably, if the exception stands, the rule falls. The argument that an exception proves there must be rule for there to be an exception from it is of very doubtful logic. The common use of this saying to justify inconsistency suggests the expression should be abandoned altogether.
The longest journey begins with a single step	However intimidating the task, make a start.
The opera isn't over till the fat lady sings	Do not assume something is finished until you are certain it has ended. The allusion to the fat female songstress refers to some operas in which an aria by a rotund soprano is often a reliable indication that the opera is about to end.
The pen is mightier than the sword	Words and ideas are more powerful than physical strength or military might
The Peter Principle	Employees tend to rise to their own level of incompetence. The justification for this proposition is that, in any hierarchical organisation in which employees are promoted on merit, employees who prove competent are promoted until they reach a level where they are no longer competent, at which point they remain where they are. The Software Peter Principle states that there is a tendency for software to become so complex over time that, in the end, even the software developers no longer understand it.
The road to hell is paved with good intentions	Good intentions must lead to good actions; otherwise one is on the road to damnation. It does not mean that many people are damned because, although their intentions are good, the results are bad.

EXPRESSION	MEANING
There's no such thing as a free lunch	You can't get something for nothing. Although something may appear free, there is always a hidden cost.
What can't be cured must be endured	If it is impossible to rectify or improve a situation, you must accept it.
What you see is what you get	Originally a computer term, meaning that what you saw on the screen was exactly how it would appear when printed on paper. It now has a much wider application. Acronym: WYSIWYG
When one door shuts, another door opens	When we lose or are denied something we have become accustomed to, a new opportunity presents itself. The pessimists version is: "When one door shuts, another door closes".
When the going gets tough, the tough get going	When things get difficult, those who can handle it respond with vigour.
You can't make a silk purse out of a sow's ear	If you start with poor materials (literally or metaphorically), you cannot make something fine.
You can't make an omelette without breaking eggs	It is necessary to accept some damage as the price for achieving a desired end.
You win some; you lose some	Consolation for losers.

10.3 TRICKY WORD GUIDE
10.3.1 Criteria for advice on tricky words

There is a strong trend amongst contemporary writers on English usage to adopt a descriptive rather than prescriptive stance. In other words, rather than condemn a particular form of expression as incorrect, they prefer simply to describe and explain the expression and locate it amongst that class, community or group which uses such expressions.

In business writing, which requires clarity, there is a very strong argument for a rather more prescriptive approach and that is the one adopted here. At the same time, if we are to condemn an expression as incorrect it is only fair to set out the criteria we have used. So here are the grounds on which such expressions are condemned:
- avoidable ambiguity
- evident illogicality
- grammatical inconsistency
- unjustifiable verbicide

We give the simplest of examples of each type of transgression below, not because any reader is likely to make such mistakes but in order to illustrate the criteria on which we have tried to base our recommendations:

- **Avoidable Ambiguity**

"He only seems to put in some effort when under pressure."

Does this mean his effort is apparent, not real?

Or does it mean that, even when under pressure, he only puts in some effort, not all his effort?

Or does it mean he puts in effort only when under pressure?

Of these three possible interpretations, the third is probably most likely but that is no reason for excusing the ambiguity. After all, the first interpretation is the 'correct' one (because, according to its position, the 'only' qualifies 'seems') and that might be precisely the thought which the writer wished to express.

- **Evident Illogicality**

"He has not got no sense."

Logically this must mean he has at least some sense, which is not the writer's intended sense and therefore nonsense.

- **Grammatical Inconsistency**

"We was outraged by his prescriptive attitude to English usage."

'We' is plural; 'was' is singular.

"I, together with my entire team, are disappointed with your attitude."

It is the "I" that governs the verb and since "I" is singular, the verb should be singular.

"He said he had dismissed the salesman which had let us down."

'Which' is neuter. The salesman, for all his faults, is a person, not a thing, and deserves a 'who'.

"None of the managers are competent."

'None' means not one and therefore takes a singular verb.

- **Unjustifiable Verbicide**

"Although I made every effort to present my case as persuasively as possible, the manager was entirely disinterested."

Assuming that here 'disinterested' means 'not interested', this is an example of what seems to be a concerted effort either to eliminate 'disinterested' from the language or to make it a synonym for 'uninterested'.

While the meaning of disinterested (i.e. impartial) survives, the example given here is highly ambiguous. Does it mean the manager was 'not interested' or that he remained 'impartial'.

There is a fifth and admittedly rather dubious criterion for passing judgement, namely the consensus of educated people. Since the purpose of business writing is to communicate as clearly and efficiently as possible, it is not unreasonable to argue that, in our writing, we should adhere to the form of language understood and approved by our target readers. In the past, this criterion was the over-arching principle which would have embraced all the specific criteria set out here - and, no doubt, some others.

Today, we can be less sure of our ground. One of the consequences of the descriptive, as opposed to the prescriptive, approach to the language, is a weakening of consensus on correct usage and a fragmentation of the language itself. It is also the case that a new generation of young people is often more at ease with non-literary forms of communication, such as the oral, the visual or televisual.

Nevertheless, the elite (i.e. those who run government, the civil service and large corporations) continue to maintain agreed standards of English usage, quite simply because they need a precise form of communication, and words, correctly used, remain unrivalled whenever complex ideas call for clear expression.

Whether you plan to impress, or indeed join, the elite, or simply wish to communicate as efficiently as possible, we hope the criteria we have set seem reasonable and the advice we have given will prove helpful.

10.3.2 Tricky Words and Verbiage

There are many words in English which it is easy to confuse or misuse. In some cases, such errors simply offend against agreed conventions; in other cases, they derive from false etymology or failures of logic. Here we are primarily concerned to assist the writer in achieving clarity and avoiding ambiguity.

Using such words incorrectly is not a cardinal sin. Indeed almost every writer (including this one) will misuse a word or offend against some rule of grammar at some time. Nevertheless, in a business environment, especially at more senior levels, such mistakes can diminish the clarity of your discourse and may seriously damage your image. **And you will never know because no-one will ever tell you.**

There are also a number of words and phrases which are used as a means of avoiding clarity or in order to give the impression the author is more intelligent or saying something more important than is the case. These we place in the verbiage category (a vague and muddled land where there are more words than sense).

Below, we provide a list of the most common problems arising from such tricky words with advice on how best to deal with them. Where words have been paired, the explanations attached to the words are not conventional definitions. They are intended to focus on the differences between the words to help the user to distinguish between them.

Expression/ Term	Comment	Forms/ Tenses
at about	It is arguable that **about** in such expressions as: "The meeting will take place at about 11 a.m. tomorrow." is incorrect. 'At' is precise; 'about' is imprecise. The meeting will take place either at 11 a.m. or about 11 a.m.	

Expression/ Term	Comment	Forms/ Tenses
above	In written work, there is a convention that **above**, as in 'See the quotation above' invites the reader to look at previous pages, as well as higher up the same page.	
abrogate/ arrogate	**abrogate** = to cancel or get rid of in a formal sense **arrogate** = to claim or seize without justification of legal right.	abrogates/ abrogated/ abrogating; arrogates/ arrogated/ arrogating
accessary/ accessory	**accessary** = a person implicated in a crime but not the perpetrator. "'By helping the killer to escape, he became an accessary to murder." **accessory** = a useful but inessential addition to something else (a car accessory; a fashion accessory). Also now used in law as an alternative spelling of 'accessary'.	accessaries accessories
accommodate	Two 'c's and two 'm's - 'accommodate' and 'accommodation' are two of the words most commonly misspelt, even by estate agents.	accommodates/ accommodated/ accommodating
according	'according **to**' but 'in accordance **with**'.	
actual/ actually	**actual** = existing in the real world. Actual and actually should be avoided unless the author wishes to draw attention to the difference between what happened and what might/should have happened: e.g. "Despite guarantees as to its reliability, the car actually exploded on its first outing."	

Expression/ Term	Comment	Forms/ Tenses
acronym	An acronym is a set of initial letters that make up a word (e.g. Nato = **N**orth **At**lantic **T**reaty **O**rganisation; Opec = **O**rganisation of **P**etroleum **E**xporting **C**ountries). It is not just a set of initial letters. The BBC is not an acronym nor, for that matter, is the Beeb.	
addendum	The plural of addendum is addenda.	
addressing a problem	**addressing a problem** should be reserved for situations in which you intend to take a look at the different aspects of a problem with a view to attempting to find a solution. It is not a superior way of saying 'solving a problem' or 'dealing with a problem'. If you intend to deal with or solve a problem, why not say so?	
adduce/ deduce	**adduce** = to bring forward as evidence **deduce** = to draw a conclusion from the evidence	adduces/ adduced/ adducing; deduces/ deduced/ deducing
adverse/ averse	**adverse** = hostile (adverse conditions) **averse** = opposed, disinclined, not in favour of ("What cat's averse to fish?" Thomas Grey). 'Averse to' is correct, although logically it should be 'averse from'. Both *ad* and *ab* can be abbreviated to a before certain consonants in English word formation.	Latin *ad* = to Latin *ab* or *a* = from
aetiology/ etiolate	**aetiology** is the study of causation. It is most commonly used in the context of diseases. **etiolate** = to make weak; to make pale by denying light.	Greek *aitiologia* *aitia* = cause; *logia* = study

Expression/ Term	Comment	Forms/ Tenses
affect/ effect	**affect** (v) = a) to influence: 　"The bad weather affected ice-cream sales adversely." b) touch, move emotionally: 　"The collapse in the share price affected him deeply." c) put on a show of, pretend: 　"He affected to be upset by the redundancies his actions had caused." **effect** (v) = to bring about: 　"It was he who effected the company's recovery." **effect** (n) = result of a cause: 　"His rash actions had the effect of destroying the company." 　"Although he had effected (brought about) the collapse of the company, he affected (pretended) to be unconcerned by the effect (result) of his actions."	
agenda	an **agenda** is a list of matters to be dealt with at a meeting. It is the plural form of the obsolete agendum.	
aging/ ageing	Either spelling is acceptable, although 'ageing' probably has the edge.	
aggravate	Strictly means to make worse: 　"His wounds were aggravated by lack of care." 　"The poor condition of the UK economy was aggravated by the global recession." Its use to mean 'to irritate'; 　"He found all forms of snobbery aggravating." 　"You really are aggravating" is not generally approved, although in common use.	

Expression/ Term	Comment	Forms/ Tenses
agree	**agree to** = to accept what someone has proposed. "I agree to your proposal." 'Agree' itself is often followed by an infinitive which again produces the 'agree to' juxtaposition but here the 'to' is part of the infinitive.. "I agree to implement your proposal." **agree on** = to accept what someone has proposed "We agree on this matter." **agree with** = to concur with someone "I agree with you about your proposal." A noun and a verb are said 'to agree' with each other when, for example, they both appear in plural form.	agreeing agreed
algorithm	Strictly speaking, an **algorithm** is a mathematical formula designed to solve a defined problem, not merely a clever word for a way of doing something.	algorithms
all together/ altogether	**all together** = all in a single group "We went to the management all together." **altogether** = as a whole, entirely "The management's response was altogether unsympathetic."	
all right/ alright	Although both **all right** and **alright** are in common use, in formal writing 'all right' is to be preferred.	
alleviate/ ameliorate	**alleviate** = to relieve, lessen the burden or pressure **ameliorate** = to make better, to improve "He set out to alleviate the poverty of the people and succeeded in ameliorating the conditions in which they lived.".	alleviates/ alleviated/ alleviating; ameliorates/ ameliorated/ ameliorating

Expression/ Term	Comment	Forms/ Tenses
allude / elude	**allude** = refer to, to make casual or implicit reference to, without mentioning by name **elude** = escape, evade, cunningly to avoid "In passing, I alluded to Mr. Smith's extraordinary ability to elude responsibility for any of the company's problems."	alluding eluding
alone	**alone**, like 'only', can create ambiguities. 'The Marketing Manager alone can save the company.' This could mean only the Marketing Manager can save the company (i.e. there is no-one else who can do it) or that he/she can do it without help from anyone else. The meaning would be clearer if we said: "Only the Marketing Manager can save the company." or "The Marketing Manager can save the company without help from anyone." depending on the intended sense.	
a lot allot	**a lot**, meaning a considerable amount or number of something, should be avoided in formal writing, since it fails to quantify the amount or number and is therefore vague and imprecise. '**to allot**' means to allocate and is similar in meaning to apportion or to assign, but suggests the sharing is less precise and possibly less fair.	allotted
alternately/ alternatively	**alternately** means in turn. "John and I hit the nail head alternately (i.e. in turns) to drive it into the wood." **alternatively** means 'as another option'. "You can agree with me; or, alternatively, you can go to hell".	

Expression/ Term	Comment	Forms/ Tenses
alternative	one of two, usually mutually exclusive, options or possibilities. Now widely used in the same way as 'option', ignoring the origin of the word, so that now there can be any number of alternatives from which we can choose. It seems a pity to lose the 'one of two' meaning when we have several words (choices, options, possibilities) which have no numerical limit.	Latin *alter* = other, of two
alumnus (m) alumna (f)	Masculine plural: alumni Female plural: alumnae	Latin *alumnus* (m), *alumna* (f) = a pupil
ambiguous/ ambiguity/ ambivalent/ ambivalence	**ambiguous** = capable of bearing more than one interpretation **ambivalent** = experiencing or expressing opposite or conflicting judgements or emotions. 'My ambivalent feelings about the European Union probably explain the ambiguity of my voting record.'	ambiguities ambivalences

Expression/ Term	Comment	Forms/ Tenses

among/ amongst/ between	**among/amongst**
	There is no definable distinction in meaning, at least none observed by the broad community of good writers. The choice is yours. Some favour 'amongst' before words beginning with a vowel.
	    e.g. amongst all those who voted
	        among his colleagues
	
	amongst/between
	In cases of dividing something up:
	• between is used of two people or things
	• among/amongst is used of more than two
	
	'Between' is applied to more than two in such expressions as "Between them, they created a pig's feast of the operation" but, in general, because 'between' contains the Old English root 'twa' (two), it should be reserved for dividing things into two parts.	

amoral/ immoral	**amoral** = outside the scope of morality **immoral** = morally wrong Greek and Latin prefix '*a-*' negates the word it introduces: hence 'a-gnostic' (*a+gnostos*: not knowing), 'a-pathetic' (*a+pathos*: not feeling), 'a-theist' (*a+theos*; no god). The Latin prefix '*im-*' (like '*in-*', '*il-*', '*ir-*') converts the meaning of the word to which it is attached into its opposite: e.g. 'im-practical' (cf. '*in-capable*', '*il-legal*', '*ir-responsible*').	
amount	In most instances, in writing business reports, **amount** should be quantified.	

Expression/ Term	Comment	Forms/ Tenses
an	**an** is the form of the indefinite article 'a' which is used before a word beginning with a vowel. It is generally accepted now that words such as 'hotel' and 'hierarchy' should be preceded by 'a', rather than 'an'. Words beginning with a completely silent 'h' (e.g. honest, hour) should be preceded by 'an'.	a hotel a hierarchy an honest an hour
analogous	'analogous **to**', not 'analogous **with**' **analogous** is stronger than 'like' or 'similar to'. It is used to denote a close and sustained similarity between two things. There is a sense in which analogous indicates some degree of parallelism between one thing and another: i.e. this is to this, as that is to that. The Eucharist contains an analogy in which the wine is to blood as the bread is to flesh. Sustained metaphors depend on analogies.	
analysis/ analyses	**analysis** is singular; **analyses** is plural	
anarchy	strictly speaking, **anarchy** simply means 'without rules' or without government. Such a state may be one of chaos (which is what the word is often used to mean) but is not necessarily so.	
angry	'angry **with**', rather than 'angry at'	
anticipate	Strictly speaking, **anticipate** means to 'forestall', not to 'expect'. "The convicted murderer anticipated his execution by committing suicide, an outcome no one had expected."	anticipates/ anticipated/ anticipating

Expression/ Term	Comment	Forms/ Tenses
any/ some	'**any**' means one or more of several and 'some' means an amount of something. "Is there/are there any (one or more) here who will give me some (an indeterminate portion of) support?" **some** is used in positive statements: "I have some money." **any** is used in negative statements: "I don't have any money". We would not say: "I don't have some money" or "I have any money". We use 'any' with 'hardly' and 'scarcely' because these words contain a negative connotation: "I have hardly any money". "I have scarcely any money".	
apparently	often misspelt as 'apparantly'	
appeal	You don't appeal a decision; you appeal **against** a decision.	
appearance	often misspelt as appeerence	
appendix/ appendices	When referring to additional information supplied at the end of a report, the plural of 'appendix' is 'appendices'.	
appraise/ apprise	**appraise** = assess the value or quality **apprise** = inform 'Having appraised the antique table, I apprised him of its value.'	appraises/ appraised/ appraising apprises/ apprised/ apprising
arrogate	See 'abrogate'	

Expression/ Term	Comment	Forms/ Tenses
a priori/ prima facie	These two Latin expressions are sometimes confused: ***a priori*** means 'from assumed premises' i.e. from premises neither proved nor based on experience ***prima facie*** means 'on the face of it', 'at a first glance'	
argument	often misspelt as ''arguement'	
as a consequence	consider 'therefore' as a less verbose alternative.	
at the end of the day	consider 'finally'	
at this moment in time	You probably mean 'now'. At least cut it down to 'at this moment' or 'at this time'	
aural/ oral/ verbal	**aural** = relating to the ear **oral** = relating to the mouth. An agreement that is based on the spoken word is an oral agreement. (All contracts are verbal.) **verbal** = relating to words	
autarchy autarky	**autarchy** = absolute rule; adj. autarchic **autarky** = independence; adj. autarkic **autarkic** is used to describe a country that is self-sufficient	
averse	**averse to** (although 'averse from' would seem more logical). See also Adverse.	Latin '*a*' or '*ab*' = 'from'.
axis	plural 'axes'	

Expression/ Term	Comment	Forms/ Tenses
bacteria/ bacterium	**bacteria** is plural. The singular is 'bacterium'. "He was struck down by a noxious bacteria" is therefore incorrect.	
barely	**barely** has a negative force and should not be used with another negative word. "He hadn't barely time to finish the report" is incorrect. It should be "He barely had time…"	
basis	Such expressions as 'on a provisional basis' and 'on a temporary basis' are often unnecessarily wordy. 'Provisionally' and 'temporally' will often serve as well or better.	bases (plural)
bated/ baited	In the expression 'with bated breath', 'bated' is often misspelt 'baited'. The 'bated' in 'bated breath' is a contraction of abated, which means 'reduced'. **baited** means equipped with a bait or, metaphorically, as a verb, to provoke or tease.	
because	The expression 'the reason is because' is tautological. Say either 'the reason is that' or 'because'.	
bare/bear	**bare** = uncovered 'Bare' carries a range of meanings including 'naked', 'unconcealed' (laid bare), 'lacking' or 'stripped of' (bare of all social graces), unadorned (bare facts) and 'thin' or 'slim' (the barest chance of success). **bear** = to carry 'Bear' has an even wider range of uses, in an even wider range of expressions: 'to bear a grudge' (i.e. to feel), to bear false witness (i.e. to testify), to bear a child (i.e. give birth to), 'to bear fruit' (to produce), 'to bear pain' (to endure), 'to bear the cost' (to incur or accept), to bear right (to move in a direction) - and many more.	

Expression/ Term	Comment	Forms/ Tenses

begs the question	**to beg the question** is to put forward a proposition which assumes as true the point it is making. In other words, it fails to prove the assumption on which the proposition is based. In yet other words, begging the question is one form of a circular argument.
	
	Here are some simple examples:
	   "I am more intelligent than most people because clearly most people are not as bright as me."
	   "Abortion, the killing of a human being, should, like other forms of murder, be made illegal."
	The argument assumes that a foetus is a human being, an essential premise if abortion is to be equated with murder.
	
	There is an element of question begging in the following:
	   "This reactionary government is the main obstacle to social progress."
	
	The expression 'begs the question' is often misused, and is variously construed to mean 'raises the question', 'avoids the question' or even 'ignores the question'.
		beg
		begged
		begging

behalf of	**on behalf of** = for the benefit of, as representative of. It is not a synonym for 'by' or 'on the part of'.
	   "This offer of a generous redundancy package, presented on behalf of the company, is one the workers would be well advised to accept."
	
	In this case, assuming the company itself is making the offer, 'by', instead of 'on behalf of', would be correct.
	
	It is correct to say:
	   "The redundancy package offered by the company was rejected by the shop steward on behalf of his members.	

Expression/ Term	Comment	Forms/ Tenses

better/best	**better** of two;
	best of more than two
	
	e.g.
	   "Of Paul and Mary, Mary was the better motivator."
	   "Of Peter, Paul and Mary, Peter was the best motivator."	

biannual/ biennial	**biannual** = twice a year **biennial** = every two years This distinction is not widely understood. Probably best to say 'twice a year' and 'every two years'.	
bona fides bona fide	Latin for 'good faith', 'sincerity'. ***Bona fides*** (n) looks plural but is singular; ***bona fide*** (adj.) which might look like the singular of bona fides is in fact an adjective meaning 'sincere'. Probably best to use 'good faith' for one and 'sincere' for the other.	
born/borne	**born** = given birth to **borne** = carried, conveyed "As soon as the baby was born, it was borne away to be placed in an incubator."	
between	When choosing between one thing and another, only 'and' will do. "He had to decide **between** raising prices and (not 'or' or 'against') cutting costs."	

Expression/ Term	Comment	Forms/ Tenses
between you and I / between you and me	Common errors in the use of "I" are found in the expression "between you and I" which should be "between you and me". 'Between' is a preposition that takes the objective case which means it should be followed by 'me', 'us' and 'them', not 'I', 'we' and 'they'. See also 'from'. Those who jubilantly point out that Shakespeare used 'between you and I' in *The Merchant of Venice* ("All debts are cleared between you and I": *Antonio's letter, Act III, Scene ii*) prove nothing, except that, if you are a genius, then a character in your play who has already proved himself a foolhardy and unlucky businessman may be excused the odd grammatical solecism. (Maybe I'm overdoing the point.)	
betwixt and between	**betwixt and between** is an idiom meaning 'neither one thing nor the other'.	'Betwixt' = 'between' and is archaic, deriving from Middle and Old English.

Expression/ Term	Comment	Forms/ Tenses

both	Use of **both** with plural nouns
	
	Be careful when using 'both…. and' with plural nouns.
	   "Both the salesmen and the researchers have reached the same conclusion."
	
	If there are just two salesmen, it would be best to say: "The two salesmen etc."
	
	If there are more than two salesmen, it would be best to omit the 'both' and say: "The salesmen and the researchers etc."
	
	Both with prepositions
	
	If the preposition follows the 'both', it should be repeated after the 'and'.
	
	   'Both on the one hand and on the other'	

both	but if the preposition precedes the 'both', it would be wrong to repeat the preposition after the 'and'. It should be: 'On both the one hand and the other'	
breakdown	**breakdown** is a useful word for an analysis of information, especially its division into categories, and should be confined to this meaning. Insensitive use of the word can lead to solecisms: "As the new managing director, I am eager to see a complete breakdown of all the company's operations."	
broach/ brooch	You 'broach' a subject (i.e. you open it up for discussion; you wear a 'brooch' (an item of jewellery or an ornament pinned to clothing): "Suspecting the jewellery was stolen, be decided to broach the subject of the provenance of the diamond-studded brooch she was wearing."	broaches/ broached/ broaching
bureau	plural bureaux	

Expression/ Term	Comment	Forms/ Tenses
By	**by** is a preposition with many uses. One of its uses is as an indicator of agency: e.g. "He was attacked **by** a dog". It is also used to denote place: e.g. "The dog was **by** the lake." This can lead to unintended ambiguities: e.g. "Dzhokhar Tsarnaev,19, was arrested late on Friday after he was found seriously injured by a suburban house." (BBC website, 20/04/2013)	
burned/ burnt	**burned** and **burnt** are equally acceptable as the past tense of burn.	
calendar (n) calender (v) colander (n)	a **calendar** is a display in table form of the days, weeks and months of a year, often misspelt as calender 'to **calender**' is to press between rollers or plates to produce thin sheets of some material a **colander** is a perforated bowl used for draining or straining food.	

can/ may	**can** is concerned with ability or knowledge
	   "Can we win?"
	   "Can you repair this car?"
	
	may is concerned with permission, possibility, wishing
	   "You may go = You have my permission to go"
	   "He may go or he may stay. I don't know."
	   "May you live a long and prosperous life."
	
	In modern usage, there is some overlap between 'can' and 'may' but in formal writing it is better to retain the distinctions of meaning.	

canvas / canvass	You use canvas, a tough fabric, for clothes or sails. You canvass for votes. Just to confuse you, the plural of canvas is canvasses; i.e. the same as the third person singular of the verb to canvas.	

Expression/ Term	Comment	Forms/ Tenses
cartel	a **cartel** is a group of independent commercial enterprises that conspire to manipulate prices or maximise profit, typically by agreeing amongst themselves levels of output. A group of illegal drugs barons can properly be described as a cartel only if their actions meet the above definition.	
catalyst	A **catalyst** speeds up a process; it is not one of the principal elements in the process. In general use, a catalyst prompts, provokes or inspires something; but it is not a synonym for cause. "The foreman's absenteeism was a *catalyst* for general discontent in the workforce which *caused* us to lose the government contract."	
catholic/ Catholic	**catholic** = embracing a wide range **Catholic** = member of the Roman Catholic church	
cemetery	often misspelt as 'cemetary'. Mnemonic: "We all find 'e's in a cemetery."	
censor/ censure	**censor** = to delete, or prohibit **censure** = criticise, disapprove of "He censured his editor for failing to censor the libellous publication."	censors/ censored/ censoring censures/ censured/ censuring
centred	something is 'centred on', not 'centred around'	
childish/ childlike	**childish** is pejorative, suggesting foolish, silliness and immaturity **childlike** suggests innocence	
chronic	**chronic** means long term, of long duration or frequent occurrence. It does not mean particularly bad. 'His catarrh, a chronic condition, did not interfere with his tennis playing.'	

Expression/ Term	Comment	Forms/ Tenses
circum-stances	**circumstances** are the conditions that are **around**, not **above**. It is therefore arguable that "in the circumstances" is to be preferred to "under the circumstances".	
classic/ classical	There is some overlap of meaning but: **classic** = of the highest quality, of proven and enduring excellence (e.g. a classic car) **classical** = arts and literature of ancient Greece or Rome, showing the qualities of balance; classical music as distinct from popular music	
climactic/ climatic	**climactic** = adjective from climax, pertaining to a climax **climatic** = adjective from climate, pertaining to climate	
coarse course	**coarse** is an adjective meaning rough **course** is a noun meaning a path to follow; a set of lessons to study; or part of a meal.	
collapse	**collapse** is an intransitive verb. You do not collapse something. It collapses.	
committee	often misspelt as 'commitee'	
compare	Use either 'compare to' or 'compare with' If you wish, you can try to make a distinction in meaning on the following basis: • use 'compare to' if, on balance, the emphasis is on the similarities between two things • use 'compare with' if, on balance, the emphasis is on the differences. e.g. "Shall I compare thee to a summer's day?" "If I compare you with her, there is no contest."	

Expression/ Term	Comment	Forms/ Tenses
complement/ compliment	**complement** = something that goes to make up a whole, to complete ("The baby had the usual complement of fingers and toes.") **compliment** = an expression of admiration ("He paid her a compliment on her good taste.")	
complement/ supplement	**complement** = something that goes to make up a whole, to complete ("We're delighted to report the baby still has the usual complement of fingers and toes.") **supplement** = an addition to something which can be seen as already whole e.g. a supplement to a book or magazine. "The baby's full complement of fingers and toes was supplemented by a prehensile tail." Whoops!	
complex/ complicated	**complex** = having many parts **complicated** = difficult to understand 'Complex' is also a psychiatric term which can have a precise meaning (repressed desires or memories which can adversely affect a personality) or a looser meaning of over-reaction to an experience (he has a complex about flying) or a perceived weakness (he has a complex about his ability to express himself).	
compound	Often used to mean 'make worse' but, strictly speaking, that is **not** what it means. In the common expression 'to compound a felony', it means to agree, on certain terms, not to prosecute. (You're probably as surprised as I was!)	

comprise/ consist of	These are synonyms:
	comprise does not need an 'of'.
	  "The team comprises three managers and a secretary."
	  "The team consists of three managers and a secretary."
		comprises/ comprised/ comprising; consists of/ consisted of/ consisting of

Expression/ Term	Comment	Forms/ Tenses
concluding	**concluding** can be ambiguous (meaning either ending or deducing). "He concluded by saying that television damages the brain." Was that his considered opinion or was it just the last thing he said, or both? The noun 'conclusion' has the same ambiguity.	
connote/ denote	**connote** means to imply something other than the precise or obvious meaning **denote** means to signify or indicate something The difference in meaning is clearest in the use of the noun 'connotation'. "His promise to solve all our problems once and for all carried disturbing connotations."	connotes/ connoted/ connoting; denotes/ denoted/ denoting
consensus	**consensus** = what is generally agreed, not simply a compromise or the middle ground in an argument Since consensus means general agreement of opinion, 'consensus of opinion' is tautological. 'Consensus' is sometimes misspelt as 'concensus' through confusion with census, with which it has nothing to do.	
consequence	Frequently appears in the expression 'as a consequence of'. "Because of" might serve as well, if not better.	
consist of/ consist in	**consist of** = means to be made up of **consist in** = means what something is	

Expression/ Term	Comment	Forms/ Tenses
contemporary	**contemporary** can be ambiguous, meaning either 'of the same time' or 'of the present time'. "Charles Darwin was a contemporary of Charles Dickens." (i.e. lived at the same time in the nineteenth century). "The new office was built in a contemporary style." (i.e. modern style) "The Shakespeare play was performed in contemporary dress" is ambiguous, since it could mean either in 16th century or 21st century fashion.	
continual/ continuous	There is overlap of meaning but: **continual** = occurring over and over again at regular intervals **continuous** = occurring without interruption.	
convince/ persuade	These words are not interchangeable. You **convince** someone of an argument; you **persuade** someone to do something. "As soon as I had convinced him our product was the best on the market, it was easy to persuade him to buy."	convinces/ convinced/ convincing; persuades/ persuaded/ persuading
council/ counsel	**council** = an assembly of people **counsel** = advice.	
credible/ credulous	**credible** = believable **credulous** = easily persuaded to believe, naive	
crescendo	the process of building up noise to a higher level. To build up to a crescendo is therefore to build up to a 'build up', so to speak.	
crisis/ crises	**crisis** is singular; **crises** is plural	
criterion/ criteria	**criterion** is singular; **criteria** is plural 'The criterion is....' 'The criteria are....'	

Expression/ Term	Comment	Forms/ Tenses
critique	**critique** is a noun but is sometimes used now as a verb. The use of nouns in place of verbs is not to be encouraged, especially when there is a perfectly good verb (in this instance, criticise) available.	
crucial	**crucial** = decisive, critical. Not simply 'very important'. A crucial decision is one that marks a turning point and/or determines the outcome.	Latin *crux*, a cross, where two lines intersect
current	**current**, like 'contemporary', can be ambiguous. It can be used to mean the present time (e.g. currently the dollar is worth …i.e. today the dollar is worth…), or it can mean a particular time in the past (e.g. current prices in 1980). 'current' can also mean a flow of air, electricity or water. 'currant' is a dried grape.	
curriculum	plural curricula	
dated	In the expression "your letter dated 12th March', the 'dated' is unnecessary. 'Your letter of 12th March' will do.	
datum/ data	**datum** is the singular of data but data is now treated as singular so often that datum (i.e. a single item of data) is almost obsolete in general discourse. Use of the singular with data - 'The data is (rather than 'are') inconclusive' - is so common now, it is acceptable and can be justified by interpreting data as 'a set of data'.	

Expression/ Term	Comment	Forms/ Tenses
day, in this day and age, at the end of the day	The expression 'in this day and age', is an overworked cliché. 'Nowadays' or 'today' are better alternatives. 'At the end of the day' can mean exactly what it says but it is often used as a cliché for 'finally', 'in conclusion' or 'taking everything into account'. If you have a penchant for cliché-ridden prose, try "At the end of the day, when all's said and done, clichés rule in this day and age". The expression 'back in the day' has gained popularity relatively recently. It refers, usually fondly, to a past time in the speaker's life or experience. "I was a bit of a lad back in the day." Popular with quite young celebrities who wish to give their brief lives epic proportions. Probably best kept for informal discourse with friends from back in the day.	
debar/ disbar	**debar** = stop, prevent or exclude **disbar** = to expel a barrister from the Bar	debars/ debarred/ debarring; disbar/ disbarred/ disbarring
decimate	Although the word comes from the Roman practice of executing every tenth legionnaire if the Roman army had failed to perform well in battle, it is now widely used to mean total destruction of a group of people or even a thing. If you use the word, there is no need to qualify the thing decimated. You would not say: 　"The decline in profits has decimated most of the sales force." since 'decimated' now means 'most', if not 'all of'.	decimates/ decimated/ decimating

Expression/ Term	Comment	Forms/ Tenses
deduce/ infer	There is overlap of meaning but: **deduce** = derive a conclusion strictly from the evidence **infer** = reach a conclusion by reasoning/intuition/ guesswork.	deduces/ deduced/ deducing; infers/ inferred/ inferring
defective/ deficient	**defective** = faulty **deficient** = inadequate, insufficient in quantity "Christmas dinner was disappointing, partly because of a deficiency of food (the shop had sold out of turkeys) and partly because of a defective cooker (it didn't work)."	
definite & definitely	These words are often used to strengthen what is already an absolute. "He made a definite decision to resign." Strictly speaking, if it was not 'definite', it was not a 'decision'. "There can be no doubt that this competitor is definitely a danger to our profitability." Either it is a danger, or it isn't! 'Definitely' is often misspelt as 'definately'.	
definite/ definitive	**definite** = precise, firm **definitive** = comprehensive, conclusive, final	
defuse/ diffuse	**defuse** = to remove the fuse from a bomb; to remove the cause of tension in a situation **diffuse** = to spread out widely; to thin out	defuses/ defused/ defusing; diffuses/ diffused/ diffusing

Expression/ Term	Comment	Forms/ Tenses
delusion/ illusion	**delusion** = a firm conviction that something which is untrue is true. "Despite all the evidence to the contrary, he remained deluded that he was Catherine the Great." **illusion** = an impression that something which is false is true. "The growth in sales proved to be an illusion."	
deny/ refute	**deny** = assert as untrue, declare untrue **refute** = *prove* to be untrue You can 'deny' but you cannot 'refute' without evidence.	denies/ denied/ denying; refutes/ refuted/ refuting
dependant/ dependent	dependant (noun) = a person who depends on someone or something else dependent (adjective) • depending on someone or something else (She is dependent on state benefits.), • contingent upon (e.g. Your promotion is dependent on good sales figures.)	
deprecate/ depreciate	**deprecate** = disapprove of, deplore **depreciate** = fall in value, belittle, disparage I deprecate (i.e. deplore) your indifference to the depreciation (i.e. decline in value) of our currency. I deprecate (i.e. deplore) your practice of depreciating (i.e. belittling) the talents of your peers".	deprecates/ deprecated/ deprecating; depreciates/ depreciated/ depreciating

Expression/ Term	Comment	Forms/ Tenses
derisive/ derisory	There is overlap, with both words meaning 'mocking'. The response of the audience to his attempts at wit was derisive/derisory (i.e. mocking). But derisory also means 'worthy of mockery'; e.g. a derisory pay increase (i.e. one so small it could only be seen as a cross between a joke and an insult). Through this usage of the word, 'derisory' has come to mean 'very small' (as in 'a derisive pay increase'; i.e. a very small, contemptible increase.	

despite the fact that	'although' will often serve as well and save space.
	
	Reserve 'despite the fact that' for occasions when there is an element of real surprise that **a** is happening, despite **b**.
	
	Even then, make sure you need 'the fact that'. For example:
	    "He promoted me despite that fact that he was unable to understand what I had achieved."
	could probably be reduced to:
	    "He promoted me despite his inability to understand my achievement."
	without any discernible loss of meaning but with a reduction of verbiage.	

determine	**determine** has two main meanings: a) to find out ("He quickly determined the cause of failure.") b) to decide ("Just as quickly he determined appropriate remedial action.") A third meaning, 'to set a limit to, to bring to an end', is a legal term.	determines/ determined/ determining

Expression/ Term	Comment	Forms/ Tenses
diagnosis/ prognosis	**diagnosis**, the identification of a disease or other medical condition on the basis of symptoms **prognosis**, the predicted outcome of a medical condition and its treatment if any.	plurals: diagnoses prognoses
dichotomy	a split into two (but not more than two) completely separate, mutually exclusive groups, not simply a difference.	dichotomies
different	'different from', not 'different to' or 'different than'	
dilemma	a situation in which there is a choice between two equally undesirable alternatives. Although the 'di-' comes from the Greek for 'two', 'dilemma' is now often used to cover situations where there are more than two alternatives. 'Dilemma' does not mean simply 'a difficult problem'. dilemma is often misspelt as dilemna	dilemmas
disclose	'disclose' means to reveal. It is not a synonym for say or tell.	discloses/ disclosed/ disclosing
discreet/ discrete	**discreet** = tactful, prudent, circumspect **discrete** = distinct, separate His assistant was always discreet about the Managing Director's discrete (i.e. various, separate) business operations.	
disinterested/ uninterested	**disinterested** = impartial, unbiased **uninterested** = not interested This distinction is worth keeping. Otherwise, 'disinterested' is redundant.	

Expression/ Term	Comment	Forms/ Tenses
dissociate	The negative form of 'associate' is 'dissociate', not disassociate.	dissociates/ dissociated/ dissociating
distribute	'distribute **among**', not 'distribute **between**'

Because 'between' retains some notion of 'two-ness', it is better to 'divide' between two. Distribute implies a larger number than two, so it is best to distribute 'among'. | distributes/ distributed/ distributing |
| doubt | 'doubt whether', not 'doubt if'

In the negative 'doubt' is followed by that:
   "I don't doubt that he will succeed."
since, in this construction, there is no doubt. | |
| doubtful | 'doubtful whether', rather than 'doubtful if' | |
| due/due to | due, as an adjective meaning 'just' or 'deserved', is straightforward. "He got his due punishment."

Problems arise with 'due to'. Purists criticise the general use of 'due to' to mean 'on account of' or 'because of'. They argue it should be used only immediately after copula verbs (e.g. be or seem) or immediately before nouns.

   "The earth slide was due to heavy rain."
   "Premature death, due to bad lifestyle choices, is a significant drag on population growth."

Given the now widespread use of 'due to' and 'owing to' in the sense of 'because of', this would seem to be a battle the purists will lose, especially as the purists' rules seem particularly arcane. For any who wish to preserve a distinction, consider using 'due to' only when you want it to mean precisely 'attributable to'. | |
| due to the fact that | 'because' or 'since' will often serve as well and save space. | |

Expression/ Term	Comment	Forms/ Tenses
each	**each** takes a singular verb "Each of the products was [not 'were'] thoroughly tested before launch."	
each and every	= every	
each other/ one another	Some argue we should use 'each other' to refer to two individuals or things and 'one another' if there are more than two but there seems to be no sound basis for such a distinction.	
earlier on	The 'on' is redundant and illogical in this expression. It would be more logical to write 'earlier back' - in which case the 'back' would merely be redundant. Of course, the 'on' in 'earlier on' is not redundant in a sentence such as: "He arrived earlier on his bike."	
economic/ economical	**economic** = relating to the economy, or economics **economical** = thrifty "Reviewing the state of the country's finances, he was economical with the truth in his economic analysis."	
ecstasy	often misspelt as 'ecstacy'	
effectively/ in effect	**effectively** means 'done well, achieving a goal. e.g. "He cleared the ground effectively with his chain saw." **in effect** means 'more or less', 'done but not in the perfectly correct manner'. 'The land was, in effect, cleared by crowds trampling all over it.'	

Expression/ Term	Comment	Forms/ Tenses
effective/ effectual	**effective** = having the power to achieve a goal **effectual** = producing a desired effect Effectual is more common in its negative form, 'ineffectual', which is often applied to individuals. "The Chancellor proved ineffectual in his efforts to prevent the devaluation."	
e.g./ etc.	**e.g.** = for example (appears at the beginning of a list and indicates that there are other items not listed) **etc.** = and the rest (appears at the end of a list and indicates there are others of the same kind not listed) You should not use both terms on the same list since 'e.g.' indicates the list is not exhaustive.. You should not use 'and' before 'etc.' since 'etc.' means 'and the rest'.	e.g. stands for the Latin *exempli gratia* (for example) 'etc.' is short for the Latin *et cetera* (and the rest).
e.g./ i.e.	e.g. See above i.e. = that is (an explanation of a previous statement, a repeat of a previous statement in different words). 'You are surplus to requirement: i.e. you're fired.'	i.e. stands for the Latin *id est* (that is).
either/ or	If the alternatives are both singular, the verb should be singular. 'Either partner, John or Mary, is able to run the company.' Even when 'either' is followed by a plural noun, the verb should be singular, since either refers to one or other of the two: e.g. "Either of these plans is practical."	

Expression/ Term	Comment	Forms/ Tenses
elder/ eldest	**elder** is to be used when comparing the age of two people or things. "Of Peter and Mary, Peter is the elder." **eldest** is to be used when the age of more than two people or things are being considered: "Of Peter, Paul and Mary, Peter is the eldest."	
elicit illicit	**elicit** means to draw out something (usually a response) **illicit** means not permitted by law, illegal	
embarrass	often misspelt as embarass	
emotional/ emotive	**emotional** = relating to the emotions **emotive** = arousing the emotions, provocative "Her emotive remarks prompted an emotional response from him."	
ensure/ insure	**ensure** = make certain **insure** = to take out insurance "You should ensure you are insured."	
enervate	**enervate** = to weaken, not to strengthen. Derived from Latin '*e*' = '*ex*' meaning 'out of', and '*nervus*' = 'sinew'. Enervate means to extract the sinew or strength. It is the opposite of invigorate.	enervates/ enervated/ enervating
enormity	**enormity** has a negative connotation. "All condemned him for the enormity of his sin." It is not a synonym for immense. You would not say "He was knighted for the enormity of his good works."	
epitome	**epitome** = a perfect example of something 'Epitome' does not mean an extreme of something. Someone could be the epitome of moderation.	

Expression/ Term	Comment	Forms/ Tenses
equable/ equitable:	**equable** = even-tempered, moderate (He had an equable temperament) **equitable** = fair, just (an equitable solution) "His suggestion of an equitable solution contributed greatly to the equable atmosphere at the meeting."	
especially/ specially	There is considerable overlap but some writers make the following distinction: **especially** = to an unusual/extraordinary degree (The Managing Director tried especially hard to build a team spirit.) **specially** = for a particular purpose ("I chose this present specially for you.")	
etc./ et cetera	etc. = and the rest. Do not write 'and etc.' since this it tautological. Do not use 'e.g.' at the beginning and 'etc.' at the end of a list. 'e.g.' tells the reader at the start of the list that the list is not complete; 'etc.' at the end of the list is therefore tautological.	
everybody	**everybody** = everyone Everybody and everyone are interchangeable. Both words take a singular verb: "Everybody loves everyone who is a winner."	

Expression/ Term	Comment	Forms/ Tenses

everyone/ every one	**everyone** = everybody, every person
	
	every one = each person or thing in a group
	
	Both are singular:
	e.g.
	   "Everyone enjoys a holiday."
	   "Every one gives what he/she can."
	
	In the latter example, there is perhaps a case for using 'they' to avoid 'he/she': i.e. "Everyone gives what they can".	

evince/ evoke	**evince** = display or show clearly **evoke** = to bring to mind, to bring back or bring out a feeling or memory "He evinced contempt for the fear that memories of the last recession evoked."	evinces/ evinced/ evincing; evokes/ evoked/ evoking
evoke/ invoke	**evoke** = to bring to mind, to bring back or bring out a feeling or memory **invoke** = to call upon, to appeal to a law or rule "When the dictator invoked the harsh discipline of ancient Rome, he evoked all the fears associated with that cruel period."	evokes/ evoked/ evoking; invokes/ invoked/ invoking
ex-	**ex-** meaning former, needs to be precisely positioned. The 'ex-President's wife' is rather different from the 'President's ex-wife'. In the former case, the wife's husband has lost the presidency but kept his wife; in the latter case, the wife has lost the President but he still holds the presidency. These comments apply equally to the use of 'former'.	

Expression/ Term	Comment	Forms/ Tenses
exaggerate	**exaggerate** = to represent something as more (e.g. bigger, more important) than it is. To intensify the word, 'exaggerate greatly' is preferable to 'over-exaggerate' which comes close to tautology. Sometimes misspelt with only one 'g'.	exaggerates/ exaggerated/ exaggerating Needs two 'g's, because of Latin *agger*, meaning heap.
excellent	sometimes misspelt as 'excelent', perhaps because excel has only one 'l'.	
excepting	**excepting** is used only in such expressions as 'always excepting', 'not excepting' and 'only excepting'. Elsewhere 'except' should suffice. "Always use 'except', only excepting the exceptions noted above."	
exercise exorcise	**to exercise** is to take part in physical activity generally to improve fitness **to exorcise** is to drive out evil which may or may not involve exercise.	
existence	often misspelt as 'existance'	
extract/ extricate	Both words mean to draw out or remove. **extract** = to draw out, remove **extricate** = to get (usually oneself) out of a difficult situation; or to get out of a situation with difficulty. "He extricated himself from financial disaster." 'Extricate' conveys a sense of difficulty.	

Expression/ Term	Comment	Forms/ Tenses
factoid	the word has two meanings.

The original and still most common meaning is a statement presented as a fact but, lacking supporting evidence; i.e. not actually a fact.

A secondary meaning is a novel fact that, although to some degree relevant to the subject, does not form part of the main narrative. | |
| factor | Strictly speaking, 'factor' is something that contributes to a result. ('His marketing expertise was undoubtedly a factor in his success as Managing Director.')

'Factor' is not a synonym for 'component', 'element' or 'part' which are words which denote something which simply forms part of a whole without any suggestion of causation. | |
| farther/ further | Despite efforts by etymologists and others to define a distinction between the two words when referring to distance, it is probably not worth the effort. 'Further' is generally more popular and will serve on all occasions.

Purists could restrict 'farther' to distance and use 'further' in all other cases. "He went many miles farther down the road of pedantry in order to further his pet project, namely to distinguish the meanings of the two words."

'Further' is used in expressions such as "Further to my memo of..." | |

Expression/ Term	Comment	Forms/ Tenses
feel comfortable with	While this expression occasionally has a useful meaning, it has been so overused that it has become a cliché. There are alternatives. Try "I find your attitude acceptable". Or "We seem to be in agreement". Or "Our views seem compatible". In passing, it is worth commenting that this expression is often an excuse for woolly thinking or a desire to avoid critical scrutiny. You may feel comfortable with two entirely inconsistent attitudes or arguments but who cares how you feel? If the attitudes or arguments are inconsistent, they should be exposed, however comfortable you may feel before or uncomfortable after. Well, it's a view!	
fewer/ less	**fewer** refers to numbers ("There are fewer typing errors than before.") **less** refers to quantities ("He showed less sense than I had hoped.") "Since he now earns fewer pounds each week, he has less money to spend." If so minded, mention to checkout staff at the supermarket that "10 items or less" is incorrect.	
flammable/ inflammable	Both words mean liable to catch fire. Because 'inflammable' could be wrongly taken to mean 'not flammable', 'flammable' is to be preferred on most occasions.	

Expression/ Term	Comment	Forms/ Tenses
flaunt/ flout	**flaunt** = show off, display ostentatiously **flout** = disregard (e.g. the law) "She flaunted the ill-gotten gains she derived from flouting the law."	flaunts/ flaunted/ flaunting; flouts/ flouted/ flouting
flaccid	should be pronounced flaksid, although common practice and onomatopoeia would suggest otherwise.	
focus	plural foci or focuses	he/she focuses
for the purpose of	The expression 'for the purpose of' can often be cut to 'for' or 'to' without any discernible loss of meaning.	
forbear / forebear	**forbear** means to refrain from an act or resist an impulse a **forebear** is an ancestor	
forego / forgo	**forego** = 'going before' as in 'foregone conclusion'. Now used only in this expression and in the present participle 'foregoing'. **forgo** = give up, relinquish, renounce "The banker's foregoing (i.e. immediately preceding) admission of systematic misselling of financial products means he must surely forgo any hopes of a knighthood." You wish.	foregoes/ foregoing/
foreword/ forward	**foreword** is a noun meaning an introductory note or preface to a book **forward** is an adverb or adjective meaning 'towards the front' or 'in an advanced position'.	
formula	plural formulae or formulas	
former	**former** is the first of two, not of three or more	
forty	often misspelt as fourty	

Expression/Term	Comment	Forms/Tenses
forward on	In the sense of sending something, the 'on' is superfluous. You can just 'forward the message', no need to 'forward it on'. Of course, you can still 'move forward on a plan'.	
fraction	**fraction** = a part of a whole. 'Fraction' is often used to mean "a very small part". We should remember that 9/10ths is a fraction. In business reports, it is best to qualify ('a small fraction') or quantify (e.g. one fifth).	
free from/ free of	There is some overlap of usage but: **free from** = implies 'escape from' **free of** = without, not subject to "Although you have not paid me, I declare you free from debt because I give my advice free of charge."	
from	When followed by a pronoun, 'from', like 'between' takes the objective case. It is "Best wishes from my wife and me", not "Best wishes from my wife and I".	
garner	**garner** = 'to store', but now also widely used in the sense of 'to gather'.	'garner' can also mean a 'granary'
gender	**gender** is a grammatical term to denote whether a word is masculine, feminine or neuter. Humans are distinguished by their sex, not their gender. In some contexts, however, gender can be useful where 'sex' might seem to suggest the act rather than the 'gender'. In the sentence, "Sex is a major factor in determining an appetite for chocolate", it might be better to use gender, instead of sex, unless the meaning is that copulation heightens the appetite for chocolate.	

Expression/ Term	Comment	Forms/ Tenses
genus	plural genera	
get	**Get** is a useful but overworked word which has got a reputation for getting writers who just want to get on with the job out of the requirement to get stuck into the task of finding more precise words, thus enabling the lazy writer, who wishes only to get by, to get away with a lack of clarity. Almost always, there is a word which, when used to replace 'get', will make the writer's meaning clearer: e.g. 'Get' is a useful but overworked word which has acquired a reputation for enabling writers, eager to put pen to paper, to avoid the effort of finding more precise words, thus enabling the lazy writer to muddle through at the expense of clarity.	got
gourmand/ gourmet	gourmand = glutton gourmet = someone who appreciates fine food	gourmands/ gourmets
'h'	The letter 'h' does not begin with an aspirate. It is spelt and pronounced 'aitch', not 'haitch'.	
hang/ hanged/ hung	In the present tense, you hang a picture and you hang a man. But in the past tense, the picture was 'hung' and the man was 'hanged'. "The picture of the murderer being hanged was hung in the hall."	hang hanged hung
happen/ occur	These words are best used to indicate the incidence of an **unplanned** event. For planned events 'take place' is correct. "The sales conference took place (not happened or occurred) in April."	happens/ happened/ happening; occurs/ occurred/ occurring

Expression/Term	Comment	Forms/Tenses
harass harassment	often misspelt with two 'r's	harassed harassing
hardly	**hardly** already contains a negative force. "He hadn't hardly" is therefore incorrect.	
historic/ historical	**historic** = momentous **historical** = having happened in the past	
hoard/horde	**hoard** = a stock or supply of something preserved for future use **horde** = a tribe (e.g. the Golden Horde) or a large crowd	hoards hordes
Hobson's choice	**Hobson's choice** is a choice between one thing and nothing (i.e. take it or leave it). It is not a choice between two equally unacceptable alternatives; that is a dilemma.	
hoi	*hoi polloi* = the many, the masses, the common people. It is sometimes mistakenly used to mean the opposite - i.e. the wealthy, the elite - probably through association with the colloquial expression 'hoity toity' meaning snobbish, pretentious. Strictly speaking, 'the' in the expression 'the hoi polloi' is redundant (since 'hoi' means 'the') but it is now accepted in common usage.	*hoi polloi* is the Greek for 'the many'.
homosexual	the word comes from the Greek word for 'the same' (not the Latin word for man) and therefore applies equally to males and females who are attracted to their own sex. 'Gay' is the term now generally used to denote both male homosexuals and lesbians	

Expression/ Term	Comment	Forms/ Tenses

hopefully	hopefully = in a hopeful way.
	
	The use of hopefully at the start of a sentence, to mean 'It is hoped' or 'It is to be hoped' is now common in speech but best avoided in business documents. It can cause ambiguity:
	   e.g. "Hopefully, he tried his best."
	
	This could mean:
	   "In trying his best he was hopeful he would succeed."
	or
	   "It is to be hoped he tried his best."	

however	**however** is an adverb with two meaning:
	
	- in whatever way, to whatever extent
	- nevertheless
	
	The following pairs of sentences illustrate the two usages. Punctuation makes the intended meaning clear.
	   "However much I should like to, I cannot support you."
	   "However, much as I should like to, I cannot support you."
	   "I think it is impossible. However you try, you will fail."
	   "I think it is impossible. However, you try. You will fail."	

humorous	often misspelt humourous	
hyper-/ hypo-	**hyper** = above, beyond, excessive (e.g. hyperactive) **hypo** = below, under, deficient (e.g. hypothermia - abnormally low body temperature)	Greek *hyper* Latin *super* Greek *hypo* Latin *sub*
hypothesis	plural hypotheses	
idiosyncrasy	often misspelt as 'idiosyncracy'	idiosyncrasies

Expression/ Term	Comment	Forms/ Tenses
I can see where you're coming from	This usually means "I know the nature of the prejudices on which you are basing your opinion". If the expression is sincerely meant, consider "I see your point of view" or "I understand why you feels as you do" as alternatives.	

if/ whether	**if** introduces conditional clauses
	
	 whether introduces an indirect question or a clause expressing choice or doubt
	
	 Although 'if' is commonly used for 'whether' in informal speech, in formal writing, it is best to use each in its precise meaning:
	    "He said he would resign if the plan failed."
	 but
	    "I was unsure whether (not 'if') the plan would succeed."	

immanent/ imminent	**immanent** = existing, inherent **imminent** = impending, about to happen	
immoral	See 'amoral'.	
imply/ infer	**imply** = suggest indirectly. "His silence implied indifference to the plight of the victims." **infer** = to deduce, conclude. "I inferred from his silence he was indifferent to the plight of the victims."	
impracticable/ impractical	see practicable/practical	
in any way, shape or form	'in any way' probably covers it.	

Expression/ Term	Comment	Forms/ Tenses
in reality	a favourite of politicians who, when using it, intend to suggest that whoever disagrees with the view about to be expressed is living in a parallel universe or indeed in one that does not, 'in reality', exist. Has the same flavour as a sentence qualified by "with respect".	
inchoate/ incoherent	**inchoate** = at an early stage of development **incoherent** = not logically or intelligibly organised	
include	**include** should not be used if the list or set is complete. "He fielded a three-person team including Paul and Mary" is correct. "He fielded a three-person team including Peter, Paul and Mary" is incorrect. If the list or set is complete, use 'comprises' or 'consists of'.	includes/ included/ including
imply	See 'infer'.	imply implies implied implying
incidentally	often misspelt incidently	
independent	often misspelt independant	
index	plural indices or indexes	
ingenious/ ingenuous	**ingenious** = clever **ingenuous** = simple, naive "It seemed unlikely that anyone so ingenuous could devise a strategy so ingenious."	
inside of	The 'of' is generally redundant, as in: "He went inside of the building." although it is of course correct when used as follows: "He painted the inside of the building."	

Expression/Term	Comment	Forms/Tenses
intense/ intensive	**intense** = extreme in quality or degree **intensive** = concentrated, thorough "He maintained an intense dislike of intensive methods of cultivation."	
intensely/ intently	**intensely** = with strong emotion **intently** = with concentrated attention "I was intensely irritated when he persisted in staring at me intently."	
inter/ intern	**inter** = to bury **intern** = to detain in a limited area	Interred interned
inter-/ intra-	**inter-** is a prefix meaning 'between', 'among' (international = between nations) **intra-** is a prefix meaning 'within', 'inside' (intracontinental = within a continent; company intranet = network within a company)	international internationally intranational intranet
in the circumstances/ under the circumstances	'in the circumstances' is still preferable to 'under the circumstances', since the former is more at home with the Latin origin of 'circumstances' ('circum' = around), and the latter offers no advantages over its rival.	
it	when using **it**, watch out for ambiguity. In the sentence "He chose the curry because it was hot", it is unclear whether it was the curry or the weather which was hot. "Take the hammer. I'll hold the nail. When I nod my head, hit it." This type of ambiguity can be a headache.	

Expression/ Term	Comment	Forms/ Tenses
its/ it's	**it's** = it is; all other 'its' manage without an apostrophe. The confusion is understandable. 'Its', without an apostrophe, means 'of it', so you would expect it to have an apostrophe to indicate the possessive, but it doesn't. So tough.	
judgment/ judgement	judgment, judgement judgmental, judgemental These words may be spelled with or without an 'e'.	
judicial/ judicious	**judicial** = pertaining to the law, the courts and the administration of justice **judicious** = finely judged, discerning, wise, "His judicious use of diplomacy enabled us to avoid the judicial process entirely."	
kind	**kind** = sort or type The number of the verb following 'kind of' should be consistent with any demonstrative adjective attached to 'kind'. e.g. "*This* kind of sales pitch *is* unethical." "*Those* kinds of sales pitch *are* unethical."	
last	**last** means either the 'final' one or the 'most recent' one. "I heard him deliver his last lecture" could mean either his final lecture or his most recent lecture. It is generally better to use 'final' or 'most recent', depending on the intended sense, to avoid ambiguity.	
later on	In the expression 'later on', the 'on' is redundant, except in sentences such as "He refused to accept the fine later on principle."	

Expression/ Term	Comment	Forms/ Tenses
latter	'Latter' is the second of two (not the third of three, etc.). If there are more than two, consider 'the last named/mentioned'.	
lay/ lie	**lay** = to place on a surface: lay is generally transitive (you lay something). The past tense is 'laid' – 'She laid the book on her lap'. **lie** = to assume a horizontal position, to be at rest: lie is intransitive (you lie down). The past tense of 'lie' is 'lay', hence the confusion - "He lay down yesterday". Lain is also a past participle of lay There is also the verb 'to lie' = to tell untruths. The past tense is lied. "When I laid my cards on the table, he lied, telling me he had lain with her when he lay down yesterday."	lays/ laid/ laying lies lay/lain lying lies/ lied/ lying
less	See under 'fewer'.	
liable/ likely	**liable** = legally responsible. "The husband used to be liable for the debts of his wife." **liable** = predisposed to, have a strong tendency to; "He is liable to lose his temper." "Whenever he was reminded he was liable for his wife's debts, he was liable to lose his temper." In the second sense, the meaning is 'very likely to' or 'in the habit of' and is synonymous with 'apt to'.	
liaison	often misspelt as liason	
libel/ slander	Both words mean to defame someone. **libel** = written or broadcast defamation **slander** = oral defamation	libels/ libelled/ libelling; slanders/ slandered/ slandering

Expression/ Term	Comment	Forms/ Tenses
licence/ license	**licence** is the noun. **license** is the verb.	licences/ licensed/ licensing
lightening/ lighting	**lightening** = making lighter **lightning** = electrical discharge "When the lightning and thunder stopped, we all felt a lightening of mood."	
like	**like** = similar to 'Like' is best reserved to denote resemblance. "He is very like his father." "He acted like the tyrant he is." In the following sentences: "He has learned to manipulate his staff like we did." "It looks like we have lost the initiative." It would be better to replace 'like' with 'as' in the former and 'as though' in the latter. The use of 'like' as a meaningless, like, interjection, is to be, like, avoided, like, even in casual, like, conversation.	
like/ such as	**like** denotes similarity 'such as' introduces one or more examples of the topic to which it relates. e.g. "Business disciplines **such as** market research and advertising research are very **like** each other."	

Expression/ Term	Comment	Forms/ Tenses
literally	**literally** means precisely in accordance with the meaning of what is said: e.g. "He arrived at the conference literally with only minutes to spare." We should not use 'literally' if what we say is not literally true: e.g. we should not say: "He was so angry he literally exploded with rage".	
loath/ loathe	(adj.) loath (also loth) = unwilling, reluctant. "I am loath to pay my parking fines." (v) loathe = hate. "I loathe parking meters."	loth/loathes/ loathed/ loathing
loose / lose	**loose** means to untie or set free **lose** means to be unable to find something	
lot	as in 'a lot'. Quantify, if possible.	
majority	The context determines whether you should use a singular or plural verb with 'majority'. When the majority denotes a numerical calculation (the larger or largest number) or when the emphasis is on the majority as a single group, use a singular verb: "At the end of the vote, his majority was substantial." "On many issues, the majority is wrong." but, when the majority indicates a large number of individuals, use a plural verb: "The majority of people are well-meaning." Majority refers to a number of people or things. If we are talking about the greater proportion of an amount of something, 'most' is the right word.	majorities
masterful/ masterly	**masterful** = authoritative, dominating, domineering **masterly** = highly skilled, highly professional	

Expression/ Term	Comment	Forms/ Tenses
matrix	a much used and over-used word in business circles. Mathematically, a matrix is a table of numbers, symbols or other elements, arranged in rows and columns that, when appropriately manipulated, can, for example, be used to solve sets of simultaneous equations. The word also has other specific meanings in other fields (e.g. the tissue at the base of the fingernail from which new nail grows; an impression of a gramophone record to be used as a master for mass reproduction; something on which fungus or lichen grows). Given the words versatility and its intellectual appeal (it sounds impressive), it is not surprising that the word is now also used to denote any complicated network of inter-related factors, items or substances.	matrices/ matrixes Origin: Latin *matrix* meaning female used for breeding or parent stem. Later the word came to mean womb.
maybe/ may be	**maybe** = perhaps. This is a colloquialism to be avoided in formal writing **may be** is a verbal construction, expressing possibility or permissibility: e.g. "The word 'maybe' may be excluded from formal writing without regret."	

Expression/ Term	Comment	Forms/ Tenses
may / might	There is a fair amount of overlap but they are not always interchangeable. 'Might' is used in the present and past tense; 'may' is confined to the present; e.g. "I may/might give up trying to define the difference." "I might have tried too hard to define the difference in the past." 'May' also has the meaning of permissibility: e.g. "You may go." i.e. you have my permission to go. whereas;	
may / might	"You might go." simply means there is a possibility you will go. There is also a subtle distinction centring on a degree of possibility; e.g. "He may have been killed'" simply means there is a possibility he has been killed. "He might have been killed" would usually be taken to mean that, although there was a possibility he could have been killed, he survived.	
medium/ media	Television is a medium, as are the press, radio and the internet. The plural of medium is media. The media include television, radio, the press, the internet and any other form of communication. When you use 'media' use the plural form of the verb.	
meet/ meet up/ meet up with	**meet** on its own will do. Appending 'up' or 'up with' adds nothing.	

Expression/ Term	Comment	Forms/ Tenses
meet with	On most occasions you just 'meet', without a 'with'. e.g. "I met her on the corner." 'Meet with' is generally reserved for negative situations: e.g. "He met with an accident." but not always: "If you can meet with **triumph** and disaster, And treat those two imposters, just the same." *'If'*, *Rudyard Kipling*	meet met
moot	moot means 'open to debate', 'debatable': You can 'moot' an idea for discussion. e.g. "In questioning whether the money was well-spent, the MP raised a moot point." It is often incorrectly used in the sense of relevant.	**moot** goes back to the Old English *mot*, a meeting for discussion
most	**most** = the greater part **majority** = the greatest number e.g. "The majority of the voters thought the independent candidate deserved most of their support." But note that 'most' can also be used of number: "Most of the people supported the independent candidate."	
mean	**mean** does not need a 'for' after it. "I did not mean this to happen", not "I did not mean for this to happen".	means meant meaning

Expression/ Term	Comment	Forms/ Tenses
media/ medium	**media** is the plural form of medium. "The most powerful of the mass media is the medium of television." (That's a moot point. See 'moot' above.)	
memo- randum	plural memoranda	
meretri- cious/ meritorious	**meretricious** = superficially and garishly attractive **meritorious** = praiseworthy	Meretricious is derived from **mer- etrix**, the Latin for prostitute.
metal/ mettle	**metal** = a mineral substance which conducts heat and electricity **mettle** = courage, determination, strength of character "A sword may be made of metal but it is the mettle of the swordsman which will determine how well it is used."	
militate/ mitigate	**militate** = work against, conflict with, fight (The recession will militate against the firm's speedy recovery.) **mitigate** = reduce, make less bad (e.g. 'mitigating circumstances' which may reduce the seriousness of a crime) "In passing sentence, the Judge remarked that the defendant's lack of contrition militated against the defense counsel's plea of mitigating circumstances."	militates/ militated/ militating; mitigates/ mitigated/ mitigating

Expression/ Term	Comment	Forms/ Tenses
momentary/ momentous	**momentary** = of the instant (a momentary lapse) **momentous** = of great significance (a momentous event) "Gerald Ratner's momentary lapse in a speech in 1991 turned out to be a momentous event in the life of his company, wiping £500 million from the value of its shares."	
moot/ mute	**moot** = debatable. "Whether he ever fulfilled his potential is a moot point." **mute** = silent	
more/most	Generally, we are advised to use 'more' when comparing two people or things; and to use most when comparing one person or thing with more than one other person or thing. "Of Peter and Mary, Mary was more (or the more) experienced." "Of Peter, Paul and Mary, Paul was the most experienced". On the other hand, it is correct to say: "John was more intelligent than all the others" when we mean that, if you compared John with each of the others, we would find, in every case, he was more intelligent.	

Expression/Term	Comment	Forms/Tenses
most	As well as being a superlative, **most** can also mean 'very' or 'exceedingly'. This can lead to ambiguities. In the following sentence: "I am pleased you have come up with the most satisfactory solution." It is unclear whether the solution is the best of the solutions under consideration or simply an extremely satisfactory solution. If the former, we could say: "I am pleased you have come up with the most satisfactory solution of all." If the latter, we could say: "I am pleased you have come up with an exceedingly satisfactory solution."	
mutual	Strictly speaking, **mutual** involves the concept of reciprocity: i.e. it means something said or felt by all those involved about all the others involved. "As the parties to the dispute discussed the crisis, it was clear that the distrust felt was mutual" (i.e. all the parties distrusted each other). 'Mutual' is not a synonym for 'common' or 'shared'. According to this definition, the statement, "You and I have a mutual interest in marketing", is incorrect, since there is no reciprocity. Instead, we could say: "You and I have a common/shared interest in marketing".	

Expression/ Term	Comment	Forms/ Tenses
necessary	often misspelt neccessary	
neighbour-hood	'in the neighbourhood of'. Verbose? What about 'about'!	

neither/ nor	If both the 'neither' subject and the 'nor' subject are singular, the following verb should be singular:
	    e.g. "Neither Peter nor Paul **has** the necessary skill."
	
	When there is only one noun and the noun is plural, the verb should still be singular:
	    e.g. "Neither of the salesmen **has** the necessary skill."	

never/ not	**never** = not ever
	
	It is increasingly common for writers to use 'never' as an emphatic form of 'not'.
	
	    "He never attended this year's sales conference although he was product manager for one of the products we were launching."
	
	This is a pity because 'not' means 'not' and 'never' means 'not ever'. If all that is meant is 'not', use 'not', not 'never'.
	
	In the example above, it would be possible to give even greater emphasis to the irresponsibility of the product manager by writing:
	    "He even failed to attend...."	

nice	now over-used as a bland word of approval. It is a word to be avoided in serious writing. Its meaning of 'precise' or 'fine' is obsolescent.	

Expression/ Term	Comment	Forms/ Tenses
none	**none** = not one 'None' takes a singular verb, although it is frequently and, in less formal contexts, perhaps excusably attracted to a plural verb by the plural noun to which it relates: e.g. "None of these products *meet* our requirements."	

no one	**no one** is singular. The only possible excuse for treating it as plural is to avoid the gender problem:
	    e.g. "No-one has successfully completed **their** course."
	is probably preferable to:
	    "No-one has successfully completed **his/her** course."
	
	But a better solution might be:
	    "No-one has successfully completed **the** course."	

notable/ noticeable	**notable** = worthy of note (e.g. a notable achievement) **noticeable** = perceptible, catching the attention; e.g. "The improvement in profits was noticeable". 'noticeable' is often misspelt 'noticable'	
nucleus	plural nuclei	
oblivious	Oblivious means forgetful or unaware of. You are 'oblivious of', rather than 'oblivious to'.	
occur	See under 'happen' occurred and occurrence are often misspelt occured and occurence (or even occurance)	

Expression/ Term	Comment	Forms/ Tenses
official/ officious	**official** = authorised, recognised **officious** = exceeding what is required or appropriate, interfering	
older/ oldest	**older** is to be used when comparing the age of two people or things. "Peter is older than Mary." **oldest** is to be used when the age of more than two people or things are being considered: "Of Peter, Paul and Mary, Peter is the oldest."	
on/ upon	The words 'on' and 'upon' are interchangeable in most cases. "'Upon' is considered rather more formal, but is hanging on to its place in informal speech through such formulaic expressions as 'once upon a time' and 'upon my soul'.	
only	While some argue that concern about the positioning of "only" is pedantic, there is a strong case for placing the word where it will make the writer's meaning clear. In a sentence such as: "I will only give bonuses to those who deserve them", the meaning is clear, although it would have been better expressed as: "I will give bonuses only to those who deserve them." But a sentence such as "The present decline in profits can only be slowed by appointing a new Chief Executive" can be interpreted in two ways. Will the appointment of a new Chief Executive slow down but not reverse the decline in profits? Or is the appointment of a new Chief Executive the only way to slow down the decline in profits? If the latter, we could make this meaning clear by saying: "The present decline in profits can be slowed only by the appointment of a new Chief Executive".	

Expression/ Term	Comment	Forms/ Tenses
onto	The 'on' and the 'to' should be written separately when the 'on' forms part of a verb (in the infinitive form). e.g. "He went on to explain his position."	
onus	**onus** = duty, responsibility 'Onus' generally has a negative connotation of burden or blame: e.g. "The onus is on you to prove your innocence." It is not a synonym for 'aim' or 'objective'.	Latin ***onus probandi***, the burden of proving
oral	See 'aural'.	
ordinance/ ordnance	**ordinance** = a decree, a religious edict **ordnance** = mounted guns or government stores of military guns, ammunition, vehicles, etc.	
overestimate/ underestimate	It is easy to become confused in using these words, especially when using a negative formulation. The following error is not uncommon: "The importance of this product launch to the future of the company cannot be underestimated." (Presumably, it should be "cannot be overestimated".)	overestimates/ overestimated/ overestimating; underestimates/ underestimated/ underestimating
owing to	**owing to** = because of **due to** = caused by "***Owing to*** problems ***due to confusion*** between 'due to' and 'owing to', some writers avoid both terms, preferring 'because of' and 'caused by." Who can blame them?	

Expression/ Term	Comment	Forms/ Tenses
pacific/ specific	**pacific** means peaceful; **specific** means clearly, precisely defined	
pair	**pair** takes a singular or plural verb depending on whether the pair *is* seen as a **unit** or *are* seen as **two distinct entities**: e.g. "That pair of gloves has disappeared." "That pair are forever at each other's throats." and of course the sentence introducing these examples.	
panacea	**panacea** is a cure for all ills or problems. It should not be used to describe a remedy for a single problem.	From the Greek *pan* = all and *akos* = remedy.
paradigm	now used, and over-used, as a more sophisticated word for model or pattern	pl. paradigms adj. paradigmatic
parenthesis	An explanatory note inserted into a passage, usually delimited by punctuation marks and, most commonly, brackets.	parentheses
partially/ partly	**partially** places the emphasis on degree; **partly** indicates a division or a fraction of something. e.g. "This building has been partly devoted to ophthalmic services and has been specially equipped for the partially-sighted."	

Expression/ Term	Comment	Forms/ Tenses
passed/ past	It is not surprising these words are sometimes confused. **passed** is the past participle of 'to pass'. **past** is an adjective: "I am troubled by past memories". **past** is a preposition: "She walked past me." **past** is an adverb: "She walked past". And, as a noun 'the past' denotes 'times before' or history. "In the past, I have passed over the fact that I have often seen him walk past those in need without a second glance, despite his own past experience of abject poverty."	
per capita	**per capita** is the Latin for 'per head' or more precisely 'per heads' since it is the plural form of 'caput'. There is a bit of a problem here. Per capita, a term used by lawyers correctly when distributing an inheritance between a number of individuals, is now used to mean 'per head' so widely that it is accepted usage. Those who baulk at the Latin mistranslation often recommend 'per head' but they have to face the criticism that they are advocating a hybrid expression in which a Latin preposition is bonded to an Anglo-Saxon word. 'Per diem' (each day) and 'per annum' (each year) don't present the same problem because 'annum' and 'diem' are singular. Anyone for 'per caput'?	

Expression/ Term	Comment	Forms/ Tenses
peninsula/ peninsular	**peninsula** is the noun **peninsular** is the adjective	pl. peninsulas. The Latin plural form ***peninsulae*** is, according to the Oxford Dictionary, obsolete.
perquisite/ prerequisite	**perquisite** = an ancillary benefit (hence 'perks') **prerequisite** = a condition which must be fulfilled if something else is to happen or be true.	
perfect	**perfect** is an absolute. Something cannot be 'more perfect'.	
perpetrate/ perpetuate	**perpetrate** = to perform or implement something bad (e.g. a crime) **perpetuate** = to cause to continue or to last indefinitely "We have no wish to perpetuate the publicity he has derived from the crimes he has perpetrated."	perpetrates/ perpetrated/ perpetrating; perpetuates/ perpetuated/ perpetuating
phenomenon/ phenomena	**phenomenon** is singular; phenomena is the plural form	
photo	plural photos; unlike potato, plural potatoes	
plus	When 'plus' is used to add to a subject, whether the verb is singular or plural in form is still determined by the subject alone. "This product launch, plus the other products recently introduced, was highly successful." Note "Two plus two equals four," where the first 'two' is taken to be a single entity, whereas two plus fours (i.e. two pairs of knickerbockers) would require a plural form of the verb.	

Expression/Term	Comment	Forms/Tenses
pore/pour	**pore** over = to examine intently (to pore over a document) **pour** = to cause a liquid to flow in a stream	pores/pored/poring; pours/poured/pouring
possible	**possible** is not interchangeable with 'likely'. Something may be 'very likely' but, strictly speaking, it cannot be 'very possible' because possible is an absolute. In any case, if it's 'very possible' it's probably 'probable'.	

pp	**pp** = per pro (Latin for 'through the agency of' and equivalent to 'as represented by':
	
	This means that, if an assistant is signing on behalf of a manager, the correct form is:
	    Manager,
	    pp Assistant
	and not, as is often seen, the other way round.	

practicable/practical	There is overlap in the meaning of these words but: **practicable** = usable, feasible, possible **practical** = sensible, realistic, useful A plan or a solution can be both practicable and practical but it is possible to draw a distinction is some cases. "It may be practicable to replace the salesmen's cars with bicycles but it is scarcely practical."	
practice/practise	**practice** is the noun. "Practice makes perfect." **practise** is the verb. "If you wish to be perfect, to must never forget to practise."	practices practises practised practising

Expression/ Term	Comment	Forms/ Tenses
precede/ proceed	**precede** = go or come before **proceed** = continue	precedes preceded preceding; proceeds proceeded proceeding
precipitate/ precipitous	There is an overlap of meaning but some try to make a distinction along the following lines: **precipitate** = hasty, happening sooner than expected **precipitous** = very steep, dangerously steep	adv. precipitately adv. precipitously
prefer	'prefer a) **to** b)', not 'prefer a) **than** b)' preferred and preferring are often misspelt prefered and prefering	prefers preferred preferring
preferable	**preferable** is an absolute. Something cannot be 'more preferable'	
preposition/ proposition	**preposition** = a word, such as 'at' or 'on', which combines with a noun to form a phrase in order to indicate direction, manner, position, time, etc. **proposition** = proposal, a statement to be considered "He put forward the proposition that a preposition is the type of word that you should never stop a sentence at or end a sentence with."	
prescribe/ proscribe	**prescribe** = recommend, specify **proscribe** = ban, condemn	prescribes/ prescribed/ prescribing

Expression/ Term	Comment	Forms/ Tenses
presently	In British English, 'presently' means 'soon but not yet', "I will give you a hand presently." The American sense of 'presently', meaning at this present time, is covered by 'currently' or 'now' in British English. Presently is used in some circumstances to mean currently in British English in expressions such as "He is presently filming in Spain", although 'currently' would be more common.	
preventative/ preventive	Both words mean the same. 'Preventive' seems to be superseding 'preventative'.	
principal/ principle	n. **principle** = a standard, a rule, a fundamental law n. **principal** = a person who is in charge of an organisation (the principal of a college); adj. **principal** = foremost in importance (the principal objection) "Taking a principled stand, the Principal of the school said it was his principal objective to promote his personal principles amongst the students."	adj. principled = based on principles
program/ programme	**program** is the American spelling on all occasions, and the British spelling for computer software.	programs/ programmes
pronunciation	**pronunciation** is spelled this way and pronounced this way. It is incorrect to spell it or pronounce it 'pro**noun**ciation'.	
prophecy/ prophesy	**prophecy** is the noun. **prophesy** is the verb. "He confidently prophesied the prophecy would not be fulfilled."	prophesies/ prophesied/ prophesying

Expression/ Term	Comment	Forms/ Tenses
proposition	Both 'proposition' and 'proposal' mean putting forward an idea or a plan for consideration. 'Proposal' generally has a sense of being more formal. 'Proposition' often implies the idea of bargaining, either as the basis for a proposal or as a necessary condition for accepting a proposal. After all, a man will 'propose' marriage; but he will 'proposition' for an affair. 'Proposition' is also a term in mathematics for a statement which has to be proved.	propositions
protagonist	You can't have more than one protagonist. In the words of the Highlander, "there can be only one".	
Protest / protest against or at	You can protest your innocence (i.e. strongly assert) your innocence and you can also protest against/at (i.e. strongly criticise) the punishment.	
providing/ provided that	'Providing' and 'provided that' can both be used to set a condition. 'Providing that' is regarded by some as incorrect but why is not entirely clear.	
publicly	**publicly**, not publically	
purposefully/ purposely	**purposefully** = with a clear objective, with determination **purposely** = with that intention, on purpose. "He purposely released news of the fall in profits, just before he purposefully confronted the Unions with his redundancy proposals."	

Expression/Term	Comment	Forms/Tenses
quantity	Strictly speaking, **quantity** takes a singular verb: e.g. "The quantity of widgets delivered meets our requirements." but the use of a plural verb is excused by some on the dubious grounds of attraction (i.e. the plural 'widgets' calls for a plural verb). Such an argument is really more an explanation of the cause of the error than a justification for it.	quantities
quantum	plural quanta	
quite	**quite** seems to be an inherently fuzzy word, since it can be used to intensify or moderate the word it qualifies: e.g. "His performance was quite extraordinary." indicates an outstanding performance. "She was quite kind to me after I lost my job" indicates her kindness was strictly limited. (If it is so, be thankful English is your mother tongue!)	
rack/ wrack	**rack** (n) = an instrument of torture, involving the stretching of the body **rack** (v) = to torture on the rack **wrack** (n) = collapse or destruction (as in' wrack and ruin') For obvious reasons, the meanings of these words have become confused. Strictly speaking, someone is 'racked (not wracked) by pain' and parents will be 'racked (not wracked) by grief' at the loss of a child. Except in the company of 'ruin', 'wrack' is obsolete.	racks/ racked/ racking
radius	plural radii	radii

Expression/ Term	Comment	Forms/ Tenses
rarely	In the expression 'rarely ever' the 'ever' is redundant, since 'rarely' means 'hardly ever'.	
reaction	**reaction** = a fast or immediate response to a stimulus. When describing a considered reply to some event, 'response' is a better choice.	reactions
real	**real** is a useful word with several precise meanings but, when 'real' and 'really' are used simply as intensifiers, they are generally best replaced by 'very' or left out altogether. "**Real** is a really useful word which can really change the meaning of a sentence." The two 'reallys' add nothing to the meaning of the sentence.	
reason is because/ reason was because	The expression "the reason is because" is tautological. Use either 'the reason is' or 'because'.	
refer (back) to	In the expression 'referring back to', the 'back' fulfils no purpose, unless you are also 'referring forward to' or referring to something for the second time. referred and referring are often misspelt refered and refering	refers/ referred/ referring
refute/ rebut	When you rebut a proposition, you argue against it and reject it. When you refute it, you *prove it* to be *wrong*. The words refute and rebut are not interchangeable. See also 'deny'.	
regard/ regards	'with regard to' but 'as regards'	

Expression/ Term	Comment	Forms/ Tenses
regardless/ irregardless	**regardless** (adj.) means 'careless' 'without regard to'. As an adverb, 'regardless' means 'despite everything'. 'irregardless' does not exist, and is presumably formed through a mistaken analogy with 'irrespective' which means 'without regard to'	
regrettable/ regrettably/ regretful/ regretfully	You are 'regretful' when you are sorry you have done something 'regrettable'.	regretted
reign/ rein	**reign** = the period during which a monarch is on the throne **rein** = one of a pair of straps used with a bit to control a horse "Following the excesses of his royal father's reign, Parliament was determined to rein in his wayward son."	reigns reins
reiterate	**reiterate** = repeat "Reiterate again" is therefore tautological unless perhaps you are doing something for the third time.	reiterates reiterated reiterating
religious	often misspelt religous	
reluctant/ reticent	**reluctant** = disinclined, loath, unwilling **reticent** = reserved, taciturn, holding back 'Reticent' does not mean 'reluctant'. The two words are correctly used in the following sentence: "Although the defendant was reticent, refusing to furnish an alibi, the jury was reluctant to bring in a guilty verdict."	

Expression/ Term	Comment	Forms/ Tenses
remuneration/ renumeration	**remuneration** = reward, pay **renumeration** = renumbering Remuneration, meaning reward or pay, is often misspelt as and/or confused with renumeration.	remuneration' is derived from Latin '*munus*', a gift or favour
repeat	**repeat** = to say, do, or experience something again. "Repeat again" is therefore tautological unless perhaps you are doing something for the third time.	repeats/ repeated/ repeating
replace/ substitute	While 'replace' and 'substitute' both mean changing one thing (A) for another (B), they use different constructions. You replace A with B. You substitute B for A.	replaces/ replaced/ replacing; substitutes/ substituted/ substituting
repel/ repulse	**repel** = to drive back; to disgust **repulse** = to drive back, to reject coldly There is some overlap but the sense of disgust associated with 'repel' and cold rejection with 'repulse' justifies some degree of distinction. If you are repelled by someone or something, you are disgusted. If you are repulsed by someone, you are rejected coldly. "She was so repelled by him that she repulsed his overtures immediately."	repels/ repelled/ repelling; repulses/ repulsed/ repulsing
report on/ report into	Best to report **on**. Your investigation **into** the subject can always from part of your report **on**.	

Expression/ Term	Comment	Forms/ Tenses
re-present/ represent	**re-present** = to present again **represent** = to convey an impression of, to be a sign of	re-presents re-presented re-pre-senting represents represented representing
respectively	Referring to two or more people or things in the order in which they have been mentioned. "Peter and Mary won £100 and £50 respectively in the salespersons' competition." (i.e. Peter won £100 and Mary won £50). Respectively is sometimes used tautologically.; "The prizes of £100 and £50 were awarded respectively to Peter who took the £100 prize and Mary who won £50."	
reticent	See 'reluctant'.	
revert	**revert** = to go back to a former (often inferior) practice In the expression 'reverts back', the word 'back' is usually redundant.	reverts/ reverted/ reverting
ring	meaning 'to sound resonantly', has two past tenses; 'rang' (transitive) and 'rung' (intransitive) "He rang the bells; for sure, the bells were rung." There is also 'ringed' which is the past participle of 'ring', meaning 'to form a ring around'. "Ringed by admirers, he rang the bells; for sure the bells were rung."	rings/ rang/ rung ringed

Expression/ Term	Comment	Forms/ Tenses
route	There is a case for retaining the 'e' when 'routeing', to avoid confusion with 'routing' and 'being routed'. "The captain decided on routeing us through mountainous country, following our thorough routing by the enemy."	routeing routing
rural/rustic	**rural** = of the countryside **rustic** = quaintly or clumsily of the countryside	
's/ s'	When '**s** is used to denote possession, the apostrophe which must accompany it is often misplaced. '**s** is used to indicate the possessive in the singular **s'** is used to indicate the possessive in the plural "I have provided the money for the salesperson's prize" = one salesperson "I have provided the money for the salespersons' prize" = two or more salespersons; one prize. "I have provided the money for the salespersons' prizes" = two or more salespersons and two or more prizes.	
scarcely	**scarcely** has a negative force and should not be used with another negative word. "He hadn't scarcely arrived before he was subjected to a verbal onslaught." is incorrect. It should be "He had scarcely…" The clause following 'scarcely' can be introduced by 'when' or 'before', but not by 'than'. "Scarcely had I spoken before the audience burst into applause."	

Expression/ Term	Comment	Forms/ Tenses
seeing/ seeing as how	**seeing as how** is incorrect and can generally be replaced by 'since' or 'seeing that'. "Seeing as how he can't organise his own domestic affairs satisfactorily, it is unlikely he will be able to run a public company effectively." Try: "Since he can't organise his own domestic affairs satisfactorily, it is unlikely he will be able to run a public company effectively."	
seem	**seem** can be used with an infinitive to moderate the force of a following verb: "You don't seem to understand what I am saying to you." which is less blunt than: "You don't understand what I am saying to you."	seems/ seemed/ seeming
sensual/ sensuous	Both words describe what we experience through our senses: **sensual** relates more to the physical (sex, food, drink, etc.). "He was determined to satisfy his sensual appetites." **sensuous** relates more to the aesthetic and emotional. "The dancer aroused his sensual appetites with her sensuous movements."	
series	**series** is both singular and plural	
serum	plural sera	

Expression/ Term	Comment	Forms/ Tenses
shall/ will	There is a subtle distinction in the use of 'shall' and 'will' which is probably fading away but, for those who wish to preserve it, here is the rule: Simply to indicate the future, use 'shall' with 'I' and 'we'; use 'will' elsewhere. "I shall go tomorrow. They will go the day after." To indicate determination or command, use 'will' with 'I' and 'we'; use 'shall' elsewhere. "I will demand my rights although they have told me they shall resist."	
should	Grammatically, 'should' is the past tense of 'shall', but it generally means 'ought to': e.g. "You should go." = "You ought to go." It also fulfils the role of a subjunctive in expressions such as: "I should like you to go."	
significant	If you say something is 'significant', it should be clear what you think it is significant of. It is not simply another word for 'important'. There is also the term 'statistically significant' which has a precise meaning (i.e. the result could not have occurred simply by chance).	
similar	'similar to', not 'similar as'	
simplistic	**simplistic** = too or over simple, invariably with a negative connotation. 'Simplistic' contains negative implications. The word 'over' in the expression 'over simplistic' is therefore redundant or, if it suggests there is a simplistic condition that is acceptable, illogical.	

Expression/Term	Comment	Forms/Tenses
sing	The past tense of **sing** is 'sang'; 'sung' is the past participle. "The song he sang had been sung by others."	sang/sung cf. ring
situation	**situation** = physical position, state of affairs 'Situation' is a much overused word. 'Crisis situation', for example, can generally be reduced to 'crisis' without loss of meaning.	situations
some	**some** = an unspecified number or quantity In business reports, quantify if possible. "In our research, 5% of responses were negative." is clearly better (more informative and precise) than "In our research, we had some negative responses."	
somebody/someone	Both 'somebody' and 'someone' take a singular verb.	
sometime	**sometime** = at an unspecified point in time **some time** = an unspecified period of time. "It was sometime after the committee meeting that he asked if he could have some time off." 'Sometime' can also mean erstwhile, previous: "The sometime Chairman of X, now Chairman of Y."	
sometimes	**sometimes** = on occasions 'Sometimes' is always written as one word - except in sentences such as: "Corruption is more common in some times than in others".	

Expression/ Term	Comment	Forms/ Tenses
sooner	'no sooner than', not 'no sooner when' "No sooner had he resigned than (not 'when') his deputy applied for his parking space."	
sort	The number of the verb following 'sort of' should be consistent with any demonstrative adjective attached to 'sort'. e.g. "*This* sort of excuse *is* unacceptable." "*Those* sorts of excuse *are* unacceptable."	sorts
sorts	**sort** has a plural form which should be used when writing of more than one type: e.g. "These sorts of misdemeanors are unforgivable."	Cf. kind
specially	See 'especially'.	
species	**species** is both singular and plural	
speed up	The past tense of 'speed up' is 'speeded up', not 'sped up'.	speeded up
stationary/ stationery	**stationary** = immobile **stationery** = paper, envelopes, etc.	
stimulus	plural stimuli	
storey / story	**storey** is a level in a building **story** is a narrative	
stratum/ strata	**strata** is the plural of stratum and takes a plural verb. "The strata of society are many."	stratum
strategy/ tactics	**strategy** = a long-term plan for the achievement of a defined objective **tactics** = the detailed manoeuvres executed to fufil a strategy	strategies

Expression/ Term	Comment	Forms/ Tenses
strim	to use a strimmer. The past participle is strimmed, although 'strummed' is somehow tempting.	strimming strimmed
subsequent	'subsequent to'. 'After' might well do and do well.	
superior	'superior to', not 'superior than'.	
supersede	**supersede** = replace, supplant

often misspelt as 'supercede'

The word comes from the Latin '*sedere*' = to sit (i.e. supersede = to sit over or above) and has nothing to do with 'ceding' (yielding). | supersedes superseded superseding |
syllabus/ syllabuses	Should the need arise for a plural form of 'syllabus', 'syllabuses' is to be preferred over 'syllabi'. The word syllabus is said by some etymologists to owe its existence to a misprint of the Greek sittybos (plural of Sittyba meaning a parchment label) which became legitimised through a spurious Latinisation to syllabus; hence the often used plural syllabi. (Too much information?)	syllabuses
synopsis	plural synopses	
synthesis	plural syntheses	adj. synthetic
technical/ technological	**technical** = having or involving specialised, often mechanical, knowledge or skill

technological = of a technical nature (technological advances) | |
| temporary/ temporarily | **temporary** is an adjective

temporarily is an adverb

    e.g. "He was temporarily absent from work because of a temporary illness." | |

Expression/ Term	Comment	Forms/ Tenses
terms/ in terms of	'in terms of' should be used when there is a relationship between one thing and another. "He explained his success in terms of good planning and the commitment of the sales team." It is not simply an alternative to 'about' or 'as regards'.	
than	Because 'than' can be seen as a conjunction or a preposition, confusion can arise. "I like her more than you" can mean either "I like her more than you like her" (where 'than' is a conjunction) or "I like her more than I like you" (where 'than' is a preposition). To avoid ambiguity, it is probably best to say what you mean in full.	
that/ who/which	There is some confusion in the use of **that** and **who/which**. **that** introduces *defining ('restrictive')* relative clauses; **which** introduces both *defining ('restrictive')* and *commenting ('non-restrictive')* relative clauses **that**, as a relative pronoun, is used to introduce *defining* clauses (a clause that forms an essential part of the noun to which it refers): e.g. The salesman that won the prize was given a standing ovation." Without knowing we are talking about the prize winner we could not know which salesman we were referring to. This use of 'that' is sometimes called *restrictive* in that it contains information that is strictly an essential part of the noun to which it refers.	

Expression/ Term	Comment	Forms/ Tenses
that/who/ which	**who/which** are used to introduce either *commenting* or *defining* clauses. e.g. 　"The top salesman, who had been trained by me, was given a standing ovation." Here 'who' introduces a commenting clause. This use of which is sometimes called *non-restrictive*. The essence of the above sentence is "The top salesman was given a standing ovation." This is a complete and meaningful sentence. The 'who' clause simply adds some additional information. If in doubt, use 'who'/ 'which'.	
the fact of the matter	another favourite of politicians, keen to correct the ignorance or deceit of an opponent. 'In fact' will generally serve as well, although "You are wrong…" is often what is meant.	
there is	The verb used with 'there' should agree with the subject it introduces: 　"There is a man at the door." 　"There are two men at the door." If a man and a woman came to the door, we should write: 　"There are a man and a woman at the door." but no-one is likely to object to: 　"There is a man and a woman at the door."	there are, there was, there were
thesis	plural theses	theses
till/ until	**till** and **until** both mean 'up to the time that' and are interchangeable, except at the start of a sentence where 'until' is preferred. 'til' is an incorrect spelling of 'till'.	

Expression/ Term	Comment	Forms/ Tenses
times	When defining quantities remember that three times more than 100 is 400. Three times as much as 100 is 300.	
titillate / titivate	**titillate** means to arouse interest **titivate** means to make someone or something look smarter or more attractive	
together with	When 'together with' is used to add to a subject, whether the verb is singular or plural in form is still determined by the subject alone. "This product launch, together with the other products recently introduced, *was* (not '*were*') highly successful."	
too	When **too** is used to denote 'to an excessive degree', it should be applied only to adjectives: "He was too clever for his own good." Many argue it should not be used with past participles and the following: "He felt he had been too criticised by the panel." is clearly wrong. 'Excessively' or, in this case, 'unfairly' should replace 'too'. There are, however, many past participles (generally expressing mood or condition) which have come to be regarded as adjectives: e.g. disappointed, delighted, exhausted, pleased, tired With such words, 'too' is acceptable.	

Expression/ Term	Comment	Forms/ Tenses
transpire	Strictly speaking **transpire** means to become apparent or become: "It transpired he was an incorrigible womaniser." It is often used as a pretentious synonym for 'happen'. Don't use it in this way. Given that 'transpire' is shorter than either 'become apparent' or 'become known', and no-one wants to be thought pretentious, why not reserve it for its strict meaning?	transpires/ transpired/ transpiring
troop/ troupe	**troop** = a group of soldiers or any other individuals **troupe** = a group of actors or other entertainers	troops/ troupes
try	'try to do something' not 'try and do something', although 'try and' is common in spoken English. Of course 'try and' can be correct but it has a different meaning. "I will try and kill him" doesn't mean "I will try to kill him"; it means "I will try and I will kill him" (i.e. I will try and I will succeed).	tries/tried/ trying
ultimate	strictly speaking, ultimate means the last or final. It is widely used, especially in advertising, to mean the best, presumably on the argument that the most recent version of a product is sure to be an improvement. Sadly, experience informs us that all too often 'new and improved' simply means the manufacturer has found a way of reducing costs and/or increasing price and profit.	

Expression/ Term	Comment	Forms/ Tenses
uncharted/ unchartered	**uncharted** = not surveyed **unchartered** = unauthorised, unregulated	
underprivileged	**underprivileged** is open to the criticism that it is an emotive word with no clear meaning. A privilege is a special favour. If I have never had that privilege, I could be described perhaps as unprivileged. If I lose a privilege, I could be described perhaps as deprivileged. But underprivileged seems to suggest that being privileged is the normal state of affairs which surely contradicts the meaning of the word privilege.	
unexceptionable/unexceptional	**unexceptionable** = inoffensive **unexceptional** = average, mediocre	
unique	**unique** is an absolute. Something cannot be 'more unique', or 'rather unique' or 'very unique'.	
universal	**universal** is an absolute. Something cannot be 'more universal'.	
until such time	In the expression 'until such time', the 'such time' is redundant.	
up until	In such expressions as "We will continue the advertising up until completion of the initial distribution of the product", the 'up' is redundant.	
verbal	See 'aural'.	
vertex	plural vertices	vertex vertices

Expression/ Term	Comment	Forms/ Tenses
very	**very** is one of a number of adverbs denoting degree which, strictly speaking, should be used only to qualify adjectives. The use of 'very' with past participles, such as 'angered' (as in "He was very angered by the audience's response") is open to criticism. In this example "He was greatly angered..." is preferable. There are, however, a number of past participles which have been accorded adjectival status (e.g. disappointed, disturbed, tired). In these cases, the use of qualifiers such as 'very' is acceptable. 'very' is also implicated in cases of tautology or verbiage. e.g. "It was very evident that his days were numbered." It could hardly be "not very evident".	
volcano	plural volcanoes	
waste/ wastage	Both words mean anything unused or not fully used: **waste** is the thing itself; **wastage** is the process of wasting. 'Waste' is the word usually used when the cause is human action or error. "Trying to help him was a waste of my time." 'Wastage', often combined with 'natural' is used to describe a reduction in a workforce through normal staff turnover, including retirement.	
weird	often misspelt wierd.	

Expression/ Term	Comment	Forms/ Tenses
were	In hypothetical statements ("If I were to make a decision now, we could complete the project within six months."), it is now commonplace to use 'was' rather than 'were'. There is, however, a case for retaining 'were' as confirmation of the hypothetical nature of the statement. (And a neat riposte to those who use 'was' when they should use 'were'.)	
when	**when** relates to time. It should be avoided when there is no reference to time. e.g. "A coherent strategy is one in which (rather than when) each of the components of the campaign plays an integrated role."	
when all's said and done	try 'in the end' or 'after all'	
whence	**whence** = from where 'from whence' is therefore tautological. 'Whither' (to which place) and 'whence' (from which place) are described by dictionaries as 'chiefly formal'; i.e. not in common use.	
where	**where** relates to place and is best avoided when there is no reference to place. "This seems to be a problem where no-one has the answer." would be better expressed as follows: "This seems to be a problem for which no-one has the answer."	

Expression/ Term	Comment	Forms/ Tenses
who/ whom	**who** is the subject form. **whom** is the object form. "There were many at the conference whom I had previously met." "I, who have spent all my working life in marketing, ask to whom I should defer in marketing matters." Those who argue that it is pedantic to use 'whom' in the former example are challenging a basic feature of English grammar, as in I/me, he/him, she/her, they/them.	
who's/ whose	**who's** = who is **whose** = 'of whom' or 'of which' e.g. "Who's to know whose book this is?"	
with regard to	'with regard to', not 'with regards to'	

10.4 QUIRKY WORDS

For word buffs, here are some words which seem eccentric in some way.

10.4.1 One-hit words

Here are some words which now seem to be restricted to a very narrow field of use. These words listed on the left rarely if ever appear in any expression other than the one listed on the right.

Word	Expression
amok	run amok
begone	woe-begone
betide	woe betide
concerted	concerted effort
crock	crock of gold
crux	crux of the matter

Word	Expression
dereliction	dereliction of duty
dudgeon	high dudgeon
duress	under duress
effacing	self-effacing
fangled	new-fangled
fettle	fine fettle
figment	figment of the imagination
foregone	foregone conclusion
forlorn	forlorn hope
grist	grist for the mill
halcyon	halcyon days
luke	luke-warm
manna	manna from heaven
paragon	paragon of virtue
petard	hoist with one's own petard
poke	pig in a poke
trice	in a trice
wend	wend one's way
wrack	wrack and ruin

10.4.2 Un-Positive words

Here are a few words which exist or have survived only in their negative form. Their positive form is obsolete or obsolescent - or never existed. We have given a few examples of how the positive form of these words might have been used, had they ever existed.

dishevelled	Why not, "She combed her hair until she looked well and truly 'hevelled'", - or would it be 'shevelled'?
inadvertent	inadvertent = unintentional. There is no 'advertent' = intentional.

unabashed	unabashed = not to be embarrassed or ill at ease. There is a word 'abash' which means 'to cause someone to feel disconcerted or ill at ease' but only unabashed remains in current use.
unassuming	unassuming = modest. There is no adjective 'assuming' meaning immodest.
uncouth	Sadly, there are no 'couth' youths with which to compare the 'uncouth' variety.
undaunted	undaunted = not discouraged. 'Daunted' would mean 'put off, discouraged', perhaps someone whose confidence has been dented.
unkempt	unkempt = untidy, disorderly. What happened to: "In his DJ, he looked really kempt."?.
unwieldy	unwieldy = unbalanced, awkward, difficult to handle. Why not "The two handles made the case extremely wieldy"?
unwitting	unwitting = unintentional. Why not "You have insulted me wittingly"?

10.5 GRAMMATICAL/VERBAL HAZARDS

We must tread carefully here. In matters of grammar, the descriptive approach has supplanted the prescriptive. It is wrong to judge people by their grasp of grammar, partly because any "mistakes" are not really errors; rather they are simply "non-standard". In any case, it is wrong to judge people in matters of grammar, just as it is unacceptable to distinguish between the deserving and the undeserving poor.

We do not need to debate the moral standing of the above propositions but we do need to recognise that, at least in the case of grammatical solecisms, educated people are making judgements the whole time. When a man says: "We was having a good time on the beach", the word "was" immediately marks the speaker as uneducated and lower class. Of course it's terrible. He may be a truly wonderful person; he may be highly intelligent (although this is less likely) but wonderful or not, intelligent or not, he has placed himself in the lower reaches of the social hierarchy. Any who deny this is so, however well meaning, are not being honest.

Do not kritisize spelling miss takes or gramer tickle croars; their just come on egg samples of non standerd Inglish."

Of course, in a business document or academic essay, you would not expect to see "we was" too often but there are some grammatical errors which do occur, frequently perpetrated by those desperate to show they are not "ignorant". Of these, the most frequent is the use of "I" instead of "me" in such expressions as:

"Between you and I, we would be well advised to keep quiet."

The reason for the use of "I" in the expression "between you and I" seems to be a neurotic fear of using "me" when "I" would be grammatically correct.

"Me and my mate John went down to the pub."
is a common formulation in which "me" is incorrectly used instead of "I".
In eagerness not to make this type of error, the person who says "between you and I" sadly makes the opposite mistake, exposing a lack of basic grammar. The key question is whether we are dealing with a subject or an object. "I" is the subject form, so the correct version must be:

"My mate John and I went down the pub."

On the other hand, in the sentence "Between you and I, my mate John is a bit of a nutter", between, a preposition, takes the object case, so it should be "between you and me".

"Between you and me, my mate John is a bit of a nutter."
So it's always "between you and me".

We should add, before we go any further that, although there are grammatical rules that can be used to explain the flaws in each of the examples we provide, a knowledge of grammar is not essential to avoiding the errors. If you read through carefully what you have written, with an open mind, alert to the meaning of the words and the sense of each sentence, you will spot most, if not all, of these solecisms (assuming there are any.)

10.5.1 Ambiguity

Ambiguity is almost always to be avoided in business communications where the general aim is simplicity, clarity and precision.

Below, we give a number of examples: some are obvious, some more subtle; some invite misinterpretation, others will resent it; some result in nonsense, others are funny. In all cases, they fail the test of simplicity, clarity and precision.

"As the town's leading chemist, we dispense with accuracy."

'We launched the product which sadly has failed as you intended.'
(This should perhaps read: 'We launched the product as you intended. Sadly it has failed.')

"The young lady sat on the chair with crossed legs."

"Never knowingly undersold."
(Does this mean that the store has 'never knowingly been undersold' or that it has 'never knowingly undersold anyone else'?)

She served pizza to her husband cut into four pieces

"Fine for parking"
Not so fine, if fined!

"I caught the hooligan stealing my wife's car in my underwear."
Who was wearing the underwear?

"He stopped the man with a blunt instrument."
(Was the blunt instrument instrumental in stopping the man or merely additional information about the man who was stopped?)

He is unlikely ever to compete so well again after an accident.

(Presumably we can expect only modest performances after accidents in future.)

"I will not resign because of your incompetence."

(If not for the incompetence, why will you resign? Alternatively, whose incompetence will suffice to elicit a resignation?)

"I do not accept your argument and condemn those who have furnished evidence."

(How far does the 'not' extend? Does he, or does he not, condemn those who have furnished evidence?)

Record profits warning

This headline does not make it entirely clear whether the subject is a warning about *record profits* (perhaps unlikely) or a *record warning* about (presumably declining) profits.

"The Prime Minister realised he needed the support of the Unions more than the CBI."

(Who needs whose support?)

In all cases, the author should be aware that, in employing words, he is dealing with an infinitely subtle, crafty and sometimes subversive medium. Always be on your guard against the playful tendencies of words and syntax!

Of course, ambiguity can be used to devastating effect for comic purposes. Here is the exchange between Jack Cloth and Anne Oldman in the television spoof crime thriller A Touch of Cloth:

Jack Cloth: "I haven't laughed since my wife died?"
Ann Oldman: "Why did you laugh when your wife died?

10.5.2 Dangling Participles

Adjectival phrases should have a noun or pronoun to describe within the sentence where they appear and it should be clear, generally through positioning, which noun or pronoun 'owns' the adjectival phrase. When using adjectival phrases containing a participle, readers can become confused. The previous sentence is an example of a dangling participle. Who is doing the 'using'? Not the reader. Here is another example:

"Peter stood up. On reaching the podium, the applause rose to a crescendo."

But we have not mentioned Peter in the second sentence, so we attach the adjectival clause to the first available noun - the applause (which is not what we meant and is nonsense).

Here are some more examples:

> "When downsizing an organisation, the remaining staff may well become demoralised."

It is not, or is it, 'the remaining staff' who have down-sized the organisation? This is perhaps a more serious example of this type of error, because it is possible the meaning could be misunderstood.

> "Walking along the shore, the Gormley statues seemed almost lifelike."

Well, I guess they would, if they were walking along the shore! 'Walking along the shore' needs to be attached to a noun to which it belongs. Try: "Walking along the shore, I thought the Gormley statues looked almost lifelike."

> "Hovering motionless in the sky, we could only admire the mastery of the hawk."

It's possible we are in a hot air balloon or hanging from a stationary hang glider but it's more likely that the hawk is doing the hovering. Try: "We could only admire the mastery of the hawk, hovering motionless in the sky."
(Is the 'only' misplaced in the above sentence?)

> "After a thorough beating, the chef was ready to turn the six eggs in to a superb omelette."

Surely no way to treat a competent chef even if it is the only way to ensure a decent omelette!
There are one or two participles that add a dash of ambiguity to the dangling problem.

> "Considering the appalling sales figures, massive redundancies are the only way forward."

'Considering' might lead us to look for a noun that is doing the considering but the only available noun is 'redundancies' which are not capable of thought. Here 'considering' does not really signify thinking; it is used to mean 'given'. It might be better to write:
"The appalling sales figures mean that massive redundancies are the only way forward."
but, to be honest, this use of 'considering' in the sense of 'given' is now so common in business and other written documents that is unlikely to cause confusion or prompt criticism.

10.5.3 False Ellipsis
False ellipsis arises when we omit a word to avoid seemingly unnecessary repetition but what remains is not strictly grammatical.

> "I have not nor will I ever forgive you."

If we wrote this in full, it would read:
"I have not forgiven you nor will I ever forgive you."

The abridged version is ungrammatical because we cannot say:
"I have not forgive you."

In the following example, the missing 'with' leaves 'disillusion' to struggle on with the inappropriate 'for':
"He expressed his disillusion and contempt for your attitude."

In longer sentences the problem of false ellipsis is even greater. Wherever you insert the required 'with' in the following sentence, you will simply make a poorly constructed sentence even more awkward.

"He found himself at variance in almost every respect and in opposition to all the ideas and measures which the new managing director proposed."

10.5.4 Mispositioning

When using expressions which combine two parts of a sentence, it is not uncommon for the writer to misposition one of the linking words.

both...and: The use of 'both...and' is particularly problematical because the 'both' can often be taken, wrongly, to refer to a particular word in the 'both' phrase:
"He said he would support both his managers' goals and the methods they proposed to achieve them."

Does this mean that there are two managers, or that, irrespective of the number of managers, they have two goals, or that, whatever the number of goals, he will support them and the methods that the unknown number of managers has chosen to achieve them?

not only...but also: It is easy to misposition one part of the 'not only...but also' expression:
"He tried to set the record straight, not only explaining why he had not attended the last meeting but also why his results were poor."

It would be better to put the 'not only' after the 'explaining' to make it clear that the explaining covers both 'why he had not attended the last meeting' and 'why his results were poor'.

The expression 'not only...but also' also seems to invite needless repetition of some words:
"He said he would not only repair the product free of charge but would also pay me compensation for my trouble."

Since the first 'would' appears before the 'not only', the sentence construction does not require a second 'would' after the 'but'.

either...or:
'Either...or' are another pair of words that are easily mispositioned.

"She said either I could accept the terms she offered or ensure my letter of resignation was on her desk by the end of the day."

There are two problems here. Because the 'either' is placed before "I could", the 'I could' is cut off from 'ensure'. The 'or' clause is therefore incomplete. Even if we rewrote the sentence to solve that problem:

"She said I could either accept the terms she offered or ensure my letter of resignation was on her desk by the end of the day."

we would find that the 'or' clause (which would now read, if written in full, "I could ensure my resignation was on her desk") is still not right because she doesn't mean "I could ensure" etc.; she means "I should or must ensure" etc. We would have to recast the sentence as follows:

"She said either I could accept the terms she offered or I should/must ensure my letter of resignation was on her desk by the end of the day."

also, even, mainly, merely, only, really, truly
Care is needed when positioning these and some other words which can be used to qualify different parts of a sentence and thus substantially change its meaning. We need to be clear about the precise thought we wish to convey. The following sets of sentences illustrate the point:

also
Basic Sentence: "I was upset by the wording of the advertisement."

"I also was upset by the wording of the advertisement."
(i.e. I am another person who was upset...)

"I was also upset by the wording of the advertisement."
(i.e. the wording of the advertisement was something else that upset me)

"I was upset also by the wording of the advertisement."
(The wording of the advertisement was one aspect of the advertisement which upset me.)

ooo

even
Basic Sentence: "I am not reassured by the results you presented"

"Even I am not reassured by the results you presented."
(i.e. not even I am reassured, let alone anyone else...)

"I am not even reassured by the results you presented"

(i.e. I am not reassured, much less convinced...)

"I am not reassured even by the results you presented."
(i.e. even these results have failed to reassure me)

"I am not reassured by the results even you presented."
(i.e. although I hold you in high regard, even you have failed to reassure me or even your results, like the results presented by others, have failed to reassure me.)

ㅁㅁㅁ

only
Basic Sentence: "Radical measures will stabilise the present situation"

"Only radical measures will stabilise the present situation."
(i.e. nothing less than radical measures will stabilise the situation)

"Radical measures will only stabilise the situation."
(i.e. radical measures will do no more than stabilise the situation)

"Radical measures will stabilise only the present situation."
(i.e. radical measures will do for now, but not for the future)

ㅁㅁㅁ

truly
Basic Sentence: "He said I was mad."

"Truly, he said I was mad."
(i.e. it is true he said I was mad)

"He said truly I was mad."
(ambiguous because it could mean 'He spoke the truth when he said I was mad' or 'He said I was undoubtedly mad')

"He said I was truly mad."
(i.e. he said I was undoubtedly mad)

ㅁㅁㅁ

Mispositioning can also lead to confusion and, on occasions, comedy. Here are some examples:
   "Despite the hunchback, Esmeralda was fond of Quasimodo."

Surely Esmeralda was perfectly formed! Perhaps we should write:
   "Esmeralda was fond of Quasimodo, despite the hunchback."

Or, because of the gender difference, if we are lazy, we could simply replace 'the' with 'his' in the original sentence:

"Despite his hunchback, Esmeralda was fond of Quasimodo."

¤¤¤

"I rushed downstairs and caught the burglar in my pyjamas."

Here is a longer example:

"No sooner had John taken the leaflet from the book, yellow with age, and read out loud to Peter the printed message which declared 'This is the property of Ealing Library' than he decided that it must be returned forthwith."

All very confusing. We can assume it is the book, not the leaflet, that must be returned, but who is going to take the book back, Peter or John? Is it the book or, more likely but not certainly, the leaflet that is yellow with age? Or both? This is an ungainly sentence but we can at least make the meaning clear.

"No sooner had John taken the leaflet, yellow with age, from the book, and read out loud to Peter the printed message which declared 'This is the property of Ealing Library' than Peter decided the book must be returned forthwith."

¤¤¤

"He was relieved to read his lost umbrella had been found in the local newspaper."

□□□

"The old lady sat down at the piano with finely carved legs."

10.5.5 Problems with Negatives
Double Negative

While it is unlikely any reader would write "I ain't got no satisfaction" (which may, in any case, be Mick Jagger's way of letting us know he is at least partly satisfied), there are slightly less obvious forms of negative problems which may creep in.

In the next three examples, the writer has lost the logic of his sentence:

"I think it is impossible that, with all the investment in personnel and other resources which we have devoted to this project and with the total commitment of the board to what many saw as a high risk venture, we shall not fail."
(It is impossible 'we shall fail', not 'not fail'.

"These errors are not common and to be avoided."
(A second 'are' after the 'and' would remove any possible misinterpretation.)

"Are there any restrictions on what you're not allowed to do?
(Like Alexander the Great, cut through the 'not'.)

There is, of course, also the double negative which is meant (i.e. the two negatives that make a positive):
e.g.
- not uncommon = common
- not insignificant = significant
- not unacceptable = acceptable
- not unusual = usual

There is also the legitimate use of two negatives, the second to reinforce the first:
e.g.
"He said he would not resign, not even if profits fell again this year."

We should concede that there is a long tradition in some literature and local dialects of using double negatives to 'intensify' the negative sense but here we are concerned with standard written English. In written English (as in logic and mathematics) two negatives make a positive.

Other 'Negative' Problems

There are some truly problematical issues with negatives.

"I wouldn't be surprised if the plan didn't succeed."

This must mean "I wouldn't be surprised if the plan failed" but, perhaps because of confusion caused by the two negatives ('wouldn't' and didn't'), it can be taken to mean "I wouldn't be surprised if the plan succeeded".

"Don't smoke more than you can help."

This presumably means "Do not smoke more than you **cannot** help."

If English is your first language, just be thankful you learnt these idioms when you were too young to worry about them.

10.5.6 Problems with Pronouns

Problems can arise with the case of some pronouns following verbs and prepositions. The following pronouns have a subject and an object case:

SUBJECT	OBJECT
I	me
he	him
she	her
we	us
they	them

It is usually very easy to determine whether to use the subject or the object case.

In such sentences as "It was to John and I that he offered the bribe", we have only to remove 'John and' in order to see that the 'I' should be 'me'. We would never say "It was to I that he offered the bribe".

Common errors in the use of 'I' are found in the expressions 'between you and I' which should be 'between you and me' and 'from my wife and I' which should be 'from my wife and me'.

Another example of this common error is given below:
"His savage rebuke was intended for you and I."
which should be:
"His savage rebuke was intended for you and me."
because we would never write:
"His savage rebuke was intended for I."

It is worth getting the use of 'I' and 'me' right in any formal writing because the incorrect use of 'I' instead of 'me' strongly suggests that, in a desperate attempt to avoid using 'me' when the correct pronoun would be 'I', someone is trying, but sadly failing, to prove they are 'posh'. "Between you and I" is now common on the BBC, even, heaven forbid, on Radio 4.

10.5.7 Mixed up Figures of Speech

Mixed up figures of speech, by definition, involve some degree of incongruity:

e.g.
"He bandied accusations around like confetti at a wedding."
"He struck exactly the right note when he hit the nail on the head."
"In his efforts to reform the company, he leant over backwards to take a step forward."
"Legalising soft drugs is clearly the thin end of the slippery slope."
"To his surprise the tide of public opinion turned against him, entirely upsetting his applecart."

Mixed metaphors often have a comic effect and, if used intentionally, can enliven a speech or presentation. When used, they depend for their humorous effect on the ability of the audience to recognise them.

"MEPs spend most of their time on the EU gravy train with their mouth in the trough when they haven't got their noses in the European taxpayer's pocket."
"I offered him an olive branch. 'No way,' he said 'will I accept the hand that bites me!'"

There are of course examples where mixed-up figures of speech are not intended to be amusing and do not have a comic effect. Shakespeare tells us that Hamlet wondered whether:

"to take arms against a sea of troubles."

The balance of Hamlet's mind was disturbed, so that may account for the mixed metaphor. Or it might be a device to point out the futility of any attempt by Hamlet to deal with his problems. Or, perhaps more likely, it is an example of how the greatest of writers can break any rule in the book with impunity.

10.5.8 Number errors

Here 'number' refers to whether the verb should be in the singular or plural form.

In general, collective nouns take singular verbs.

1. **Collective Nouns**

   As a starting point, we can say that collective nouns (e.g. committee, family, flock, team) should take a singular verb:

   e.g.
   "The committee has decided..."
   "The family is in agreement..."
   "The flock is safe..."
   "The team has won..."

While you are always safe with the singular form of the verb, there is a good case for using the plural form where the emphasis is on the individual members of the group rather than on the group as a single entity:

e.g.
"The committee have failed to reach agreement."

"The family are now dispersed all over Europe."

Whichever form of the verb you use, you should try to be consistent in any particular document. Avoid the following:

"The committee which **has debated** for four hours **are** in total agreement."

"The herd of cows, which **were** under threat, **is** now safe."

2. **Singular and Plural Forms of Greek/Latin Words**

Watch out for words like 'criteria' and 'data'! Criteria is the plural of criterion and therefore takes a plural verb. "*My criterion **has** been rejected but your criteria **are** acceptable.*"

The situation with 'data' is less clear. 'Data' is the plural of 'datum' but is now widely used as a collective noun. As a collective noun, it takes a singular verb: "The/this data is controversial", although it is also correct to say: "The/these data are controversial".

10.5.9 Prepositions
10.5.9.1 *Which to use*

Many writers, especially those whose first language is not English, have problems with prepositions. Here are just a few examples of prepositional problems:

according	'according to', 'in accordance with'
acquaint	'acquaint' someone 'with' something
acquiesce	'acquiesce in', not 'acquiesce to'
aim	'aim at' a target; 'aim to do' something
allude	'allude to' something, not 'allude at'
analogous	'analogous to', rather than 'analogous with'
angry	'angry with', rather than 'angry at'
averse	'averse to '(although 'from' might seem more logical)
annoyed	'annoyed with', rather than 'at'
behalf	"on X's behalf", not "for X's behalf"
bored	'bored with' or 'bored by', not 'bored of'
borrow	'borrow from', not 'borrow off'
compared	'compared to' when comparing unlike things 'compared with' when comparing similar things
comprises	'comprises', not 'comprises of'
conducive	'conducive to', not 'conducive of'
different	'different from', not 'to' or 'than'
distribute	'distribute among', not 'between'

distribute	'distribute among', not 'between'
equal	'equal to' not 'equal as' or 'equal with'
indifferent	'indifferent to'
inferior	'inferior to', not 'inferior than,
in respect of	'in respect of', not 'in respect to'
mean	'mean', not 'mean for' ("I didn't mean this to happen.")
oblivious	oblivious to (or, more rarely, oblivious 'of')
part	"for X's part", rather than "on X's part"
prefer	'prefer a to b', not 'prefer a than b'
protest	'protest against', rather than 'protest at'
proud	'proud of', not 'proud about'
similar	'similar to', not 'similar as'
superior	'superior to', not 'superior than'
tolerant	'tolerant of', not 'tolerant to'

10.5.9.2 *Ending sentences with prepositions*

Winston Churchill famously derided a pedantic aversion to ending a sentence with a preposition by commenting;

"This is the sort of English up with which I will not put."

(In some versions, 'English' is replaced by 'bloody nonsense' which, given Churchill's character, sounds more authentic.)

Nevertheless, when possible, the practice is to be avoided:

"The industry conference is one I really have to go to."

is easily recast:

"The industry conference is one I really must attend."

In some cases, it is awkward, difficult, if not impossible, to avoid such a sentence construction:

"This is one trade secret which I would rather not give up."

If an attempt to avoid the prepositional ending results in:

"This is one trade secret up which I would rather not give."

then, as Winston suggested, it is surely best left alone (or perhaps reformulated to:

"This is one trade secret which I would rather not relinquish."

10.5.9.3 Prepositional Overstretching

"My experience of setting priorities and adhering to deadlines will be suited and best developed in a challenging environment."

Assuming we wished to persevere with this sentence, we would at least have to insert a 'to' after 'suited', since the 'in' which goes with 'developed' cannot also serve 'suited'.

10.5.10 Split Infinitives
Split Infinitive

As a general rule, it is best not to split an infinitive.

It is better to say:

"He decided to respond promptly"

than to say:

"He decided to promptly respond."

(If we were to say "He decided promptly to respond", we would have either changed the meaning by attaching 'promptly' to the 'deciding' rather than to the 'responding' or created an ambiguity by leaving the reader unsure as to which verb the 'promptness' should be applied.)

There are some occasions when, if the writer has any sensitivity to the natural flow and rhythm of the language, he will tend to split the infinitive:

e.g.

"Although he knew there was evidence against him, he found it difficult to publicly admit his guilt.", rather than "publicly to admit his guilt" or "to admit publicly his guilt".

On the other hand, it would be perfectly satisfactory to say: "to admit his guilt publicly" which would retain both the natural rhythm of the sentence and the undivided infinitive.

10.5.11 Tautology

Tautology is the unnecessary repetition of a word or an idea. Some are obvious; some less so; some excusable, even justifiable, some less so or not.

"**All** the salesmen performed well **without exception**."

'All' means 'without exception'.

"**Both of the twins** talked **continuously without a break**."

'Both of the twins' is just about excusable, but 'continuously without a break' is not.

"He **rushed quickly** to her aid."

'He rushed to her aid' or 'He came quickly to her aid'.

"He said that in all **probability** it was **likely** to happen."

'He said that in all probability it would happen' or 'He said that it was likely to happen'.

"If we **co-operate together**, we shall surely prevail."
'If we co-operate, we shall surely prevail' or 'If we work together, we shall surely prevail'.

"**I myself** have done this often enough."
When am I not myself, other than in the expression 'I am not myself'?

"**I personally** find it difficult to disagree."
When do I express anything other than personally?

"I trust this type of irresponsible behaviour will not **recur again**."
Either 'recur' without 'again', or substitute 'happen' for 'recur'.

"It is ten years **ago since** she started her career."
'It is ten years ago that...' or 'It is ten years since...'

"It's **just exactly** what's required."
Either 'just' or 'exactly' but not both.

"**Looking back in retrospect**, I think I may have repeated myself."
'Looking back' or 'in retrospect'.

"**Previously** we have never charged so high a price for this type of service **before**."
Either 'previously' or 'before' but not both.

"She **wept** uncontrollably at the verdict with **tears in her eyes**."
Is there any other way of weeping?

"**Speculation** about the **possibility** he might resign was rife."
'Speculation that he might resign was rife' is adequate.

"The **reason** for my indignation is simply **because** he clearly set out to insult me."
Either 'The reason for my indignation is that he clearly set out...' or 'I am indignant because...'.

"This service is **absolutely free** and **completely without charge**."
At least doubly tautologous!

"The word 'amok' **invariably** appears **only** in the expression 'run amok'."
This one merits a bit of exegesis. The combination of invariably and only appears tautologous but can be defended in that invariably tells you where it always appears and only tells you not only where it does appear but also where it doesn't. On the other hand, the statement that amok invariably appears in the expression 'run amok', while self-evidently true, is a bit pointless. After all the word 'bit' invariably appears in the expression 'bit pointless'. Enough!

"We will **continue** to abide by last year's agreement this year **too**."
The 'too' is redundant.

Tautological expressions are not only inelegant; they are wasteful of space, reduce clarity and indicate a sloppy or undisciplined mind. So there!

11 Advanced Techniques

There are many ways in which authors, once they have mastered their material, can employ techniques to influence, persuade or appeal to their audience.

Some of these techniques involve the careful selection of words in order to use their connotations to move the reader's mind in a certain direction.

Others involve changes in sentence structure or sentence sequencing to effect delicate shifts in emphasis which will help to bring or keep the reader 'on message'.

Yet others are designed to enrich the content of the document in order to hold the reader's interest.

We will explore a few of these advanced techniques in this section.

11.1.1 Emphasis
Fine-tuning a sentence, a paragraph or a document, in order to ensure that you have placed the emphasis correctly, is as much an art as a science.

SENTENCES
Although word order is critical in English, there is still room for manoeuvre in constructing sentences. We can exploit this room for manoeuvre in order to shift the emphasis in a sentence and to bring variety to our composition. The following examples illustrate just how flexible English can be, despite the absence of inflexions (word endings to identify the function of words).

e.g.
"Variety and the shifting of emphasis are two of the benefits that changes in word order can bring to our compositions."

"Variety is one of the benefits that changes in word order can bring to our compositions. The shifting of emphasis is another."

"Two of the benefits to be derived from changes of word order are the shifting of emphasis and variety."

"Two benefits we can bring to our composition by changes of word order are shifts of emphasis and variety."

"We can bring two benefits to our composition by changes of word order; variety and shifts of emphasis."

"Changes in word order bring two benefits: shifts of emphasis and variety."

We can use this flexibility to change, shift or increase emphasis:

"If we continue on our present course, undeterred by the seemingly adverse effects on sales, we shall eventually reap very great rewards."

This sentence comprises three strong elements. A condition, an elaboration of the condition, and a consequence. As it stands it is a powerful, evenly balanced sentence, with each of the three elements being given equal weight.

If we wished to place more emphasis on the positive outcome, we might write:

"We shall eventually reap very great rewards if, undeterred by the seemingly adverse effect on sales, we continue on our present course."

If we wished to place more emphasis on what we must do to reap the very great rewards (i.e. remain undeterred), we might write:

"We shall eventually reap very great rewards if we continue on our present course, undeterred by the seemingly adverse effect on sales."

or

"If, undeterred by the seemingly adverse effect on sales, we continue on our present course, we shall eventually reap very great rewards."

(Note that in this example, although we have relegated "undeterred etc." to the subordinate clause, because it breaks into the "if" clause so early, it draws attention to itself. What a language!)

If we wished to emphasise how long it may take to reap the rewards, we could move 'eventually' into a more prominent position:

"If we continue on our present course, undeterred by the seemingly adverse effects on sales, eventually we shall reap very great rewards."

or

"Eventually we shall reap very great rewards if, undeterred by the seemingly adverse effects on sales, we continue on our present course."

And so it goes on. We have scarcely begun to tamper with the syntax of the sentence but already we have changed or increased the emphasis in several ways. An experienced practitioner will always be sensitive to the opportunities word order presents, and routinely exploit them.

PARAGRAPHS

In the section on composition, we looked in some detail at how best to determine the paragraph structure (we argued for balance and approximately equivalent 'weight') and how to ensure that paragraphs are clearly linked together (we listed nine types of linkage).

That said, those who are in complete control of their material can often, to great effect, break the rules in order to achieve the right emphasis. For example, a one word paragraph can have very great impact and entirely justify its isolation.

> "We have followed every recommendation proposed by the consultants. We have restructured the company, a process which caused considerable hardship to some of our employees, traumatised at least one of our managers and dislocated the normal running of the business for many months. We discontinued some of our oldest product lines and introduced an entirely new product range in months when everyone thought it would take years. We retained a marketing organisation to 'rebrand' us and a public relations agency to enhance our image. All this we have done; and all this has brought us to where we are today."
>
> "Bankrupt!"

NOTE FOR DOCUPRAXIS® USERS ON OVERALL STRUCTURE: The techniques used for determining how best to achieve the correct emphasis are valid at all levels of composition (sentence, paragraph, chapter, section). The DocuPraxis® program has been designed to help you find the right balance. By presenting a clear structure of your document at all times and allowing you to adjust and manipulate each part of the structure at any time, it could not be easier to experiment and test each version until the right emphasis is achieved. And while you experiment and test, DocuPraxis® will hold your composition together, adjusting heading levels automatically, so that when you order a draft, it will appear as a finished document for you to assess and, if need be, amend.

11.1.2 Digressions

Throughout this guide, we have emphasised the two essential qualities of simplicity and clarity. What follows may contradict these principles but, when used by writers who are in complete command of their material and their medium, digressions can enrich the narrative, entrance the reader and subtly persuade the audience to the author's view.

Perhaps the greatest and certainly the best known exponent of the digression was Jesus. The parable is a clever device for presenting an argument, a proposition, a moral judgement, in the form of a story. The use of narrative catches the reader's attention and the plot of the story effortlessly carries the argument.

When someone says:

> "If I work hard, am always conscientious, and prove myself totally trustworthy, and he is lazy, careless and unreliable, surely I should enjoy all the rewards and he should be excluded?"

the reply could either be a long, carefully argued, rather obscure moral tract covering questions of merit, altruism, justice, reward and punishment - or it could be the parable of the prodigal son. Given that you wish to reach, challenge and persuade a large audience, it is not a hard choice.

Anyone who listened to the late Alistair Cook's "Letter from America" on BBC Radio 4 over the decades will have experienced the art of digression performed by a master.

We should perhaps emphasise that this type of digression is entirely distinct from rambling. This digression is intimately linked to the core of the subject being treated. Indeed, in the right hands, it becomes the core of the subject.

11.1.3 Bending the rules

There are a number of techniques which experienced practitioners can use to achieve their ends.

These techniques can fall anywhere between the slightly devious and the outright dishonest. Nevertheless, they can be highly effective in enabling the writer to manipulate the reader.

11.1.3.1 Analogy/False Analogy

Of all the techniques employed to present a case and to persuade others of its validity, there is none more common or more open to abuse than the analogy.

> "We workers are treated like mushrooms - kept in the dark, fed manure and expected to produce results overnight."

While this may be a pithy statement of a point of view, it is not an argument. The sustained analogy ("We are not told what is going on; what we are told is of doubtful value; and yet we are expected to perform miracles") may make it sound like an argument but it is not.

Some analogies are presented as arguments. Many of these are false, simply because the subject itself and the thing to which it is supposedly analogous are essentially different.

> "Our company is one great family, happily working to achieve our goals."

While this is perfectly acceptable as a piece of maudlin nonsense in an after-dinner speech winding up a sales conference, the analogy does not bear scrutiny. A company is not like a family (not even family businesses are like families). In a family (or good ones at least), we come closest to the communist ideal of selfless co-operation based on the principle of "From each according to his abilities; to each according to his needs". In a business, there are sure to be rivalries within and between departments; and all employees are likely to seek reward commensurate with their work, their effort and their value - not on the basis of need. At the same time, a company will have corporate goals which it will expect its employees to recognise and devote their energies to achieving; whereas in a family, each member has his/her own goals and the family, if it is a good one, will endeavour to help each member to succeed. In other words, in certain essentials, the analogy between a business and a family fails.

The falsity of an analogy does not mean it cannot be an effective weapon in the persuader's armoury. Many people have some difficulty in exercising their critical faculties and, in the right context, especially when emotions are running high, a skilful operator can get away with murder. (Is this last sentence an example of a metaphor, an analogy, a false analogy, or all three?)

11.1.3.2 Cause/Effect reversal

Cause/Effect reversal involves twisting the truth so that the effect becomes the cause and the cause becomes the effect.

"The product failed because the sales campaign was totally ineffective."
is easily reframed to suggest:
"The sales campaign failed because the product was totally ineffective."

Many propositions can easily be reversed or reformatted to say or imply the opposite.

For example, if it is statistically proved that more single men commit suicide than married men, we can conclude that:
"Being single inclines men to suicide."
or that:
"Men inclined to suicide remain single."
In the former case "being single" causes men to commit suicide; in the second case, a predisposition to suicide leads men to remain single.

It is possible to 'turn' many propositions in this way.

In war situations, the most intense battle is often conducted in the media where rebels fight for recognition as freedom-fighters, while the authorities insist they are terrorists. Over and over again, those who can control the media are able to represent every action either as provocative or as a legitimate response to an earlier provocation. In any cycle of violence, we have only to shift the cause/effect analysis one stop forward or back to reverse the entire sequence of cause and effect:

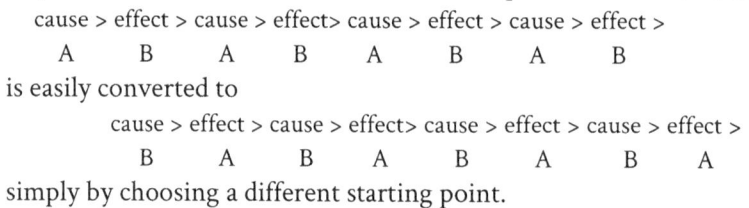

simply by choosing a different starting point.

In producing reports on past performance, the technique of ordering data in order to suggest a causal relationship can be extremely useful. For example, a managing director may choose to give an account of general economic difficulties (e.g. a recession, a squeeze on profits, higher taxes, increasing unemployment) before announcing a large number of redundancies. This will imply a causal relationship between the economic difficulties and the redundancies. Such a relationship may or may not exist. It may be simply that the company has been over-staffed for years, and the managing director wishes to trim the 'excess fat'. Whatever the truth and whatever the author's objective, the skilled report writer will be well aware of the importance of selecting and ordering his material to guide his reader along the path of his chosen narrative.

11.1.3.3 Correlation & Causation

While on the subject of cause/effect, we should say a bit more about correlation and causation. In philosophy, causation is worthy of a book in its own right; and there is an entire branch of statistics concerned with determining the existence and significance of correlations. Here I just want to look at the basics as they relate to report writing.

When two phenomena appear together, we have a tendency to consider whether there is a causal relationship between them. In some cases, there is strong evidence that one is the cause of the other: i.e. A causes B. For us to draw this conclusion the two phenomena have to appear together invariably and B needs to follow A.

If the two phenomena invariably appear together but we cannot be sure of the time sequence, we must also consider the possibility that B causes A.

There is a third possibility; that the causal relationship is reciprocal; i.e. that A and B cause each other. The relationship between heat and pressure is a good example. Increased pressure will cause a gas to heat up; heating up a gas causes increased pressure.

Yet another possibility is that A and B are not causally linked but both are caused by a third factor C. There is lightning; then there is thunder; but lightning does not cause the thunder. They are both the result of an electrical discharge in the atmosphere.

And finally, there is the possibility that, although the two phenomena appear together with great frequency, it is all just a coincidence.

When writing a report, we will often need to explain outcomes by identifying and defining causes but when we do this, we need to be conscious of the possibility of false inferences. When asserting a causal relationship, if we are trying to be objective, we should routinely consider all five of the possibilities outlined above. If we don't, the critical reader will.

11.1.3.4 Emotivation

We are using the term 'emotivation' to denote the exploitation of the known emotional predisposition of the reader to bring them on board.

The best examples of 'emotivation' are to be found in the speeches of politicians. In recent times in particular, the rational underpinning of political discourse has been largely replaced by fairly crude, but nonetheless effective, rhetorical techniques.

Amongst such devices are repetition of words and phrases, either on a single occasion or on innumerable occasions:

"[We] will fight, and fight, and fight again." (Hugh Gaitskill)

"Education. Education. And Education." (Tony Blair)

"Tory sleaze"

"Tony's cronies"

The intention here is not to persuade by reasoned argument but to trigger an emotional response in the listener or reader by pushing a sensitive button.

Another technique is the employment of catch phrases: The last two examples of repetition also fall into this category. Other examples are:

"[You've] never had it so good."
"the People's Princess"

The former includes a nudge in the ribs and a suggestion of "Come on, admit it". This has the effect of establishing an intimacy between the speaker and the listener which is more common and certainly more genuine amongst family members at home or amongst friends in a pub than between politician and voter.

The second example is more complex in that in contains an element of paradox. While a princess can be so popular that the people take her to their hearts, a 'princess' is, by definition, not one of the people. This apparent reconciliation of opposites in a more inclusive embrace has become particularly common in the last few years. Banks routinely portray themselves as friendly and on the customer's side, despite the fact that it is abundantly clear that their primary purpose is to relieve their clients of as much of their money as possible without breaking the law or indeed, on occasions, while breaking the law.

Then there is the whole question of terminology. Students of media coverage will be familiar with the way in which the choice of words can affect the response of the audience. Cases of influenza can be described as 'incidence', an 'outbreak' or an 'epidemic'. Government action on an issue can be described as 'proactive', 'a measured response', 'a reaction' or 'panic'. As we have noted elsewhere, in a continuing war situation, almost any military incident can be presented as aggression or retaliation. The same person, performing the same act, can be described as a freedom-fighter, a patriot, a nationalist or a terrorist.

Even without such obviously emotive labels, the audience can be pointed in the right direction by words such as 'perpetrate' which have negative connotations. (You 'perform' an act of heroism; you 'perpetrate' a heinous crime) or by words such as 'progress' and 'reform', both of which have positive connotations but are often used as synonyms for 'change'. And a government of which you disapprove can quickly become a 'regime'.

Such techniques are of most use in situations in which emotions run high - but they can have a place in business discourse. In particular, the pithy phrase can often help to focus attention and carry others along with its author in a way that a detailed rational argument cannot. A phrase such as "entrepreneurial zeal" may sum up the ethos of a new company so well that all employees begin to think like zealous entrepreneurs, or at least see themselves as such.

Those who master words have at their disposal an extraordinarily powerful weapon.

11.1.3.5 Verbal Latitude
A skill in which many politicians (and others who make their living by persuasion) excel is what we have called verbal latitude. A statement is made; its meaning seems clear:

"We have no plans to increase taxes"
"There will be no need for further redundancies in the foreseeable future."

But when we give the proposition further thought, what seemed to be a firm commitment slips away. If the politician and the businessman were totally honest, they would expand a little as follows on the two propositions above:

> "We have no plans to increase taxes today but we might of course formulate such a plan tomorrow, or indeed increase taxes anyway in a spontaneous, unplanned sort of fashion."
>
> "We are currently unable to foresee the need for further redundancies but foreseeing is notoriously difficult. By tomorrow, we may have a clearer view of the future, or indeed, still unseeing, be overtaken by changed circumstances."

The employment of this type of sense-bending calls for the combined skills of a lawyer and an orator. This may help to explain why so many of today's politicians studied law and were active in the student union debating societies at university.

12 Preparing Business Documents

12.1 General guidelines for reports
In preparing the contents for a report, the author should apply the guidelines set out in this document.

PLANNING: The key to success is grasping and organising the total content of the report **before** you start to write the report. (There is always a temptation to get started as quickly as possible. Resist the temptation.)

STRUCTURING: First, prepare the Structure, using the techniques of grouping, ordering and linking.

For users of the DocuPraxis program: Use the Build function to develop your structure. The Build function allows you to manipulate and control all the parts that make up the whole. You can change the order of the components; you can promote or demote them; and you can move them from one part of the outline to another. While you perform these tasks, the results will be clearly displayed in the outline. At any time you can view the Structure as a whole or, by suppressing lower levels in the hierarchy, you can check that the main components are holding together, that the links between sections make sense, and that, when you start writing, you will be able to move seamlessly from the start to the end of the Structure.

BE A GOD: Another advantage to this approach is that, from the very start of the document, you will be thoroughly familiar with the total content of the document and all the parts that make it up. Obviously, your document will follow a sequence and is therefore a temporal entity - but, with DocuPraxis®, you will be able to achieve a god-like state, outside time, knowing the beginning and the end, and everything in between, throughout the entire process of creating your document.

CONSISTENCY: Elsewhere we have mentioned consistency as a powerful aid to good writing. If you are writing in the past tense, do not suddenly change into the present. If you are using capital letters for names of organisations, use them whenever the organisation is mentioned. If you are using double quotation marks for direct speech, do not suddenly change to single quotation marks. If you are giving dates, use the same format throughout.

If you are writing a manual of any kind, define your terms, and then use the terms consistently throughout. It may be clear to the writer, for example, that 'structure', 'outline' and 'framework' mean the same thing and refer to the same feature - but, in a manual, the use of different terms may well confuse the reader.

LOGIC: In most cases, logic provides another powerful aid to good writing. Double negatives are illogical. (Each negative cancels out the other, creating a positive rather than the intended emphatic negative.) A singular verb with a plural subject is illogical. Intensified absolutes (e.g. very unique) are illogical. Logic is not an infallible guide because, as we have seen, language is not always logical but, in general, especially in matters of grammar, it will help in identifying and removing errors.

12.2 Components of a report

A good business report should present its contents at a number of different levels.
- There should be a **summary** of the main results, conclusions and recommendations. (In many instances today, it is advisable to produce a summary of the summary - a bullet point list of conclusions and recommendations.)
- There should be an **introduction** which provides background to the report and explains why the report has been prepared (its purpose and specific objectives)
- There should be a **main report** which will include a full account of the results, conclusions and recommendations, together with the information from which the results, conclusions and recommendations have been derived. (The **DocuPraxis®** program will help you to ensure that each section of the report is correctly structured and that all parts are properly linked together.)
- There may be a need for a **statistical appendix** in which the reader will find the detailed data from which the main report has been distilled.
- There may be a need for a **technical appendix** in which the reader will find full explanations of the methods and techniques employed.
- There may be a need for **other appendices** which give, for example, details of the history of the company, its range of products and services, its key personnel.
- There may be a need for a **glossary** to explain any technical terms with which the reader may be unfamiliar.
- An **index** of key words may also prove a useful to the reader.

The headings/titles of all these sections of the report, and the sub-sections within them, should be laid out in a **Table of Content**s. For each entry in the Table of Contents, the relevant **page number** of the report should be shown. (You can use **DocuPraxis®** to generate a table of contents automatically.)

The Title Page of the document should state, at least, the following:

- the subject of the report
- for whom it has been prepared
- the name of the author/s
- the date it was prepared

If the report is confidential, this should be clearly stated on the title page.

12.3 Proposals
THE BENEFITS

Ensure the Executive Summary clearly states the advantages to the client of the proposal. While this may sound obvious, the client benefits can often be forgotten or under-emphasised in the proposer's enthusiasm for the project itself.

FOCUS AND BREVITY

Remember that most people with the authority to approve projects are over-loaded with information. What they want is the essence of your proposal in a form which is easy for them to grasp. It is sometimes said that the most senior people have a very limited attention span. This if often true but not because such people are necessarily intellectually challenged. It is because they have to ration their attention in order to deal with a vast quantity of issues. If you are preparing a document for such people, take into account what they want from you.

TENSES: In proposal documents, say "We shall..." or "We will..." rather than "We should..." or "We would...".

The plain future tense implies confidence on your part and security for your prospective client. "We would" sounds tentative on your part and 'not guaranteed' from the client's view point. Don't be concerned that you may sound as though you are assuming your proposal has already been agreed; it is implicit in a proposal that, until the proposal is accepted, there is no commitment.

USPs (Unique Selling Points/Propositions)

If your proposal is in competition with others from rival companies, bear in mind that the prospective client will be looking for ways to compare your offering with that of your competitors. You should help the prospective client in this task by presenting your strengths in such a way that they will either expose your rivals' weaknesses or focus attention on your strengths at your competitors' expense.

For example, if you have the longest track record, emphasise the crucial importance of experience and the benefits that accrue from fine-tuning your service over time. If your rivals have a longer track record than you, emphasise the need for innovation and at least imply that older rivals tend to be complacent and less responsive to new ideas. If you are a large company and your rivals are smaller, emphasise the security and reliability that a large, well-resourced company can provide. If you are a smaller company, place emphasis on the advantages of flexibility and lower overheads which only smaller, hungrier companies can offer.

KEY QUESTIONS
- Have I said what I wanted to say AND have I said what my audience wanted to hear?
- Have I said it succinctly enough for it to be grasped?
- Have I shown I am confident but not arrogant?
- Have I presented my case in as positive a light as possible, casting every one of my qualities as an advantage?

12.4 Checking and revising

It is essential that you check and revise any document you prepare. Here we are not just talking about normal proof-reading for typing errors and spelling mistakes. We also mean reviewing the finished draft document and asking all the questions set out in this guide. Even the best writers will rarely go through a draft without making innumerable improvements.

Remember that you are not writing for yourself. Take account of the nature of your target audience. Consider their familiarity with the subject of your document; their educational level; their intellectual capacity. These factors will influence the language you use, how you compose your sentences and the structure of your document.

12.5 Common Business Terms

Here we list and define some of the more common terms used in business.

above the line	advertising and promotion via the mass media (see below the line).
accounts	a general term for the financial documents which every company must produce and file each year to summarise its financial performance. Typically, it will include a Profit and Loss statement, a Balance Sheet, a Directors' Report and an Auditors endorsement
accounts payable	invoices from suppliers which the business must pay
accounts receivable	money invoiced for and owed to the business
accrual accounting	the method of accounting based on when an invoice is issued and when a bill is received, not when the actual invoice or bill is settled (i.e. paid). The accounting system which is based on the physical exchange of money is Cash Accounting.
advertorial	an advertisement written and presented in the form of editorial.

AER (annual equivalent rate)	AER is the interest rate you would receive on savings or an investment if the interest is calculated on both the capital and the interest earned in the course of the year (i.e. compound interest).
ageism	discrimination against an individual on the grounds of age.
Articles of Association	the legal document setting out the scope of the activities of a company, the rules governing its operation and the responsibilities of it directors and shareholders
assets	everything of value that the business owns (e.g. property, cash, monies owed)
audit	a review of the company's account by a professional accountant to ensure that, each year, the balance sheet accurately reflects the company's true financial status
authorised share capital	the maximum amount of share capital, as stated in the Memorandum of Association, that the company is permitted to issue
avatar	a persona chosen by an individual to represent him/her in a video game, website chatroom, etc.
balance sheet	a snapshot of the financial state of a company (assets and liabilities) at a single point in time
below the line	advertising and promotion effected through direct contact at a more individual level; e.g. brochures, direct mail, exhibitions, incentives, telephone selling (see above the line)
benchmark	a benchmark is an external or objective standard against which some aspect of the business can reasonably be assessed.
black economy	business transacted, usually in cash, which falls outside the government system for tracing and taxing transactions. Sometimes called the shadow economy
brand	the unique identity of a company, product or service. The identity is made up of all aspects of the company, product or service (e.g. name, logo, product/service range and quality) - but the brand is greater than the sum of its parts
breakeven	breakeven is the point in the life cycle of a product, service or company when, after a period of investment, income balances expenditure

budget	a formal estimate of the predicted costs and returns for any business or future project
business plan	a formal document which sets out the objectives of a business or a project and explains how the objectives are to be fulfilled in qualitative and quantitative term
capital assets	capital or fixed assets are property, plant and equipment owned by the business
capital expenditure	money spent on capital assets
capital	money invested in a venture by its owners
cartel	a group of independent companies which agree to use their dominant position in a market sector to manipulate the market in order to control prices
cash accounting	the method of accounting based on the physical exchange of money (i.e. cash in and cash out). This is the simplest method of accounting.
cash flow	cash flow is the changing balance of cash within the company, as money flows in and out
cash sales	sales paid for at the time, as distinct from sales on credit
CTR (click through rate)	the number of times a web viewer clicked on an web advertisement as a percentage of the number of times the advertisement was seen
cloud computing	using hardware facilities and software services provided by service providers at remote locations via the internet, thereby reducing or eliminating reliance on in-house resources
commission	money paid to an agent who facilitates a business operation; e.g. someone who helps to negotiate a contract will be paid a commission of x% of the contract's value; or a salesman will be paid x% commission on sales achieved
competitor analysis	an objective assessment of the strengths and weaknesses of your competitors, compared with your own strengths and weaknesses
corporation tax	the tax levied by government on the profits of companies
cost of sales	can either be the direct costs of materials and manufacture or it can include all the other overhead costs such as personnel, general administration and commissions

creditor	an individual or organisation to which a company owes money
current ratio	current assets divided by current liabilities
debenture	a debt instrument, usually backed only by the debtor's reputation for credit-worthiness, whereby a company raises money by guaranteeing to pay a certain fixed rate of return, irrespective of whether or not it makes a profit
debtor	an individual or organisation which owes a company money
demographics	the characteristics of different segments of a population, in terms of age, sex, social class, lifestyle, income, ethnicity, religion, social status, etc.
depreciation	the decline in the value of assets over time
diversification	extending the range of a company's products or services or extending the range of customer categories at which the products and services are aimed.
dividends	those profits of the company distributed to the owners of the company's shares
early adopters	the second of the five categories in Rogers 'Diffusion of Innovations'. Early adopters follow innovators in accepting new technology products.
earnings	earnings is used to mean different things. It can mean the 'bottom line' figure; i.e. sales less all costs, otherwise known as profit. It is also sometimes used to mean income: i.e. money coming into the company or sales.
e-commerce	business conducted via the internet (electronic business)
economies of scale	the general principle that the more you produce, the cheaper each unit becomes, either through better use of staff and equipment or because fixed costs are spread more thinly
elasticity of demand	the extent to which price changes affect demand for a product or service
electronic billing/ invoicing	transmitting bills or invoices in electronic format by electronic means
equity	shares in the assets of the business
equity financing	sale of shares to raise capital
expenses	business costs deductible against tax

feasibility study	initial assessment of a proposed project to determine whether, on the basis of available information, it seems to be viable
fixed costs	costs incurred by the business that are not proportionate to company turnover; e.g. general overheads, rent of premises, most head office functions
force majeure	a clause in a contract which relieves a party to the contract of fulfilling an obligation in the event of an act of God, or some other catastrophe, which makes insistence on fulfilment of the obligation unreasonable
gearing	the ratio of borrowings (in this case long-term debt) to equity capital
goodwill	goodwill is the difference in value between the quantifiable assets of the company and what a purchaser of the business will pay. Good will is an intangible asset.
gross margin	gross margin is the value of sales minus the costs of sales
impression	widely used as the term for each event when a member of the target audience sees an advertisement for a company's product
innovators	The first of the five categories in Rogers's 'Diffusion of Innovations'. Innovators are the first group of customers to purchase new technology products
issued capital	the amount of share capital issued to shareholders
Keynesian economics	the view that government can most effectively influence the national economy by judicious use of taxation and public expenditure and that, by using these tools to determine demand, can bring about full employment.
leveraged buyout	The acquisition of a company which is partly or wholly financed by borrowings which are secured, partly or wholly, on the basis of the company's own cashflow or assets.
liabilities	debt that must be repaid
liability insurance	protection against the risk of claims against the company for the actions of the company
licence	a legal agreement whereby, for an agreed sum of money, one company is permitted to make use of, produce or sell something owned by another company

life cycle	the four stages through which a product or brand commonly passes: launch, growth, maturity and decline
liquid assets	assets of the company that are in the form of cash or which can easily be converted into cash
liquidation	the process of realising the net value of a company's assets usually triggered by the need to pay debtors
macro-economics	the study of economies on the large scale, analysing national and international economic statistics and processes
mail order	a type of retailing involving the selection of products from a printed catalogue or a website, the placing of orders via the internet, telephone or order form and delivery to the home by postal or courier services
Mainframe	a large, powerful computer
marginal costs	the additional cost of producing one more unit; i.e. excluding fixed costs
marketing	in essence, marketing is the exploitation of a company's resources to meet the needs of an identified market in such a way as to satisfy the market and produce a return for the shareholders
market research	the gathering of information about the market though desk research or survey research in order to provide a basis of evidence for business decisions
mission statement	a brief account of an organisation's core values and objectives
mixed economy	an economy in which economic activity is funded by both private capital and public investment, thus combining both capitalist and socialist economic models
netiquette	etiquette on the World Wide Web
net profit	income (i.e. money coming in to the company/sales) less all direct and indirect costs
operating expenses	all the costs of running a business, except for depreciation, interest and tax
opportunity cost	the opportunity cost of a particular course of action is the difference in value, assuming limited resources, between pursuing that chosen course and the value that could have been obtained by using the same resources to pursue the best alternative course of action

Overhead	costs not directly contributing or attributable to output production or service provision; e.g. premises, administration, human resources
outsourcing	subcontracting to another organisation an activity previously performed within the company using its own resources
page views	the calling up by a browser of a page on the internet. Page views should be distinguished from 'hits'. Because of the way in which website log analysis works, a single page view will typically register a number of hits
paid up capital	the total amount of capital in a company provided by shareholders who have paid in full for their shares
PAYE	the Pay As You Earn system, whereby an employee's tax is deducted by the employer before the employee is paid and then remitted to the government by the employer
PC (political correctness)	the term used to describe conduct of which the current political establishment approves. It applies to both speech and actions and is used as the criterion for condemning those who fail to observe its rules
Portfolio	a collection of various investment owned by an individual or an organisation
positive discrimination	a policy of favouring candidates from disadvantaged groups, as a means of countering prejudice or social inequalities
price elasticity	the extent to which a change in the price affects demand
price mechanism	the way in which the price of a product or service changes according to the balance between supply and demand
product line	a group of similar or related products within a company
profit and loss statement	a summary of income and expenses and, by subtracting expenses from income, the net profit
public relations	the function within a company responsible for communicating company messages to the company's public/s
racism	discrimination against an individual on the grounds of ethnicity
recession	a period of economic decline, often defined as two consecutive quarters of negative growth: i.e. two successive quarterly falls in GDP

return on investment	the ratio of income to the value of an asset (i.e. how much income is attributable to the asset compared to the value of the asset) or the ratio of income to the cost of an activity
revenue	the income of a company in the sense of money received by or owed to the company
royalty	a fee paid to the owner of a property for the right to use that property. Royalties are paid for works covered by copyright, inventions covered by patent, land on which companies mine, etc.
sabbatical	leave, often unpaid, given to an employee for rest, travel, or to pursue other interests. Traditionally in the academic world, a sabbatical is one year off in seven
security	a document which proves ownership of an investment or asset
self-employed person	someone who earns their living by working for themselves in order to provide a product or service
sexism	discrimination against an individual on the grounds of sex
social enterprise	businesses that have a social objective as their primary motivation
social networking	building social and business contacts by engaging in activities which afford opportunities to meet new like-minded individuals with a view to mutual social and / or commercial advantage
spin	the (dark) art of presenting information in such a way that it conveys the spinner's message, regardless of the extent to which the spinner must distort the information in order to achieve his goal
statistical significance	a mathematical measure of the likelihood that something is true. Any survey based on a random sample can be assessed in terms of its statistical significance. For example, if the survey sample shows 50% say yes, then depending on sample size as a proportion of the total population, we can apply a formula to calculate the degree of accuracy we have achieved. As a result, we might say that we are 95% confident the 'true' figure is 50%, plus or minus 2%; i.e. if we repeated the survey 20 times, we would expect the result to fall between 48% and 52% nineteen times. When assessing surveys of any type, you need to know whether or not the results are statistically significant.

stakeholders	any individual or organisation that has an interest in or is affected by the activities of an organisation
subliminal advertising	advertising which conveys its message without the target being aware of the advertising (e.g. through exposure of a product on a screen for less than one second). Subliminal advertising is considered unethical and is generally illegal.
supply chain	all the activities which move a product from producer to consumer, including manufacture, distribution and retailing
SWOT Analysis	an analysis of a the strengths, weaknesses, opportunities and threats for a company or a product
takeover	the buying of one company by another
tariff	duty imposed by government on imported goods, a means of interfering with free trade
tax allowance	the income that can be earned in a year before it becomes subject to any tax
tax avoidance	minimising tax by use of all available allowances and stratagems
trademark	a logo, a design, a word or an expression associated with a company, its products or services which is protected by law from imitation by that company's competitors
URL	Uniform Resource Locator, a url is an address for a website, documents, images or programs on the internet
USB	Universal Serial Bus, a plug and socket system for connecting other devices to a computer
user interface	the 'front end' of a website, consisting of a graphic interface, which provides the functionality that allows the user to explore the website
USP	unique selling point, the feature that distinguishes a product or service from all its competitors
VAT	value added tax is a tax on the value added to a product or service at each stage from its initiation though to its delivery to the end user
vertical integration	the process whereby a company purchases one or more companies in the chain from producer to consumer so that it can perform or control all the activities in the chain (e.g. a food retailer might acquire a farm, a haulage firm and a meat processing factory)

virus	a computer program which surreptitiously infects a computer and does damage
whistleblower	an employee who alerts the public to misconduct within the organisation that employs him/her
work-life balance	the concept that individuals should aim for an equitable division, in terms of time and energy, between work and 'life'. The concept is confusing (since work is part of life and, for many, a very large part of life). Enthusiasm for work-life balance seems to be most popular with those who, while compelled to work by economic demands, prefer leisure. A 'work/leisure' balance would seem more reasonable.
yield	the income earned by an investment in one year, often expressed as a percentage

12.6 Business Clichés and Jargon

Here we list a selection of business clichés to be avoided, or at least used sparingly and with care. Of course, some of these expressions were formerly honoured in the previous category (Proverbs and Aphorism) but, through overuse and abuse, now find themselves in the less distinguished company of clichés and jargon. Some of the definitions offered may be tarnished by a hint of cynicism.

Cliché / Jargon	Meanings/Origins
80 20 rule	a rule of thumb which proposes that in many situations, very often, there is an 80% / 20% split of the whole: e.g. 80% of a country's wealth is in the hands of 20% of the population; 80% of sales come from 20% of customers; or 80% of what we achieve is generated in 20% of our time. Early in the 20th century, an Italian economist Vilfredo Pareto observed that 80% of the country's wealth was held by 20% of the population. Since then, Pareto's Principle has been widely applied in areas outside wealth distribution (e.g. 80% of profits ensue from 20% of the products; 20% of your effort generates 80% of your success).
360 degree thinking	taking the broadest and widest possible view of all the possibilities in a business situation
across the piece	across the board, involving the entire project/organisation
agree to disagree	I've had enough of this discussion. We're not getting anywhere, anyway. (And I'm right!)
bad call	a bad decision

Cliché / Jargon	Meanings/Origins
best practice	the best example of how something should be done, as performed by the best companies doing it
big ask	a very demanding requirement or goal
blue sky thinking	allowing one's imagination free rein uninhibited by the constraints of current practicalities
bottom line	what is left on a company's income statement after the deduction of all legitimate expenses. Derived from company accounts where the Net Profit appears on the bottom line
box-ticking exercise	a pejorative expression describing an automatic or semi-automatic method of assessment which tends to provide superficial or misleading results
bringing value to the table	making a useful contribution to the efforts and/or resources of the group
cash cow	a product or service which generates substantial revenues for a company without the need for much attention or investment
client-facing	dealing directly with the customer
core competency	what it is that gives a company its key strengths when selling its products or services in the markets for which it competes
deal with it	"Stop whingeing and get on with it." Derived from the Middle English 'whingen' = 'to whine'.
do more with less	make better use of even fewer resources than you currently have to achieve even more. See 'a big ask' above
downsizing	in a business context, a euphemism for redundancies or reducing the expenses of a company in the hope of bringing them below the level of the company's income
dropping the ball	failing to see a project through to a successful conclusion because of a lapse of concentration or effort
drilling down	although it sounds technical, it generally simply means 'looking in more detail at the available information' Originally it meant exploring the data further, dissecting it in an effort to gain more knowledge and a better understanding of why the main results are as they are
empowerment	making someone feel good about taking responsibility

Cliché / Jargon	Meanings/Origins
evidence-based	widely used, and abused, to justify the superiority of any proposition. One should always ask: is there any evidence? If so, what is it? How reliable is this evidence? And is there any evidence that contradicts these findings? If the evidence passes these tests, the proposition is truly evidence-based and should be respected.
every challenge is an opportunity	we are all in favour of positive thinking and this is one business saw that will surely last forever. The less optimistic probably see every opportunity as a challenge
fit for purpose	fully functioning to fulfil the objectives for which is was designed. Usually used in the negative: i.e. not fit for purpose. Often used by politicians to describe government departments or regulatory bodies that are working so badly they need to be completely overhauled or abolished.
game changer	a person or an idea that brings about major, if not a revolutionary, change in the current business plan or model. Goes well with paradigm shift, as in: "Wow! This game changer has effected a paradigm shift!"
getting granular	focusing on the minutiae of an issue or situation. Granular is possibly a grown up version of the "nitty gritty"
giving 110%	putting in more effort than a reasonable and/or numerate person would think possible. Especially popular with American executives.
glass half full/ glass half empty	a metaphor for optimistic/pessimistic outlook
going forward	"Given where we are, let's talk about what we can do now." Similar to 'moving on', although 'moving on' often carries a hint of irritation with those who seem unwilling or unable to 'go forward'.
heavy lifting	performing the toughest, most demanding and challenging parts of any job
hit the ground running	to be so well prepared for a new challenge that you can be effective immediately. The expression has been adapted to deal with those less eager to take action, less incisive. These have been said ' to hit the ground reviewing'.

Cliché / Jargon	Meanings/Origins
it is what it is	a bland but irrefutable expression in effect advocating submission to the will of whichever god you worship. In the same class as "You get what you get".
line in the sand	a point beyond which one will not go or a point which, once passed, has inevitable consequences. This seems to be a metaphor drawn from the military whose practitioners seemed fond of drawing lines to mark critical boundaries
long grass	the lonely, seldom visited place where ideas with little or no future tend to end up
low hanging fruit	the easiest and most immediately rewarding opportunities
make it happen	a less dictatorial form of 'Get on with it'
man up	stop making excuses and show you can be as tough as the situation demands. Obviously a sexist remark but, perhaps because of its popularity as an expression directed at men by women, politically acceptable.
managing expectations	using various techniques to ensure that the result or outcome, as perceived by the client or any other interested party, is no worse, and hopefully even better, than the client or any other interested party had the right to expect
maximising leverage	can mean several different things. In its simplest sense it means making the fullest possible use of one's influence. In a financial sense, it means borrowing a relatively small amount of money to make a relatively high return. Leveraging, in this sense, involves increasing one's debt. Deleveraging is the process of reducing debt thereby improving a company's balance sheet
money rich, time poor	spending all your time making money, leaving little or no time for other things
multi-tasking	performing more than one job at a time. Generally means doing several things simultaneously - but none of them very well
my sense of it is	"I have given this matter some serious thought and I see things this way."
paradigm shift	a fundamental change in the way in which reality is perceived or understood. Has become widely over-used to mean any change in business theory or practice

Cliché / Jargon	Meanings/Origins
perfect storm	a situation in which, remarkably, everything (most of which was outside our control) that could go wrong has gone wrong
proactive	generally used to mean taking the initiative. The term is especially popular with PR people who use it to distinguish between activity launched by them as opposed to actions undertaken by them in response to media initiatives. It could be argued that the 'pro' is superfluous, or that, if 'active' requires a prefix, 'pre' might serve better but the term is borrowed from psychology where it is used to describe those who take responsibility for their own lives, as opposed to those who tend to seek explanations in terms of external factors.
putting lipstick on the pig	you can't make a silk purse out of a sow's ear (to keep the porcine metaphor). Superficial or purely cosmetic changes will not turn a bad product into a good one.
pushing the envelope	attempting to go beyond what are currently held to be the maximum or minimum limits. The envelope is not the paper kind but the mathematical concept of the limits of a particular function. What is within the envelope is the known to be possible. Outside the envelope is unknown.
rightsizing	a euphemism for large sale redundancies, favoured by those who are keeping their jobs
scalability	capacity to accommodate increasing demand without major structural adjustments
seamless integration	extra good integration; i.e. integrating two or more functions so fully that they appear to be one. Often a precursor to massive redundancies (i.e. the offering of new opportunities/career paths to those who are now surplus to requirement)
step up to the plate	to take the initiative and the responsibility for dealing with a problem. A baseball term for taking up a position to hit the ball
strong headwinds	major problems, partly or entirely outside our control, which will help to explain why we are announcing disappointing results

Cliché / Jargon	Meanings/Origins
taking a hit for the team / taking one for the team	accepting, as a member of a team, some personal damage for the benefit of the team as a whole
taking it to the next level	making a significant qualitative improvement
taking ownership	feeling the problem is all yours
the whole nine yards	You want to know what it means? It means the full Monty, the whole enchilada, the full works. Origin unknown or disputed.
there is no 'i' in team	No prima donnas in this group, please
thinking outside the box	breaking out of traditional or conventional ways of thinking in order to come up with innovative and/or unexpected solutions to problems
ticks all the boxes	meets all the criteria set for a particular task or requirement
win/win situation	a situation in which, whatever the outcome, the result is wholly positive; or a situation in which both or all parties to a deal benefit. Win/win is the opposite of a 'zero-sum game' where, if one person wins, the other person loses in the same measure
work/life balance	a profoundly popular concept with those who wish to tip the balance in favour of life. In passing, we should point out this is a false dichotomy. The contrast should be between work and leisure, not work and life. After all, work is part of life
work smarter not harder	by planning the use of available resources better, you can get more done in less time. When this exhortation is used simply to urge someone to get more done with fewer resources, it tends to irritate rather than motivate.
'yes, if..', not 'no, because'	another advocacy of positive thinking - and, in my view, a rather neat one. Are you a '*yes, if*' or a '*no because*' person?

Cliché / Jargon	Meanings/Origins
zero-sum game	the simplest type of competitive situation, in which, if one person or organisation gains, another person or organisation loses to the same extent. Gains and losses cancel each other out. Very different from the win-win scenario

13 Checklist Templates

13.1 Concept Proposal

1 : Concept

It is important to be as clear and concise as possible in describing the concept. If your description raises questions you have not answered, it is incomplete. An incomplete description will not convince anyone.

In developing the concept, friends and colleagues will have asked questions. Make sure you have coherent, consistent answers to these questions and include the questions and answers in your Concept description.

1.1 : Objectives
How does the Concept fulfil a definable need?
Who has this need?

1.2 : Success Criteria
How do you propose to measure the success of the project?
This section should provide some form of measurement which will enable you to determine objectively how well you have fulfilled your objectives.

2 : Detailed Project Description
Provide full details of the Concept.

2.1 : Refine the Concept
Explain exactly why you believe it will work (i.e. how precisely will you ensure the Concept, when implemented, will meet the needs of those at whom the Concept is aimed).

2.2 : Unique Selling Point (USP)
Does the Concept have a unique selling point?

Will it be the only product/service of its type on the market?

If not, does it have a unique advantage over its existing competitors?

3 : Target Market

This is one of the most critical parts of the process. You need to know who you are aiming at and how many there are of them.

3.1 : Qualitative

Who are you aiming the product/service at? Define your target market by age and sex.

Which socio/economic groups? Define your target market by educational standard, social class, income.

Are there any precisely definable groups that you feel will determine the success or failure of the Concept?

Customer groups are often divided into categories according to particular shared characteristics. For example:

- Loyal Customers
- Discount Customers
- Impulsive Customers
- Need-based Customers
- Wandering Customers

(Management Study Guide:
http://www.managementstudyguide.com/types-of-customers.htm

or

- Laissez-faire
- Micromanagers
- Utterly in the Dark
- Savvy and Perfect

(Small Business Trends:
http://smallbiztrends.com/2012/04/4-types-customers.html)

or

- Seasonal consumer
- Personal consumer
- Organisational consumer
- Impulse consumer
- Need-based consumer
- Discount driven consumer
- Habitual consumer

The Kenyan Entrepreneur: The Hub
http://kenyaentrepreneur.hubpages.com/hub/Types-Of-Consumers

The different schemes have different merits. The main point is that it is useful to try to divide your potential market into groups based on similar characteristics because you may well need different techniques to sell the concept to the various groups.

3.2 : Quantitative
What are the sizes of the groups you have identified as your target market?
What are the average incomes of these groups?
Which group is most likely to respond most quickly to the Concept?

4 : Market Research evidence
The more information you can provide about the market for your Concept the better.
There are many forms of market research:
- Desk Research
  - government statistics
  - published reports
  - news reports
  - magazines
  - the internet
- Survey Research
  - mail
  - telephone
  - personal interview
  - group discussion

Most desk research is available to all and there is no excuse for not knowing all the published information about your target market.

Survey research is generally confidential to the client who paid for it but often summaries are published in the media.

5 : Costs
Although you are not providing a complete marketing plan, you need to show that you have given some consideration to the costs of implementing the concept. You need to show that, given favourable circumstances, the implementation of the concept is, at least, a practical possibility.

This section provides a simple checklist of areas of cost to be taken into account.

5.1 : R & D Costs

5.2 : Direct Costs
5.2.1 : Materials
5.2.2 : Equipment
5.2.3 : Labour

5.3 : Marketing & Sales Costs
5.3.1 Sales
5.3.2 Advertising

5.3.3 Other forms of promotion
5.3.4 Travel & Subsistence

5.4 : Overhead Costs

6 : Schedule

We are not at the stages of providing a full critical path analysis for the implementation of the Concept but some overview of the main stages of development, production, distribution and marketing, with some indication of time scale, is required.

7 : Evaluation Criteria

What have you set as the criteria for the success of the Concept?
What levels of:
- market penetration
- sales
- profit

are you aiming at and when do you expect to achieve them?

8 : Conclusion

This provides an opportunity to summarise the concept; the target market; the research evidence on which your development work and your forecasts are based; your expected costs; your marketing ideas; your schedule; and the criteria you propose to use for assessing your degree of success.

13.2 Curriculum Vitae

1 : Name & Contact Details

2 : Personal Statement
Here you should set out clearly what you see as your main strengths. Be guided by what you know about the company and what is said in the job advertisement. There is no need to lie. Simply give prominence to those aspects of your character and experience that correspond with what the employer seems to be looking for.

Such characteristics as commitment, determination, loyalty and staying power are always popular with employers.

Try to avoid clichés. How many times have employers read that candidates are happy working on their own, on their own initiative but at the same time they are equally happy working as part of a team? Of course the ability to do both is desirable but demonstrate your flexibility by examples taken from your experience rather than just trotting out the cliché.

3 : Date of Birth

4 : Employment Record
List jobs in date order, most recent first.

Include all jobs which have given you work experience and, in each case, explain which skills the job enabled you to acquire or refine. Employers are keen to identify the transferable skills you can offer. Literacy and numeracy are prerequisites in most office-based jobs but there are now many other skills that it is useful for potential or actual managers or administrators to have:

- Computer literacy
  - word processing
  - spread sheets
  - database programs
- Foreign languages
- Programming
- Research skills
- Web design

If you have any of these skills, you may be able to make your job application stand out from the others.

Sadly, we live in a world in which everyone is so busy they are able to give only a limited amount of time to each activity. When a single job advertisement can elicit dozens if not hundreds of applications, it is not surprising that employers have a tendency to adopt fairly crude filtering mechanisms. Some of these filtering criteria are objective (e.g. whether you have a degree; what class of degree; which school or university you attended) but others are about the general impression your CV and covering letter create. This means that, at any one time, certain key words are in vogue and can help you to appear "switched on". Here are a few examples of the key words to which the employer is likely to respond:

Adjectives	Nouns
analytical	achievement
aspirational	change management
creative	commitment
eager to learn	determination
flexible	excellence
goal-orientated	success
innovative	
motivated	

5 : Education

5.1 : School
Name your schools and give the dates attended. Briefly mention anything about the schools of particular interest, and your time at them.

5.1.1 : Primary School
Name your school and give the dates attended.

5.1.2 : Secondary School
Name your school and give the dates attended.
Briefly mention anything about the school of particular interest.
Mention any distinctions during your time there (e.g. prizes, prefect, achool/sports captain, DOE attainment)
List here your GCSE and A level exam results.

5.2 : University
Devote a couple of lines to describing your university and its benefits/advantages.

5.2.1 : Bachelor Degree
Subject of Degree
Class of Degree
Year awarded:

5.2.2 : Master's Degree
Subject of Degree
Year awarded:

5.2.3 : Doctorate
Subject of Degree
Year awarded:

5.3: Any other academic distinctions

6 : Leisure Interests

Employers are looking for rounded individuals. Proof of academic ability is important but they will also be interested in other aspects of your life. Leisure interests can tell an employer a good deal about the character and aims of the applicant.

6.1 : Sport

Employers are keen to employ generally fit people. Physical exercise suggests an active, healthy lifestyle.

The list of sports below is a memory aid, just in case there is some sport in which you participated long ago but which you have forgotten. Come on, you must have participated in something!

6.1.1 : Athletics
6.1.2 : Canoeing
6.1.3 : Cricket
6.1.4 : Cycling
6.1.5 : Fives
6.1.6 : Football
6.1.7 : Gymnastics
6.1.8 : Hill Walking
6.1.9 : Judo
6.1.10 : Karate
6.1.11 : Keep Fit
6.1.12 : Riding
6.1.13 : Rock Climbing
6.1.14 : Rowing
6.1.15 : Rugby
6.1.16 : Running
6.1.17 : Skating
6.1.18 : Skiing
6.1.19 : Squash
6.1.20 : Table Tennis
6.1.21 : Walking
6.1.22 : Weight Lifting

6.2 : Mental/Social Activities

Employers will also be interested in any ways in which you exercise your mind in your leisure time. Here are some examples of activities which will impress and create interest:

6.2.1 : Amateur Dramatics
6.2.2 : Astronomy
6.2.3 : Backgammon
6.2.4 : Chess

6.2.5 : Creative Writing
6.2.6 : Playing in a band
6.2.7 : Reading
6.2.8 : Singing in a choir

7 : Social Contribution

Mention any voluntary or socially useful work you have undertaken. Employers like to see some evidence of social awareness.

8 : Other

This section if up to you. Is there anything else you think might persuade the employer to choose you rather than all the other applicants?

ααα

Despite the length of this checklist, try to keep your CV short (i.e. no longer than two pages). Consider including a relevant photograph to make the layout more attractive and memorable.

13.3 House Buying Questionnaire

Here is a list of questions to which you need answers from the vendors, their neighbours, the estate agents, your surveyor or your solicitors:

1: General Questions

Why are you moving?

What is included in the sale?

e.g.
- carpets
- curtains
- light fittings
- furniture

Is the house in a conservation area? If so, what are the restrictions?

How old is the house?

What are the neighbours like? How long have they lived next door? Have there been / are there now any disputes?

What are the views like?

Is there enough light in the house during the day?

Is the roof in good condition?

Have there ever been any subsidence problems?

2: Property Layout

How many rooms are there?
- reception
- dining
- kitchen
- bedrooms
- bathrooms/showers
- toilets

Check sizes

Ask for a floor plan.

Is there adequate storage?
- loft
- cupboards
- wardrobes

3: Security

Do you have an alarm system?

If so, is it connected to the police or other monitoring station?

If so, is there an automatic response (i.e. visit by the police)?

Is there much crime in the area? What is the crime level?

Is there a Neighbourhood Watch scheme in the area? If yes, are you a member?

4: Structure

Does the house have any structural problems?

- cracked walls/ceilings
- subsidence

5 : Community Charge
What is the annual Community Charge for the house?

6 : Utility Supplies
What utilities are supplied to the house?
- water
- electricity
- gas
- oil

What is the average annual bill for:
- water
- electricity
- gas
- oil

Is the house on mains drainage/sewage?
How do you switch off utility supplies when necessary?

7 : Electrics
When was the house last rewired?
Are all the electrics in working order now?

8 : Plumbing
When was the house last re-plumbed?
Is everything in working order now?

9 : Central Heating
What form of central heating do you have?
- Gas
- Oil
- Electric

Do you have?
- underfloor heating
- wall radiators
- other

What kind of boiler do you have? When was it last serviced?

10 : Communications
10.1 : Telephones
How many telephone lines do you have?
How many extensions? In which rooms?

10.2 : Broadband
Do you have broadband?

If so, who is your supplier?
What download speed do you get?
Is the service reliable?

10.3 : Television
Do you have satellite TV?
Do you have cable TV?

11 : Insulation
Is the loft properly insulated?
Does the property have cavity wall insulation?
Does the house have double-glazing?
- secondary double-glazing
- sealed double glazing
- sealed treble glazing

12 : Parking
Do you have a lockable garage?
Do you have off-street parking? If so, for how many cars?
Is this a residence parking area? If so, what are the costs and what are the rules?

13 : Garden
Is there a front garden?
Is there a back garden?
Are they a satisfactory size?
What condition are the gardens in?
How much work will be entailed in maintaining them?

14 : Neighbours
Do you know your neighbours?
Are the neighbours noisy?
Are the neighbours in any way a nuisance?
Have you or the previous owner had any disputes with the neighbours?
Which fences are you responsible for?

15 : Transport Links
How good are the transport links?
- Buses
- Tube
- Trains

16 : Shops
Where are the nearest shops?
What type of shops are local?

The Report Writer's Handbook

Do any of them stay open late?

17 : Schools
Where are the nearest schools?
What type of schools are they?
What sort of reputation do they have?

18 : Leisure Facilities
Where are the nearest facilities?
- bowling
- cinemas
- gyms
- swimming pools

13.4 MARKETING PLAN

1 : Introduction

2 : Market Research Programme
   2.1 : Market Data
     2.1.1 : Definition of the Market/Markets
     2.1.2 : Market Statistics
     2.1.3 : Competitor Data
     2.1.3.1 : Main Competitors
     2.1.3.2 : Strengths and Weaknesses of Main Competitors
     2.1.3.3 : Competitor Advertising/Promotional Activity/Costs
     2.1.3.4 : Competitor Sales

   2.2 : Survey Research
     2.2.1 : Mail/Email Surveys
     2.2.2 : Interviewer Research
     2.2.2.1 : Personal Interviews
     2.2.2.2 : Group Research

3 : Product Data
   3.1 : Description of Products
   3.2 : Strengths and Weaknesses

4 : Product Marketing Strategy for each Product
   4.1 : Product Positioning
   4.2 : Sales/Promotion Plan
   4.3 : Product-related PR
   4.4 : Schedule of Activity
   4.5 : Total Marketing Costs

5 : Sales/Profit Forecast
   5.1 : Sales Forecasts
   5.2 : Cost Forecasts
   5.3 : Breakeven/Profit Forecast

6 : Future Plans

13.5 Product Marketing Plan

1 : Introduction

2 : Market Research Programme
  2.1 : Market Data
2.1.1 : Definition of the Market
2.1.2 : Market Statistics
2.1.3 : Competitor Data
2.1.3.1 : Main Competitors
2.1.3.2 : Strengths and Weaknesses of Main Competitors
2.1.3.3 : Competitor Advertising/Promotional Activity/Costs
2.1.3.4 : Competitor Sales

  2.2 : Survey Research
2.2.1 : Mail/Email Surveys
2.2.2 : Interviewer Research
2.2.2.1 : Personal Interviews
2.2.2.2 : Group Research

3 : Product Data
  3.1 : Product Description
  3.2 : Strengths and Weaknesses

4 : Product Marketing Strategy
  4.1 : Product Positioning
  4.2 : Sales/Promotion Plan
  4.3 : Product-related PR
  4.4 : Total Marketing Costs

5 : Sales/Profit Forecast
  5.1 : Sales Forecast
  5.2 : Cost Forecast
  5.3 : Breakeven/Profit Forecast

6 : Product Development Programme

13.6 Renting a house checklist

1 : Location
Location, location, location.

You can change most things about a house. You can redecorate, rearrange, often even extend. But you can't change where the house is or the direction in which it is facing. So make sure you are happy, or can at least live with the location before you consider the many other factors that will affect your choice. If not, don't waste your time.

1.1 : General Quality of Neighbourhood
Every location has its own character and ambience. If you know the location well, you will have internalised a good deal of information about the location already. If you know little or nothing about the location, walk or drive around the area at different times of the day. Drive around at different times in the evening. You will learn a lot. Talk to the estate agent by all means but remember they are acting on behalf of the seller. Visit the nearest shops. If you have the opportunity, talk to some residents. You will find out what type of people live in the neighbourhood and what they themselves think of the place as somewhere to live. Buy and read a local newspaper. Check out the crime statistics on the police website (http://www.police.uk/).

1.2 : Shops
Is there a good range of shops within easy distance?
Is there opportunity for late night shopping?

1.3 : Schools
Are there good state schools in the area? How hard is it to get places in the good schools?
Are there good private schools in the area? What are the level of fees?

1.4 : Medical Services
Where are the nearest GP centres? Are they highly regarded by locals?
Where are the nearest emergency services: ambulance, fire, police?
Where is the nearest hospital? What services does it provide? Does it provide A&E? If not, where is the nearest A&E?

1.5 : Neighbours
Who are your neighbours? How old are they? What do they do for a living?
How long have they lived there?
Have there been any disputes? If so, have they been resolved? Are relations currently positive?

2 : House
2.1 : Total Square Feet

2.2 : Bathroom/s
How many bathrooms are there?
What are their dimensions?

How many are en suite?
Are the bathrooms equipped to modern standards?
- bath
- toilet
- bidet
- basin
- shower

Is the plumbing in good order? Do all hot taps work and do they deliver at an acceptable flow-rate?
Where is the stopcock?

2.3 : Bedroom/s
How many bedrooms are there? What are their dimensions?
How many doubles? How many singles?
How well are they heated?
Do they have air-conditioning?

2.4 : Kitchen
Is the kitchen equipped to modern standards?
Does it have mains gas?

2.5 : Reception Rooms
Number of Rooms?
Size of Rooms?

2.5.1 : Reception Room 1
Dimensions of Room: L   W   H
Number of Windows
Window Sizes

2.5.2 : Reception Room 2
Dimensions of Room: L   W   H
Number of Windows
Window Sizes

2.5.3 : Reception Room 3
Dimensions of Room: L   W   H
Number of Windows
Window Sizes

2.6 : Toilet/s
Number of Toilets?
Location of Toilets?
Size of Toilets?
Mains sewage or cesspit?

3 : Inventory
If the property is furnished, it is important to prepare and ensure both parties sign a comprehensive inventory.

At the same time, it is useful to prepare a list of any parts of the property already in need of repair (e.g. damaged furniture or appliances, damp walls). This list can be illustrated with photographs.

4 : Garden
4.1 : Front Garden
Size?
Current Layout?
Work/cost involved in maintenance?
4.2 : Rear Garden
Size?
Current Layout?
Work/cost involved in maintenance?

5 : Parking
5.1 : Garage
Dimensions: L   W   H
Security:

5.2 : Off-Street Parking
No. of spaces

6 : Security
6.1 : Locks
Front door: type of lock/level of security
Back door: type of lock/level of security
Window locks

6.2 : Alarms
Burglar/intruder alarm?
Fire alarm?
Panic alarm?

7 : Safety
7.1 : Fire
Fire Extinguishers?
Types of fire extinguisher:
- water fire extinguishers (primarily for Class A fires)
- foam fire extinguishers (for Class A and B fires)
- dry powder fire extinguishers (for Class A, B and C fires)
- CO2 fire extinguishers (for Electrical fires and Class B fires)
- wet chemical fire extinguishers (for Class F fires)

Fires are divided into six categories:
- Class A: **Solids** such as paper, wood, plastic etc.
- Class B: **Flammable Liquids** such as paraffin, petrol, oil etc.
- Class C: **Flammable Gases** such as propane, butane, methane etc.

- Class D: **Metals** such as aluminium, magnesium, titanium etc.
- Class E: Fires involving **Electrical Apparatus**
- Class F: **Cooking Oil** and **Fat** etc.

7.2 : Gas
Gas Safety Check certificates.

To check that a gas engineer is properly qualified, you can refer to the Gas Safe Register. Go to:

http://www.hse.gov.uk/gas/domestic/newschemecontract.htm

7.3 : Electricity
Check when house was wired/rewired

Are there sufficient power points?

7.4 : Escape Routes
What provision is there for escape from the building in the event of fire or other type of emergency?

8 : Heating/AC
8.1 : Heating System
Energy source:
- gas
- electric
- oil

Form:
- wall radiators
- underfloor

Insulation:
- double-glazing
- loft insulation
- wall insulation

8.2 : Air Conditioning System

9 : Rental Arrangements
9.1 : Deposit
£ _____

Terms of deposit retention

9.2 : Rental Amount/Payment Schedule
£ _____ per month

9.3 : Type of Contract

9.4 : Rental Period

9.5 : Termination

9.6 : Renewal Terms

9.7 : Bill splitting arrangements

9.8 : Rental Agreements
There are several standard rental agreements on the internet; some free, others not. Here are two useful links:

Law Depot:
http://www.lawdepot.co.uk/contracts/tenancy-agreement/?a=t&loc=GB&pid=-googleppc-reslse_gb-ft_rental_a1ft-s-ggkey_rental%20agreements&s_kwcid=rental%20agreements|6466445123

Residential Landlords Association (RLA):
http://www.rla.org.uk/landlord/documents/tenancy_agreement/doc_AST.shtml?ref=assured_shorthold_tenancy_agreement&gclid=CN2ezLD8q6sCFYIMfAodexJF5w

10 : Dilapidations Schedule
Dilapidation Schedules are documents, generally prepared by the landlord or his solicitor, setting out repairs, redecorations or other requirements for which the landlord intends to hold the tenant.

It is wise therefore for any tenant to inspect a property he/she is intending to rent very carefully in order to assess the current condition of the property and to make sure the landlord is aware of the assessment. Any major problems should be drawn to the landlord's attention in writing.

10.1 : Interim Dilapidations Schedule
An interim dilapidation schedule is served during the period of the lease to point out to the tenant any damage which the landlord considers to fall outside the terms of the lease and which he may well require the tenant to make good.

10.2 : Terminal Dilapidations Schedule
A terminal dilapidation schedule is served at the end of the lease and sets out any deterioration in the property or its contents which the landlord considers not to be normal wear and tear and for which the landlord intends to seek reparation from the tenant.

14 Terminology for Docupraxis Users

DocuPraxis®
'**DocuPraxis®** is the name of the process of grouping, ordering, linking and structuring advocated here for the creation of all forms of document. (See www.docupraxis.co.uk.)

The **DocuPraxis®** program has been devised and developed by Panarc International Ltd to assist those involved in producing documents. It combines the functions of a sophisticated Outliner, a File Manager, a Database Program and a Project Control Program. **Its primary function is to help users to select, organise and present any set of material, clearly, succinctly and logically, in written form.**

Hierarchy
'Hierarchy' means the arrangement of a set of information in a graded order which shows the relationship between all the parts which make up the set.

Level
'Level' refers to the position of a heading in the hierarchy (and the position of a node in the structure).

Structure
'Structure' is the hierarchical structure which constitutes the framework for a document. In the **DocuPraxis®** program, the Structure is located on the left side of the screen, in a tall window.

Content
'Content' is the text and visual material provided for each component of the structure. In the **DocuPraxis®** program, content is compiled on the work page, located on the right hand side of the screen.

Workpage
The 'Workpage' is the area of the **DocuPraxis**® screen where you organise the content that goes with each node in the structure. The Workpage is located on the right side of the screen.

There is a full User's Manual provided with every copy of the **DocuPraxis**® program.

15 Bibliography

Collins Thesaurus A-Z
Collins, 2005

Concise Dictionary of English Etymology
by Walter W. Skeat, Wordsworth Reference, 1993

Concise Dictionary of Proverbs
Third Edition, Oxford, 1998

Dictionary of English Grammar
Sylvia Chalker and Edmund Weiner, Oxford, 1998

Dictionary of the English Language
Longman, 1988

Dictionary of Word Origins
Edited: Julia Cresswell. Second Edition, Oxford, 2010

English Grammar
by Ron Simpson, Teach Yourself Books, 2007

Fowler's Modern English Usage
Second Edition, Oxford, at the Clarendon Press, 1972

Good English
G.H. Vallins, Pan Books, 1976

Guide to English Usage
by Sydney Greenbaum and Janet Whitcut, Longman Dixtionaries, 1988

Longman Dictionary of English Idioms
Longman Group Ltd, 1979

Oxford Dictionary of English Grammar
OUP, 1998

Oxford Dictionary of Quotations
Edited by Elizabeth Knowles, Oxford, 2001

Shorter Oxford English Dictionary
OUP 1973

Penguin Guide to Punctuation
Penguin Reference, 1997

Rediscover Grammar
David Crystal, Longman, 1988

Usage and Abusage
Eric Partridge, Penguin Books, 1987

Index

Subject, followed by section number/s

Alcohol pricing 6.1.3
Alliteration 9.5.1
Alphabetical ordering 4.1
Alternatives to over-worked words 9.4.2
Ambiguity 9.1.3; 9.5.2; 10.5.1
Analogy/False Analogy 11.3.1
Aphorisms 10.2
Apostrophes 9.3.1
Assonance 9.5.3

Bending the rules 11.3
Bibliography 15.0
Brevity 2.3
Bullet Points 9.1.5
Business Clichés and Jargon 12.6
Business Terms 12.5

Capital punishment 3.2.2
Cartoons 2.4; 3.0; 4.0; 4.1; 5.0; 6.1.3; 10.5, 10.5.1; 10.5.4
Cause/Effect reversal 11.3.2
Causal linking 5.1
Causal ordering 4.2
Causation, Correlation and 11.1.3.3
Checking and Revising 12.4
Checklist 13.0; 13.6
Chronological ordering 4.3

Clarity 2.1
Colons 9.3.2
Combining linking 5.2
Commas 9.3.3
Common business terms 12.5
Compare and Contrast 3.1
Components of a report 12.2
Concept Proposal 13.1
Conditional linking 5.5
Conflicts around the world 4.3
Correlation and causation 11.1.3.3
Consequential linking 5.3
Consistency 12.1
Contrasting linking 5.4
Criteria for Grouping 3.2
Curriculum Vitae 13.2

Dangling Participles 10.5.2
Diagrams 1.0; 5.0; 5.11; 6.0; 6.2.1; 7.0
Digressions 11.2
DocuPraxis 1.0; 6.0; 6.1.1; 6.3.1; 6.3.2; 11.1.1; 12.1; 14.0
Double negative 10.5.5

Ellipsis, false 10.5.3
Elucidating linking 5.6
Emotivation 11.1.3.4
Emphasis 11.1
Euphemism 9.5.4
Exceptional linking 5.7
Exclamation Marks 9.3.4

False analogy 11.1.3.1
False Ellipsis 10.5.3
Figures of speech, mixed up 10.5.7
Full Stops 9.3.5

General guidelines for reports 12.1
General to Particular ordering 4.4
Grammar 2.0; 9.0; 9.1.1; 10.5; 12.1
Grammatical hazards 10.5
Grouping 1.0; 3.0; 7.7
Grouping ideas 3.2.2
Grouping Principle 3.3
Grouping words and objects 3.2.1

Hierarchy: Status Equivalence 6.2.1

Hierarchy: Symmetry 6.2.2
Homogeneous Hierarchy 6.3.1
House Buying Questionnaire 13.3
Humour 10.1
Hybrid Hierarchy 6.3.2
Hyperbole 9.5.5
Hyphens 9.3.6

Infinitives 10.5.10
Irony 9.5.6

Jargon 12.6

Link Analysis 5.10
Linking 1.0; 5.0; 7.0
Litotes 9.5.7
Logic 12.1

Marketing Plan 13.4
Metaphor 9.5.8
Metonymy 9.5.9
Mind mapping 8.0
Mis-positioning 10.5.4

Negatives, problems with 10.5.5
Number errors 10.5.8

One-hit words 10.4.1
Onomatopoeia 9.5.10
Ordering 1.0; 4.0; 7.0
Over-worked words 9.4.2
Oxymoron 9.5.11

Paradox 9.5.12
Paragraphs 9.2
Paragraphs: Emphasis 11.1.2
Participles 10.5.2
Personification 9.5.13
PIM Aplications 1.0
Prepositions 10.5.9
Product Marketing Plan 13.5
Pronouns, problems with 10.5.6
Proof-reading 2.4
Proposals 12.3
Proverbs/Aphorisms 10.2
Pun 9.5.14

Purpose linking 5.8

Quality Control 2.4
Question Marks 9.3.7
Quirky words 10.4
Quotation Marks 9.3.8

Ranking ordering 4.5
Register 9.4.1
Renting a house checklist 13.6
Reports, Components 12.2
Reports, General guidelines 12.1
Revising, Checking and 12.4
Rhetorical Question 9.5.15
Rules 11.1.3

Semi-colons 9.3.9
Sentence: Achieving the right emphasis 9.1.2
Sentence: Bullet Points 9.1.5
Sentence: Cohesion 9.1.3
Sentence: Emphasis 11.1.1
Sentence: Key Questions 9.1.4
Sentence: Recognising a sentence 9.1.1
Simile 9.5.16
Simplicity 2.2
Split Infinitives 10.5.10
Status Equivalence 6.2.1
Structuring 1.0; 6.0; 7.0
Structuring: Bottom up construction 6.1.1
Structuring: Building a hierarchy in practice 6.1.3
Structuring: Top Down 6.1.2
Suez crisis 4.3
Syllepsis 9.5.17
Symmetry 6.2.2
Synecdoche 9.5.18

Tautology 10.5.11
Templates 1.0; 12.0; 13.0
Temporal linking 5.9
Terminology for DocuPraxis users 14.0
Tricky Words 10.3
Tricky Words criteria 10.3.1

Un-Positive words 10.4.2

Verbal latitude 11.1.3.5

Verbiage 10.3.2
Vocabulary: Alternative to over-worked words 9.4.2
Vocabulary: Register 9.4.1

Welfare Reform 6.3.2

Zeugma 9.5.19

www.ingramcontent.com/pod-product-compliance
Lightning Source LLC
Chambersburg PA
CBHW081354290426
44110CB00018B/2368